FINANCIAL INNOVATION, REGULATION AND
CRISES IN HISTORY

Banking, Money and International Finance

Titles in this Series

Alternative Banking and Financial Crisis
Olivier Butzbach and Kurt von Mettenheim (eds)

FINANCIAL INNOVATION, REGULATION AND CRISES IN HISTORY

EDITED BY

Piet Clement, Harold James and Herman Van der Wee

LONDON AND NEW YORK

First published 2014 by Pickering & Chatto (Publishers) Limited

2 Park Square, Milton Park, Abingdon, Oxfordshire OX14 4RN
52 Vanderbilt Avenue, New York, NY 10017

Routledge is an imprint of the Taylor & Francis Group, an informa business

First issued in paperback 2020

BRITISH LIBRARY CATALOGUING IN PUBLICATION DATA

Financial innovation, regulation and crises in history. – (Banking, money and
international finance)
1. Financial crises – History. 2. Economic stabilization – History. 3. Financial
institutions – Government policy – History. 4. Financial institutions –
Management – History.
I. Series II. Clement, Piet editor. III. James, Harold, 1956– editor. IV. Wee,
Herman Van der editor.
338.5'43-dc23

ISBN-13: 978-1-84893-504-4 (hbk)
ISBN-13: 978-0-367-66952-2 (pbk)

Typeset by Pickering & Chatto (Publishers) Limited

CONTENTS

Acknowledgements   vii
List of Contributors   ix
List of Figures and Tables   xv
Note on the Text   xvi

Part I: Introduction
  Foreword: Financial Crises – Will it be Different Next Time? – *Ivo Maes* 1
  1 Financial Innovation, Regulation and Crises: A Historical View
    – *Piet Clement, Harold James and Herman Van der Wee*   5
Part II: Episodes of Financial Innovation, Regulation and Crisis in History
  2 Contract Enforcement on the World's First Stock Exchange
    – *Lodewijk Petram*   13
  3 Co-operative Banking in the Netherlands in pre-Second World War
    Crises – *Joke Mooij*   37
  4 The Discreet Charm of Hidden Reserves: How Swiss Re Survived the
    Great Depression – *Tobias Straumann*   55
  5 The Redesign of the Bank–Industry–Financial Market Ties in the US
    Glass–Steagall and the 1936 Italian Banking Acts
    – *Federico Barbiellini Amidei and Claire Giordano*   65
  6 Regulation and Deregulation in a Time of Stagflation: Siegmund
    Warburg and the City of London in the 1970s – *Niall Ferguson* 85
  7 Financial Market Integration: An Insurmountable Challenge to
    Modern Trade Policy? – *Welf Werner*   107
Part III: Innovation, Regulation and the Current Financial Crisis
  8 Something Old and Something New: Novel and Familiar Drivers of
    the Latest Crisis – *Adair Turner*   127
  9 To Regulate or Not to Regulate: No Easy Fixes for the Financial System
    – *William R. White*   139

Notes   143
Index   169

ACKNOWLEDGEMENTS

The conception of this volume had its origin in the Conference 'Responding to Crises in the Global Financial Environment – Risk Management and Regulation', that took place in 2010 in Brussels at the National Bank of Belgium, and that was organized by the European Association for Banking and Financial History (EABH). The editors would like to express their thanks to the EABH, and in particular to Carmen Hofmann and Gunnar Marquardt, as well as to Philip Good and Stephina Clarke at Pickering & Chatto for their unfailing support.

LIST OF CONTRIBUTORS

Federico Barbiellini Amidei is an Economist at Banca d'Italia, Economic Research Department, Economic and Financial History Unit. Barbiellini Amidei obtained a degree in International Economics at Bocconi University, Milan (1993), and studied at Carnegie Mellon University, GSIA-PhD Program in Economics, Pittsburgh (1998–9). His main fields of interest are: economics of innovation, Italian economic history, FDI and MNC development, corporate finance and financial regulation in a historical perspective.

His recent publications include: F. Barbiellini Amidei and C. Antonelli, *The Dynamics of Knowledge Externalities. Localized Technological Change in Italy* (Cheltenham: Edward Elgar, 2011); F. Barbiellini Amidei and A. Goldstein, 'Corporate Europe in the US: Olivetti's Acquisition of Underwood Fifty Years On', *Business History* (2012); F. Barbiellini Amidei, J. Cantwell and A. Spadavecchia, 'Innovation and Foreign Technology' in G. Toniolo (ed.), *The Oxford Handbook of the Italian Economy Since Unification* (New York: Oxford University Press, 2013).

Piet Clement obtained his PhD in history from the University of Leuven (KU Leuven), with a study on Belgian public finance from 1830 to 1940. Since 1995 he has been employed at the Bank for International Settlements in Basel, Switzerland. His research interests span the history of international financial cooperation in the twentieth century, the history of central banking and colonial history of central Africa.

His recent publications include: G. Toniolo, with the assistance of P. Clement, *Central Bank Cooperation at the Bank for International Settlements, 1930–1973* (Cambridge: Cambridge University Press, 2005); C. Borio, G. Toniolo and P. Clement (eds), *Past and Future of Central Bank Cooperation* (Cambridge: Cambridge University Press, 2008); P. Clement, 'The Term "Macro-Prudential": Origins and Evolution', *BIS Quarterly Review* (March 2010).

Niall Ferguson, MA, D.Phil., is Laurence A. Tisch Professor of History at Harvard University and William Ziegler Professor of Business Administration at Harvard Business School. He is a Senior Research Fellow at Jesus College, Oxford University, and a Senior Fellow at the Hoover Institution, Stanford University. His research interests span world history, the history of finance and of empire and conflict. He is a prolific commentator of contemporary politics and economics, a regular contributor to television and radio and a contributing editor for the *Financial Times*.

His recent publications include: N. Ferguson, *Empire: The Rise and Demise of the British World Order and the Lessons for Global Power* (London: Basic Books, 2004); N. Ferguson, *The Ascent of Money: A Financial History of the World* (New York: Penguin Press, 2008); N. Ferguson, *High Financier: The Lives and Time of Siegmund Warburg* (New York: Penguin Press, 2010).

Claire Giordano has studied International Economics and Economics-Quantitative Methods at the University of Rome Tor Vergata. Since 2008 she has worked as an economist at the Research Department of the Bank of Italy, in the Economic and Financial History Division until 2012, and now currently in the Economic Outlook Division. Her research topics are productivity and economic growth, trade and competitiveness, economic and financial history. Her most recent peer-reviewed publications are: 'A Tale of Two Fascisms: Labour Productivity Growth and Competition Policy in Italy, 1911–1951', with F. Giugliano, *Explorations in Economic History* (forthcoming); 'Productivity', with S. Broadberry and F. Zollino, in G. Toniolo (ed.), *The Oxford Handbook of the Italian Economy Since Unification* (New York: Oxford University Press, 2013); 'The Italian Industrial Great Depression: Fascist Wage and Price Policies', with G. Piga and G. Trovato, *Macroeconomic Dynamics* (2004); 'Does Economic Theory Matter in Shaping Banking Regulation? A Case-study of Italy (1861–1936)', with A. Gigliobianco, *Accounting, Economics and Law*, 2:1 (2012).

Harold James was educated at Cambridge University, UK, where he obtained his PhD in Economic History in 1982. He is the Claude and Lore Kelly Professor in European Studies and Professor of History and International Affairs at the Woodrow Wilson School, Princeton University, where he has taught since 1986. His research interests span financial history and crises, international cooperation, European political history, modern history of Germany. His recent publications include: H. James, *Europe Reborn: A History 1914–2000* (London: Longman Pearson, 2003); H. James, *The Roman Predicament: How the Rules of International Order create the Politics of Empire* (Princeton, NJ: Princeton University Press, 2006); H. James, *Making the European Monetary Union* (Cambridge, MA: Belknap Press of Harvard University Press, 2012).

Ivo Maes holds a MSc in Economics from the London School of Economics and obtained his PhD in Economics from the University of Leuven (KU Leuven).

He is a Senior Advisor at the Research Department of the National Bank of Belgium and a Professor at the Université Catholique de Louvain (Robert Triffin Chair) and at the IHEC Brussels Management School. His research interests include the process of European monetary integration, macro-economic governance in the European Union, European financial integration and the history of economic thought.

His recent publications include: I. Maes, *Economic Thought and the Making of European Monetary Union, Selected Essays of Ivo Maes* (London: Edward Elgar, 2002); I. Maes, *Half a Century of European Financial Integration. From the Rome Treaty to the 21st Century* (Brussels: Mercatorfonds, 2007); I. Maes, *A Century of Macroeconomic and Monetary Thought at the National Bank of Belgium*, (Brussels: National Bank of Belgium, 2010).

Joke Mooij obtained a PhD in economic history at the University of Tilburg, the Netherlands (1988). She currently works as company historian at Rabobank Nederland. Previously, she was a researcher in economic and financial history at the Netherlands Bank, Amsterdam. Her research interests include banking history and the history of payment systems in the Netherlands.

Her recent publications include: J. Mooij and H. Prast, 'A Brief History of the Institutional Design of Banking Supervision in the Netherlands', in *Research Series Supervision*, 48 (Amsterdam: De Nederlandsche Bank, 2002); J. Mooij, 'Rabobank, An Innovative Dutch Bank: Automation and Payments Instruments, 1945–2000', in B. Batiz-Lazo, J. C. Maixé-Altés and P. Thomes (eds), *Technological Innovation in Retail Finance* (London: Routledge, 2011); and J. Mooij and W. Boonstra (eds), *Raiffeisen's Footprint, The Cooperative Way of Banking* (Amsterdam: VU University Press, 2012).

Lodewijk Petram studied finance (MSc, 2004) and early modern history (MA, 2006) at the University of Amsterdam. In 2011, he obtained his PhD in history at the same university with a thesis on the development of the world's first stock exchange: the market for VOC (Dutch East India Company) shares in seventeenth-century Amsterdam. He was a visiting scholar at Utrecht University in 2008–9.

His recent publications includes: L. Petram, *The World's First Stock Exchange* (New York: Columbia University Press, 2014).

Tobias Straumann studied history in Bielefeld, Paris and Zurich. His PhD dissertation investigated the growing cooperation between the Federal Institute of Technology in Zurich and the chemical industry in Basel from 1860 to 1920. Currently he is a lecturer at the History Department at the University of Zurich and at the Economics Department at the University of Basel. His research interests include European monetary and financial history, the history of city-states and the history of Swiss multinational companies.

His recent publications include: T. Straumann, 'Rule rather than Exception: Brüning's Fear of Devaluation in Comparative Perspective', *Journal of Contemporary History*, 44: 4 (October 2009), pp. 603–17; A. Ritschl and T. Straumann, 'Business Cycles and Economic Policy, 1914–1945', in S. Broadberry and K. O'Rourke (eds), *The Cambridge Economic History of Modern Europe* (Cambridge and New York: Cambridge University Press, 2010), vol. 2; and T. Straumann, *Fixed Ideas of Money: Small States and Exchange Rate Regimes in Twentieth-Century Europe* (Cambridge: Cambridge University Press, 2010).

Adair Turner has studied history and economics at Gonville and Caius College, Cambridge. He is a visiting professor at the London School of Economics and at Cass Business School, City University. He has previously held senior functions in McKinsey and Company, as Director General of the Confederation of British Industry, with Merrill Lynch Europe and with Standard Chartered Bank. Since 2005 he has been a member of the House of Lords. He was Chairman of the Financial Services Authority (FSA) from September 2008 to March 2013.

His recent publications include: A. Turner, *Just Capital, The Liberal Economy* (London: Pan Books, 2002); A. Turner, A. Haldane, et al., *The Future of Finance, The LSE Report* (London: London School of Economics and Political Science, 2010); and A. Turner, *Economics After the Crisis: Objectives and Means* (Cambridge: MIT Press, 2012).

Herman Van der Wee obtained his PhD in history at the University of Leuven (KU Leuven). He is a Professor Emeritus at the University of Leuven (Chair of Economic History). He has been a fellow and visiting professor at numerous institutions, among them at Princeton University, at the University of California Berkeley and at University of Paris-IV (Sorbonne). He has received honorary PhDs from the Catholic University of Brussels and the University of Leicester. His research interests cover social and economic history of the late Middle Ages and early modern times, banking history from the Middle Ages to the present, and history of the world economy since 1945.

His recent publications include: H. Van der Wee, with G. Kurgan-Van Hentenryk, *A History of European Banking* (Antwerp: Mercatorfonds, 2000); H. Van der Wee, 'Economic History: its Past, Present and Future', in *European Review*, Academia Europaea, 15:1 (2007); H. Van der Wee and M. Verbreyt, *A Small Nation in the Turmoil of the Second World War* (Leuven: Leuven University Press, 2009).

Welf Werner obtained his PhD in Economics from the Freie Universitaet Berlin. He is Professor of International Economics at Jacobs University, Bremen. Previously, he has held positions at the John F. Kennedy Institute in Berlin, Harvard University and the School of Advanced International Studies (Johns

Hopkins University). His research interests include international trade, Atlantic economic history, European integration and social policies.

His recent publications include: W. Werner, *Handelspolitik für Finanzdienste* (Baden-Baden: Nomos, 2004); W. Werner, 'Hurricane Betsy and the Malfunctioning of the London Reinsurance Market: An Analysis of Transatlantic Reinsurance Trade', *Financial History Review*, 14/1 (April 2007), pp. 7–28; W. Werner, 'Globalization, Social Movement and the Labor Market: A Transatlantic Perspective', J. Ahrens, R. Caspers and J. Weingarth (eds), *Good Governance in the 21st Century: Conflict, Institutional Change and Development in the Era of Globalization* (Cheltenham: Edward Elgar Publishing, 2011), pp. 235–63.

William R. White was educated at the University of Windsor and the University of Manchester. He worked as an economist, first at the Bank of England and then at the Bank of Canada, where he became the head of the Research Department. He was appointed Deputy Governor of the Bank of Canada in 1988. He joined the Bank for International Settlements in Basel in 1994 and was BIS Economic Adviser from 1995 until 2008. Since 2008 he has been Chair of the OECD Economic and Development Review Committee.

His recent publications include: W. R. White, 'Is Price Stability Enough?', *Working Papers*, 205 (Basel: BIS, 2006); W. R. White, 'Should Monetary Policy "Lean or Clean"?', *Globalization and Monetary Policy Institute Working Paper*, 34, Federal Reserve Bank of Dallas (2009); W. R. White, 'Is Monetary Policy a Science? The Interaction of Theory and Practice over the Last 50 Years', SUERF The European Money and Finance Forum, *The Financial Reconstruction of Europe* (Paris: Larcier, 2013), pp. 73–115.

LIST OF FIGURES AND TABLES

Figure 2.1: Five-day period share transfers, VOC Amsterdam chamber, 1609   14

Figure 2.2: Five-day period share transfers, VOC Amsterdam chamber, 1639   15

Figure 3.1: Member banks CCB and CCRB, 1899–1939   42

Figure 4.1: Technical and financial results of Swiss Re   59

Figure 6.1: Annual inflation rates, selected OECD countries, 1970–9   94

Figure 6.2: UK house prices, annual percentage change, 1970–9   96

Figure 6.3: *Financial Times* All-Share Index, nominal and real   97

Figure 6.4: Real net profits at Mercury Securities, 1954–94 (pounds of 1954)   103

Table 2.1: Court of Holland, extended sentences   34

Table 2.2: Court of Holland, Case files   34

Table 2.3: High Council, Extended sentences   35

Table 3.1: Development of member banks of CCB and CCRB, 1899–1936   42

Table 3.2: Distribution of local member banks by province, 1929 and 1939   45

Table 3.3: Average number of members per co-operative agricultural bank, 1905–40   45

Table 3.4: CCB's problem banks list, 1930–7   48

Table 4.1: Composition of Swiss Re's assets   60

Table 4.2: Real gain, reported gain, hidden reserves and dividends   62

Table 6.1: Merchant bank balance sheets, millions of pounds, 1973–7   103

NOTE ON THE TEXT

Currency terminology in this volume reflects the differences in the monetary systems of the various time periods discussed. Thus, both *f* and NLG are used to represent Dutch guilders, and CHF is used in addition to Swiss francs.

FOREWORD: FINANCIAL CRISES – WILL IT BE DIFFERENT NEXT TIME?

Ivo Maes

The contributions in this volume reflect not only on the history of financial crises, but also on the present financial crisis. Past, present and future flow into one another. It is a clear demonstration of the policy relevance of research in the area of economic and financial history. Two fundamental questions can be asked about any financial crisis: What went wrong? And, who is to blame?

So, what went wrong? Several factors must be advanced, some of which can be regarded as old and familiar drivers of financial crises, while others are rather new factors. The credit cycle is a familiar phenomenon in a capitalist economy. Easy money, associated with loose monetary policy, is also a familiar phenomenon. Together, these two factors may, to a significant extent, explain the real estate cycle, an important element of the present crisis.

Financial innovation clearly played a role, and such innovation is certainly not a new phenomenon. The only thing that was perhaps new this time around was the sheer volume of the transactions and the application of highly sophisticated technology. The hype around financial innovation culminated in the phrase 'this time it is different'. An illusion that is all too familiar for those who have studied financial crises throughout history. Once again, this time it was not different, and the bubble inevitably exploded, as it has before.

This time the innovations, which were inflating the bubble, were at the heart of the financial system. The bursting of the bubble demonstrated, in a very dramatic way, the inherent fragility of banks and the financial system. Adair Turner once referred to 'the secret' that Bank of England Governor Mervyn King shared with him over a dinner: 'banks are very risky'.

The inherently risky nature of the bank's intermediation and transformation function comes clearly to the fore in this volume. The importance of trust cannot be over-emphasized. Tobias Straumann's study of Swiss Re in the Great Depression – a financial company that used its hidden reserves to show constant profit results in order to stabilize trust – is in marked contrast to the present-day emphasis on transparency (Chapter 4).

Another point worth making is that economic crises, which are associated with banking crises, are significantly worse: the impact on the real economy is harder and lasts longer.

Turning to the second issue – who is to blame? – several culprits can be and have been advanced: corporate governance, regulators, central banks, governments and markets. However, there is certainly no consensus on the relative importance of these different actors and factors. This is not just bad news; it shows the importance of further research in understanding which circumstances different factors are likely to play a more prominent role in.

Corporate governance has been a fashionable issue for many years now. As human beings, including those working in financial institutions, are at least partially driven by greed, good corporate governance is important. The theme resurfaces in a number of chapters in this volume. Lodewijk Petram discusses the merits and limits of self-governance in relation to contract enforcement on the Amsterdam stock exchange in the seventeenth century (Chapter 2). Joke Mooij highlights the somewhat alternative governance culture in cooperative banking (Chapter 3).

Regulation too is a recurring theme here. It is important to clarify what purpose regulation is supposed to serve: are there prudential reasons, or re-distributional ones, or is it a moral issue?

Central banks have shared substantially in the blame for the current crisis, especially in view of their easy money policies. These have fuelled the traditional credit cycle, with booms and busts in the real estate sector.

Finally, as history demonstrates, the respective roles of governments and markets in this as in any financial crisis merits close scrutiny. Normally crises lead to a swing in the pendulum, resulting in more government intervention or in a greater role for market forces. The present crisis, however, has exposed serious problems both in the ability of governments and in the capabilities of markets to deal with such crises. Governments, in part due to financial innovations, were not able to control markets; and markets failed to control governments and allowed sovereign borrowing to increase.

The current financial crisis begs the question: could it have been foreseen, let alone prevented? Many may have been aware that a crisis was coming, but very few – be it academics, bankers or policymakers – could have predicted its scale. Among the few people who are considered the Cassandras who warned of the coming crisis, one might single out Nouriel Roubini, Alexandre Lamfalussy and Bill White. Typical for all three of them was a wider historical perspective. Roubini's and Lamfalussy's experience has been marked by the Latin American debt crisis of the early 1980s. White was very much under the impression of the Japanese experience of the 1990s. This broader historical approach has allowed them to take a step back. The three were marked by extreme experiences whereby bust had followed on boom. It made them very reticent to buy-in to the new paradigm of 'this time it is different'.

So, what lessons does history hold? We all know that history does not repeat itself. However, it can contribute to a broader perspective which can help us to see parallels and differences and to identify structural changes. What 'policy conclusions' can be drawn from this? We may at least try to avoid the mistakes of the past. Policymakers must find a consensus that can contribute to a more robust, or at least less fragile, economic policy framework. A very basic starting point must be the recognition that banks are inherently risky. Actions in different areas will have to be undertaken or stepped up. Strengthening corporate governance is a clear priority. Also an increase in banks' capital and liquidity ratio's figures prominently on the reform agenda. Moreover, a more countercyclical capital ratio framework is required. This should, to a certain degree, have an element of automaticity, while there might also be a role for independent boards.

Why was this not done earlier? Surely, different elements have blinded both financial institutions and regulators: (1) banks were happy, as they were accumulating profits; (2) central banks were happy as their primary objective of price stability was, more or less, achieved; (3) like in other booms, there was the (faulty) opinion of 'this time it is different'; and (4) economic theory was based on analytical frameworks where history was absent and crises could not happen. So explaining, or even acknowledging them, was not possible.

Where does all this leave economic and financial history? Personally, I would conclude that the political economy of economic and financial reform merits a very prominent place on the future research agenda of historians and economists alike.

The views expressed are those of the author and do not necessarily reflect those of the National Bank of Belgium.

1 FINANCIAL INNOVATION, REGULATION AND CRISES: A HISTORICAL VIEW

Piet Clement, Harold James and Herman Van der Wee

In public opinion, as in much of the academic literature, the financial crisis that started in 2007–8 has been blamed on financial innovations gone awry.[1] In a nutshell, the by-now conventional account runs like this: spurred on by a cheap-money environment, the financial boom in the years prior to the crisis generated an over-issue of new and complex financial products, such as credit default swaps (CDS), off-balance-sheet derivatives and, infamously, subprime mortgages packaged in mortgage-backed securities and collateralized debt obligations (CDO).[2] The main problem of this type of financial innovation has been that the underlying risks of these novel products were often incorrectly priced or not transparent to the ultimate creditor. This fundamental misalignment infected the global financial system on an unprecedented scale, and eventually proved lethal once the boom ended and vulnerabilities became apparent. The generalized loss of confidence and the collective run for safety (*de-leveraging* in the jargon; i.e. financial institutions' attempt to get rid of high-risk, toxic assets and to improve capital/asset ratios) have sparked a global financial crisis, which in terms of its severity and longevity has been the worst since the Great Depression.

It is no surprise that the current crisis has led to renewed interest in the work of the American economist Hyman Minsky (1919–96). Minsky argued that booms associated with financial innovation can easily lead to speculative eupho-ria, increased financial fragility and eventual collapse (the financial instability hypothesis).[3] One of the key problems is that financial innovations not only help to spread risks – thereby increasing the economy's overall capacity to bear risks – but often enough also have the potential, partly due to their complexity, to obscure the real, underlying risks.[4] That happens, for instance, when risk diversi-fication is achieved by shifting risks to naïve investors, who face insurmountable information asymmetries. In the recent crisis, such risk transfer 'proved to be the shell game of credit markets. A *short con*, quick and easy to pull off. Financial innovation did not decrease risk but increased risk significantly in complex ways.'[5]

New financial products that claim to spread risks more evenly are easily perceived as safe. Rating agencies play an important role in this process: although these new products are untested in times of market stress, they nevertheless receive a clean bill of health in the form of a triple-A rating. The underlying risks are still present, but are largely ignored.[6] Moreover, while risks with a normal distribution can be mathematically modelled and thus factored in in the pricing of financial products, uncertainty, due to the use of systematic errors, cannot. In a boom market, this potential weakness of new financial products is further compounded by their over-issue and financial institutions' over-leveraging. Because they are supposedly risk-free and at the same time promise high returns, there is a high demand for and excessive issuance of such new products.[7] Over-issuing finally contributes to a loss of confidence and a collapse. The end result is often that the economic and social value the initial innovation may have had is wiped out altogether. Some even go so far as to argue that many of the recent financial innovations had little or no economic or social value to begin with, but were mainly driven by an insatiable market appetite or, worse, merely aimed 'to give banks new instruments to allow them to profit at the expense of unsophisticated individuals and households'.[8] Indeed, Paul Volcker once famously remarked that the only socially valuable financial innovation of recent decades has been the automatic teller machine.

In short, the current crisis has cast financial innovation in a bad light. However, this should not mean that it is necessarily or always a bad or dangerous thing. In fact, financial innovation per se is not inherently bad or good. It is the use that is made of it that matters. As Michael Haliassos puts it: 'financial products have something in common with building materials. One can use a brick to build a house or to smash a window'.[9] In economic literature, financial innovation is most commonly seen as a positive force. There are plenty of examples in which financial innovation has played the positive role it is supposed to play.

First, much of the financial innovation over the past centuries has helped to expand access to credit for households and firms (and government), by tapping into new sources of funding.

Secondly, many financial innovations have indeed been aimed at improving the spread of underlying risks – market risks, credit risks, liquidity risks – and have been successful in doing so. They have thereby enhanced the capacity of the financial system and of the economy as a whole to take on more risk without necessarily jeopardizing overall stability. A good example of an institutional innovation that has achieved precisely that, is the introduction of limited liability in the nineteenth century.[10] A good example of a successful financial product innovation would be exchange-traded forward contracts (futures), which first appeared in Japan in the 1730s (Dōjima Rice Exchange, Osaka) and which became fashionable in the sector of commodity trading as of the late nineteenth century.

Third, financial innovations have tended to increase returns earned by the intermediaries who market them, and thus have often had a positive impact on the overall profitability of the financial sector. Indeed, in the decades preceding the 2007–8 crisis, banks increased their returns considerably thanks to the development of a structured credit market (credit derivatives, structured investment vehicles, collateralized debt obligations), which allowed them to move capital intensive assets off balance sheet through the direct pairing of non-bank liquidity providers (fixed income investors) with corporate and sovereign borrowers.[11] It should be immediately added that precisely because of these higher returns the incentive or justification for pushing such innovations and high-risk activities ever further proved irresistible, often enough beyond what was sustainable over the longer term.

For all these reasons, and notwithstanding repeated excesses, a strong case can be made that, on balance, financial innovation has been a positive force for economic growth, wealth creation and development globally. Joseph Schumpeter has argued that many of the technological and commercial innovations of the nineteenth and twentieth centuries would not have been possible without financial innovations such as the joint-stock company and limited liability.[12]

Given the apparent Jekyll and Hyde quality of financial innovation, the key question seems to be: how can we ensure that financial innovation remains a force for the good and prevent it from going awry? Proper risk management and regulation may seem the most logical answers. Risk management – be it in the form of collateral, hedging, hidden reserves or the sophisticated types of risk modelling currently in vogue – is at least as old as the financial system itself. Regulation too has a long history, for instance in the form of religious interdictions on usury. If unregulated financial innovations are an important cause of financial crises, it would appear reasonable to aim for tighter, or at least more effective, regulation. However, due to the very nature of innovation, regulation will practically always be behind the curve – that is to say, it will try to regulate to avoid a repetition of what already went wrong rather than to prevent things that still may go wrong.[13] There is a race between financial innovators and regulators that the regulators will always lose, 'but it matters how much they lose by'.[14] Tighter supervision and new regulations typically aim to address the deficiencies – perceived or real – of loose or outdated regulation. But regulatory reform may also hold the risk of over-regulation – particularly when it is undertaken under the impression of a severe crisis. Over-regulation tends to stifle innovation and therefore might have negative welfare-effects. In short, the difficulty is to strike the right balance. It should be clear that there are no easy fixes in this area.

A financial crisis and the almost inevitable regulatory responses to it, have longer-term effects when they shape the future path of financial development. New risk management strategies, adopted to contain a crisis situation, may in turn prompt financial innovations in the quest to achieve a better spread and reduction of risks. Regulation may block undesirable developments and undo earlier innovations, and thereby elicit new ones and open up new trajectories.

Finally, the long and winding road of financial development is marked out not only by innovation, crisis and regulation, but also by the financial policies – monetary, fiscal, institutional – pursued by central banks and governments. The result of these interlocking, and often conflicting, events, influences and interests is that the financial system does not develop linearly, but rather along a tortuous, often unpredictable, path, with many ups and downs and characterized by sometimes violent pendulum swings between financial repression and financial liberalization.

This volume explores a few stretches of this road, highlighting many of the key issues in the dynamic relationship between financial innovations, crises, risk management and regulation. When or under what conditions are financial product innovations most likely to occur? And, equally important, what makes them stick? (Chapter 2) How and when do institutional innovations arise and what is their longer-term effect? Do they give rise to alternative models in financial development that tend to lead to a better (or worse?) risk mitigation? (Chapters 3 and 5) Under what circumstances can financial innovations become a threat to financial stability? Does history suggest that there is an almost inevitable sequence from financial innovation to 'irrational exuberance' (to borrow Alan Greenspan's famous phrase) to crisis? Or does one rather have to look to misguided policies and failing oversight to explain why financial crises occur over and over again? (Chapter 6) Finally, once a financial crisis has broken, what strategies have been adopted in the past to deal with it – at company, national and international level? How have companies managed the fall-out of severe financial crises? (Chapter 4) How have national and international authorities reacted, and what has been the longer-term impact of their actions on regulation and, eventually, on further innovation? (Chapters 5, 6 and 7) Most chapters look at historical episodes of financial innovation and crisis, but there is also a conscious attempt, particularly in the final section of this book (Chapters 8 and 9), to reflect, from a historical perspective, on the current crisis.

In Chapter 2, Lodewijk Petram deals with a financial innovation that has had a durable institutional impact. Petram traces the origins of the secondary shares market to the Dutch Republic in the early seventeenth century. Secondary trading in shares of the Dutch East India Company (VOC) developed in a full-fledged financial market that allowed investors to actively manage their portfolio and thereby to diversify risks. The consistent enforcement of the related contracts through the courts was decisive in making this innovation stick. This created a larger measure of legal certainty, which reduced risk and transaction costs and consequently persuaded more investors to become active in this new market. Drawing on extensive research in the original court records,

Petram demonstrates how the Court of Holland effectively built the world's first securities law. This legal framework also included regulatory aspects, for instance through the prohibition of short-selling in 1610. What is interesting to see is that the gradual clarification of this legal framework also influenced private enforcement mechanisms on the secondary and sub-markets. Such mechanisms typically included some form of self-regulation, for instance through peer pressure or through trading clubs submitting voluntarily to adjudication in case of disputes. In short, the successful emergence of a secondary market for VOC shares and the legal framework that was created around it resulted in a relatively stable system of shares trading that enabled the VOC to meet its high capital requirements and thrive. As such it became a model to be copied.

Joke Mooij (Chapter 3) offers another story of successful financial innovation in the Netherlands, but in a very different time period and context. The creation of a network of co-operative agricultural banks in the Netherlands during the early twentieth century not only facilitated access to credit and financial services for small-scale farmers, but also made the individual, small-scale banking institutions themselves more resilient in the face of adverse conditions. This was, Mooij argues, largely because of an idiosyncratic business model, characterized by an intimate knowledge of the customer base and a built-in, high degree of mutual solidarity, whereby the network took responsibility for the individual members whenever they got into trouble. In exchange for this solidarity, a relatively high degree of centralization, strong internal safeguards and an embryonic form of prudential supervision were accepted by the participating banks from early on. These factors allowed the co-operative agricultural banking sector in the Netherlands to get through the Great Depression without any significant bankruptcies and with its market share largely intact. However, such an outcome was not a given: in Belgium, where the co-operative banking sector operated on a similar model, its evolution during the 1920s and 1930s was, by contrast, disastrous, before making a remarkable come-back after the Second World War.[15] In other words, institutional robustness is no absolute guarantee, and particular circumstances, short-term business decisions and investment practices matter a lot. Nevertheless, the Dutch case, as analysed by Mooij, provides a good example of an institutional innovation that has been successful in reducing risk.

Institutional innovation may have been helpful in mitigating risks in times of crisis in the case of the Dutch co-operative banks, but Tobias Straumann highlights other, less orthodox, strategies of risk management (Chapter 4). Straumann is puzzled by the fact that Swiss Re, one of the world's leading reinsurance companies, got through the Great Depression of the 1930s seemingly unscathed. Did Swiss Re owe this outcome to a far-sighted management taking timely action to counteract the fall-out from the crisis? Or was it thanks to the implementation of a timely strategic re-orientation of the company's business model? Based on a thorough analysis of the unpublished records of Swiss Re,

Straumann comes to a very different conclusion. The truth of the matter is that Swiss Re managed to weather the storm only thanks to the high amount of hidden reserves accumulated over the preceding decades. In that way, the company was able to report a positive result and to maintain a solid market reputation in spite of the underlying financial results being catastrophic. In other words, during the 1930s, hidden reserves allowed Swiss Re to absorb a major macroeconomic shock. This was not possible during the 2008–9 financial crisis: the primacy of shareholder value and the necessity to create full transparency over the accounts had long since done away with hidden reserves. As a result, Swiss Re took the full brunt of the crisis and suffered accordingly. In that sense, Straumann offers a cautionary tale on how the markets react to the revealed positions of financial firms – even, or particularly, when these prove to be incomplete or unreliable – and, more generally, on how the financial sector interacts with the real economy.

A severe financial crisis, such as the Great Depression or the current crisis, always produces a political and regulatory backlash, particularly when the crisis can be and is widely blamed on financial innovations – be it at the product or institutional level – having gone wrong. However, the regulatory responses are far from unambiguous. In Chapter 5, Federico Barbiellini Amidei and Claire Giordano illustrate this point vividly by comparing the re-design of the banking industry in the US and in Italy in the wake of the 1930s crisis. They convincingly refute the received wisdom that the US Banking Acts of 1933–5 and the Italian Banking Act of 1936 responded in a broadly similar fashion by splitting commercial from investment banking. In fact, both sets of legislation differed substantially in that they sought to address very different problems ('evils'). While the US legislator was mainly concerned with the risks posed by commercial banks' direct and active role in the stock exchange market, the Italian legislator primarily sought to address the problems caused by the long-term debt and equity stakes in industrial firms held by Italian commercial banks. This is a classic story of political economy and (attempted) regulatory capture. At the same time, it demonstrates that while regulatory responses to crises tend to cut off a particular path of future development, they can, at the same time, lay the foundation for a different development path (which, with time, may create new problems). Indeed, in both the US and Italy, the banking legislation resulting from the 1930s crisis profoundly changed the financial sector landscape, and for a surprisingly long period of time – until the 1990s.

An alternative vision of the potential link between financial innovation and crisis and the subsequent 'need' for regulation is offered in Niall Ferguson's contribution (Chapter 6). Ferguson strongly cautions against the idea that the supposed dangers of financial innovation can be or should be reined in by stricter regulation. This idea, he argues, stems from an overly nostalgic interpretation of the post-war Bretton Woods era, in which tight regulation and controls made for very conservative – even 'boring' – but also very safe banking. However, Ferguson argues, the UK's experience in the 1970s belies the notion that regulation is the best guarantee to prevent financial innovation from going wild, and thus to preclude a financial crisis. The 1970s were still a highly regulated decade in British banking, but nevertheless spawned a major banking crisis, a stock-market crash, a real estate bubble and double-digit inflation. Recounting the history of the City's most innovative bank during the post-war decades, S. G. Warburg & Co., Ferguson concludes that it is not deregulation or financial innovation that bears the blame for the financial instability and crisis witnessed in the 1970s, but rather the misguided monetary and fiscal policies of the central banks and governments of the time. The same conclusion, he contends, applies to the current financial and economic crisis, which has been the result not of financial innovations gone awry, but rather of a toxic combination of 'imprudently low interest rates and unjustifiably large public borrowing'.

However, regulatory changes are not only the direct result of crisis. They may also be triggered by the need to meet new institutional challenges. This is the underlying argument in Welf Werner's contribution (Chapter 7). Werner investigates how the move towards free trade and open borders since the Second World War has affected the financial services industry. Financial market liberalization and the cross-border integration of financial markets pose particular challenges which seem to set them apart from trade liberalization in the goods markets. The key reason for this, Werner argues, is that financial services liberalization and integration need not only to secure open markets, but also to guarantee the overall stability of the system. In other words, liberalization of the financial sector, and the innovations which this entails, should be managed or steered in such a way that they do not lead to a crisis. To avoid this from happening, Werner contends, regulation and supervision ought logically to be exercised at an international level too. But in reality, national authorities, foremost central banks and regulatory bodies, have jealously defended domestic authority over regulation and supervision. Harmonization of prudential regulation, while desirable, has proven a hard nut to crack.

The different case studies brought together in this volume allow one to step back from the fray of today's news headlines and to look for parallels and differences between earlier episodes of financial crisis and instability. Still, it remains to be seen how and to what extent history can inform the current debates. In the final section of this volume, two experts – practitioners from the world of central banking and financial supervision – shine their light on the current financial crisis.

From his unique position as chair of the UK Financial Services Authority (FSA), Lord Adair Turner provides a sweeping review of the current financial crisis, with ample references to history (Chapter 8). Financial innovations play a key role in his account. On the back of financial innovations, the financial intensity and complexity of developed economies have grown ever more rapidly. While the real economic benefits of this evolution remain disputed, Turner is convinced that it has led to increased volatility in financial markets and, hence, to a heightened risk of financial crisis. The challenge, then, is to strike the right balance in regulating the financial sector so that it can continue to play its crucial role and provide economic value added, while at the same time safeguarding the longer-term stability of the system. Such a stance points to the need for a policy response, which in Turner's view should focus on three broad areas: bank capital and liquidity standards, the very structure of the banking system, and the development of a truly macroprudential approach that factors in the overall stability of the financial system. Moreover, he stresses that 'the history of financial systems and financial markets has a crucial role to play' in framing such reforms. Indeed, it may have been more than a lucky coincidence that Ben Bernanke, Chairman of the Federal Reserve Board and one of the key monetary policy decision makers when the crisis broke in 2007–8, had in a previous life written extensively about the Great Depression of the 1930s.

Finally, Bill White, currently at the OECD and the former Economic Adviser of the Bank for International Settlements, was one of the few Cassandras who, starting in the early 2000s, consistently warned of the oncoming crisis. In Chapter 9, he discusses a number of hotly debated topics that all have to do with improving regulation to avoid or mitigate future crises, without, however, choking off financial innovation in the process. He focuses his attention in particular on the too-big-to-fail problem, which played such a major role in the 2008–9 banking crisis. He also discusses whether lax financial regulation was to blame for the crisis, and whether or not policymakers are now overreacting, with the risk that this will lead to regulatory overkill.

From the perspective of the current crisis, it may seem self-evident that there is, or at least can be, a strong relationship between financial innovations, (failed) regulation and financial crisis. This is certainly a relevant observation given the potential consequences of a severe systemic crisis. The Great Depression has taught us that a financial crisis like the one we are living through today might lead to a 'renationalisation of economics and politics' and a reversal of the globalization that we have come to accept as the normal state of affairs.[16] The mere fact that it took a crisis of this amplitude to remind us of these seemingly self-evident facts is testimony to our capacity to forget or ignore key lessons from history.[17] That is in itself a good reason to continue to study historical episodes of financial innovation, risk management, regulation and crisis. The study of financial history, as Barry Eichengreen puts it, should enable 'financial market participants and policymakers ... to look beyond recent events; history will remind them that what goes up can come down'.[18] This volume aims to contribute to such a reflection.

The views expressed are those of the authors and do not necessarily reflect those of the Bank for International Settlements.

2 CONTRACT ENFORCEMENT ON THE WORLD'S FIRST STOCK EXCHANGE

Lodewijk Petram

Introduction

After the founding of the Dutch East India Company (VOC, 1602), a thriving secondary market for company shares developed. The VOC was certainly not the first company in history that issued shares, but now for the first time all necessary preconditions for the development of a secondary market were present: the company stock was sufficiently large, a high number of shareholders subscribed to the stock,[1] there was a clear rule for the transfer of ownership of a share, and, perhaps most importantly, the company would stay in business for almost two centuries.[2] This was a major difference with earlier equity-financed companies. These companies, which were also for the most part shipping companies, usually existed for the duration of a single voyage only; when the ships returned from their destination, the company was liquidated and the proceeds were distributed among the shareholders.

It is not hard to see how the longevity of the VOC created an incentive for its shareholders to occasionally transfer a share. The majority of shareholders did not want their money to be locked up in the company for an indefinite period of time and they therefore traded their shares if, for example, need for cash forced them to do so. This is exactly what shareholders did in the first decade of the seventeenth century. The bookkeeper of the Amsterdam chamber of the VOC registered 368 share transfers in 1609. Figure 2.1 shows the value of these transfers and how they were spread over the year. Comparing this graph to Figure 2.2, which depicts the number and nominal value of share transfers in 1639, yields one obvious conclusion: the number of share transfers per year had almost doubled. This is only part of the story, however, since the number of active accounts[3] was lower in 1639 than in 1609.[4] Put another way, fewer shareholders now accounted for almost twice the number of share transfers.

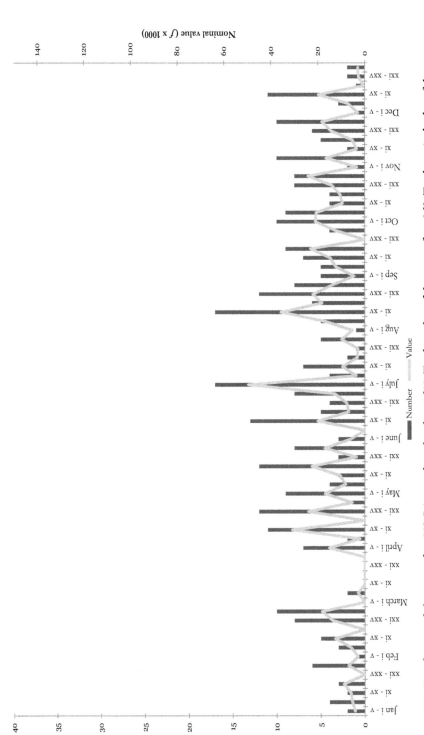

Figure 2.1: Five-day period share transfers, VOC Amsterdam chamber, 1609. Total number of share transfers: 368. Total nominal value of share transfers: ƒ785,690. Source: Nationaal Archief, The Hague, 1.04.02, Verenigde Oost-Indische Compagnie – VOC, 1.04.02, inv. nr 7066.

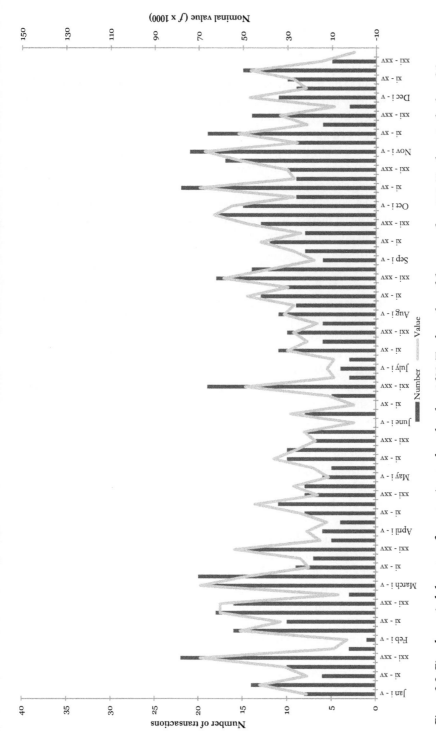

Figure 2.2: Five-day period share transfers, VOC Amsterdam chamber, 1639. Total number of share transfers: 713. Total nominal value of share transfers: *f*2,205,330. Source: Nationaal Archief, The Hague, 1.04.02, Verenigde Oost-Indische Compagnie – VOC, 1.04.02, inv. nr 7068.

A closer look at the transfer registers reveals that a small number of very active shareholders accounted for a large proportion of the total number of share transfers. In 1641, for example, the thirteen most active shareholders (with at least ten sales and ten purchases registered on their account) were involved in almost a third of all share transfers. These traders had short investment horizons; they aimed to make profits by quickly buying and selling shares.[5] Interestingly, the stock jobbers were largely new entrants to the market – they were not the same people who had dominated the market in the first decade of the seventeenth century. Most strikingly, Portuguese Jews started participating in the market from around 1640 onwards and they soon dominated the market. The transition to stock jobbing changed the nature of the stock exchange. The secondary market for shares developed from a by-product of equity-financed companies into a full-fledged financial market, which investors could use to quickly rebalance their portfolios in order to diversify risk.[6] The market thus started to resemble today's financial markets.

An active market will develop only if traders can be sure that their trades will be executed by the market.[7] A trader will be hesitant to enter into a transaction if his counterparty can renege on his obligations without suffering adverse effects. So, for the development of the secondary market for VOC shares, some kind of mechanism for contract enforcement had to be in effect. Fortunately, the Low Countries already had a long history of commercial contracting when share trading started in 1602, so merchants and legal institutions were experienced in enforcing commercial transactions.[8] Moreover, the legal system acknowledged its important role in the development of trade. In Antwerp, the commercial metropolis of the sixteenth century, legal institutions interacted with the merchant community and promoted the merchants' interests.[9]

Share trading did thus not emerge in a legal void. On the contrary, the legal principles that applied to the transactions on the share market were already in existence and hence the share transactions fitted into existing categories of commercial law. The laws that applied to the transfer of title of a share, for example, were the same as those that applied to the transfer of ownership of real estate – both were considered immovable goods under Dutch law.[10] However, not everything was clear from the start, as the large number of conflicts between share traders that ended up in lengthy court cases in the period before 1630 shows. For the period 1610–30, I have found thirty lawsuits dealing with share-trade-related court cases in the archives of the Court of Holland in The Hague.[11] This provincial court pronounced judgement in about 150 cases per year, which means that one per cent of the cases concerned share transactions.

After 1640, however, the ratio decreased to about one in every 500 lawsuits.[12] I will show in the first section of this chapter that in the earliest decades of the development of the secondary market for VOC shares, traders started litigation to test the bounds of the existing legal concepts. These litigants were convinced that there existed some space to manoeuvre within the rule of law. They were willing to enter into costly litigation – lawsuits before the appeal courts of Holland became especially costly if litigants kept adducing new evidence and appealing judgements[13] – that took up a great amount of effort; lawsuits that were ultimately brought before the Court of Holland could take anywhere between three-and-a-half and twelve years.[14]

From around 1640 onwards, however, traders no longer brought their share-trade-related conflicts before the higher courts. By then, the Court of Holland had pronounced judgement on all legal concepts that applied to the share trade. Henceforth, share traders could predict how the courts would decide in share-trade-related conflicts. Traders were no doubt abreast of the jurisprudence concerning the share trade and they regarded the Court of Holland as the authoritative institution regarding new interpretations of the law; they explicitly referred to earlier judgements of the Court of Holland if a new conflict arose.[15] The courts' jurisprudence can thus be regarded as securities law.

The legal certainty that emanated from these judgements reduced investors' hesitancy – smaller merchants and, most prominently, Portuguese Jews – to participate in the share trade. As a result of the establishment of a clear legal framework, the market grew considerably in size. Focusing on transaction costs can help to understand how legal certainty can persuade people to invest: the formation of a clear legal framework reduced the costs of protecting contractors' rights and also of costly enforcement of agreements by a third party, i.e. the court.[16]

However, the legal certainty only applied to part of the market: following the 1610 ban on short selling, shareholders were allowed to trade only shares they legally owned on the spot and forward markets.[17] The possibilities for growth were thus limited by the size of the VOC capital stock – the amount of legal shares available on the market. The sources clearly show that a number of traders performed far more transactions than their shareholdings would legally allow. Jacob Athias and Manuel Levy Duarte, for example, had monthly share turnovers on the forward market during the period 1683–4 of between ƒ200,000 and ƒ2,000,000.[18] At the same time, however, there were only very few mutations registered on their account in the capital book of the Amsterdam chamber and their nominal position never exceeded ƒ3,000. In June 1684, they liquidated their position.[19] Their forward trades generally netted out, so they did not take large short positions in the VOC, but their official ownership of shares was nevertheless insufficient to legally justify their forward sales. These were, in other words, short sales and would not be enforced by the courts. I will argue in the second section of this chapter that the participants of the forward market were aware of this. They therefore established a private enforcement mechanism that replaced the rule of law. This mechanism, which was in place in trading clubs – regular meetings where people gathered to trade shares – was based on the traders' reputations and the condition that each participant benefited from subordinating to it.

The line of argument is thus: court judgements in the first decades of the seventeenth century created a level of legal certainty that induced the entry to the market of new groups of traders. The subsequent growth could no longer fit within the legally approved boundaries of the market and created the need for a sub-market where a private enforcement mechanism was in force and where access restrictions made sure that only trustworthy traders could participate.

The two parts of this chapter build on two different fields of historiography. The first deals with the development of commercial law in north-western Europe and third-party enforcement of trade-related conflicts. In the province of Holland, the law consisted of a combination of Roman law and customary law, compiled by the famous jurist Hugo de Groot (Grotius).[20] Oscar Gelderblom has argued that this was not a static law. The *Hollandsche Consultatiën*, a seventeenth-century collection of legal advices compiled by jurists working for the provincial Court of Holland, show that this court based its judgements 'on a combination of Roman law, local and foreign customs, Habsburg ordinances, and Italian and Spanish mercantile law'.[21] It is therefore interesting to study the sentences of the Court of Holland in detail – in pronouncing judgements on share-trade-related court cases this court's judges drafted the world's first securities law. Stuart Banner has traced the origins of Anglo-American securities regulation from the eighteenth century onwards. He analysed attitudes towards the trade in securities and studied how these influenced the regulation of the trade. Banner found that although the societies and the authorities in England and the United States were often ill-disposed towards the trade in financial securities, leading to bans on the trade of specific derivatives, the courts kept enforcing the contracts. They based their judgements on general legal concepts rather than on the attitudes of the general public, thus giving legal protection to the trade.[22]

The second part focuses on private enforcement mechanisms. The most influential works on this topic have focused on international trade. The difficulty of monitoring business partners abroad required a high level of commitment by all partners involved. Avner Greif has shown for the eleventh-century trade between North Africa and Italy that traders organized themselves in coalitions. This coalition-forming created a situation in which even traders who did not know each other personally were willing to trade with one another. The system worked so well because all participants benefited from it.[23] The share market cannot be seen as an example of international trade, though. While foreign traders occasionally participated, the majority of the traders came from Amsterdam. But the trading community did not consist of a homogeneous group of traders either – particularly after the Sephardic community of Amsterdam started participating in the market from the 1640s onwards. Hence the forward market was characterized by a large heterogeneous group of traders who put very large amounts of money at stake. It is interesting to examine how they made sure that all members of the trading community lived up to their agreements.

Court cases form the most important source for this chapter's analysis. A short review of the procedure of civil litigation in the Dutch Republic is therefore indispensable. Conflicts concerning share transactions on the Amsterdam market would usually first come up before the local court of Amsterdam. The archives of this court have been lost, however, so my argument is based on the extended sentences that are available in the archives of the Court of Holland and – to a lesser extent – the High Council. The Court of Holland was the court of appeal for cases that had come up before one of the local courts in Holland. After this court had pronounced judgement, litigants could appeal to the High Council, but this court was neither more authoritative, nor more influential; the only difference was that the High Council also had jurisdiction over the province of Zeeland.[24]

The near total loss of the archives of the local court of Amsterdam is a pity, but these sources are not indispensable for the argument presented here, since my main interest concerns the development of jurisprudence on share trade. It is to be expected that the local court of Amsterdam could very well deal with most of the share-trade-related conflicts. There are indications that share traders went to the Amsterdam court to exact payment or delivery of a share from their counterparties,[25] but these were probably not the most interesting cases. However, if one of the parties was convinced that there were several possible interpretations of a lawsuit, he would appeal the judgement of the lower court to the Court of Holland. Hence, those cases are particularly important for a reconstruction of the development of a legal framework.

The procedure of litigation before the Court of Holland was as follows. The plaintiff first submitted a petition to the court, listing a short summary of the case and his principal arguments. The court then, provided that it had approved the petition, entered the case onto the scroll (*rol*), the list of cases to be dealt with by the court. Thereafter, the plaintiff could summon the defendant to appear in court. The plaintiff's solicitor then submitted his claim to the court, to which the defendant could respond within two weeks' time. Thereafter, both parties could submit a rejoinder, which could take another four weeks in total. Both parties had now set forth their positions, but the court could ask the parties to submit more information or to prove a certain argument.

Naturally, both the plaintiff and the defendant adduced evidence, for example attestations before a notary, questionings of witnesses and other forms of written evidence such as brokers' records.[26] Conflicting parties often asked other merchants or brokers – people, in sum, who were demonstrably well informed about the share trade – to attest before a notary public.[27] They attested, for instance, the customary way of trading shares or the share price at a certain date. They could also give a report as a witness.[28] Case files that contain all written evidence are available for some lawsuits.[29]

When the court had collected all the necessary information, it pronounced judgement. A report of the court procedure was included in the collection of extended sentences of the Court of Holland. This collection, as well as the collection of extended sentences of the High Council, contains reports of all cases in which the judges took some sort of action. These collections thus also contain lawsuits in which, for instance, the judges referred the litigants to mediators. This means that these sources are not biased by the selection procedure of the clerk of the court. It is true, however, that this method of research excludes those cases that reached amicable settlement before the courts' mediators. Again, this is not problematic: I have checked the reports of mediators in the years after 1672 – when a price crash led to a high number of conflicts – but the share-trade-related cases in these reports deal with relatively minor issues. The litigants whom the lower courts had ruled against simply appealed to the Court of Holland to postpone the execution of the lower court's judgement. Subsequently, the Court of Holland realized that it was no use to start a full court procedure again and referred the litigants to mediation.[30] So, to conclude, the extended sentences of the provincial courts of Holland are the right sources to use for an analysis of the development of jurisprudence on share-trade-related issues.

The Legal Framework

Conflicts about share transactions could involve three legal concepts: ownership and the transfer of ownership, endorsement and the terms of settlement of a transaction. The courts of the province of Holland refined jurisprudence on these concepts by judging on a number of court cases. All three legal concepts will subsequently be addressed in the following subsections.

Ownership and Transfer of Ownership

Clear rules for share ownership and the transfer of share ownership were crucial for the development of the secondary market. Under Roman-Dutch law, the general rule for transfer of title was that ownership passed on the basis of delivery. Since VOC shares were not payable to the bearer, however, they could not be physically delivered, so a special rule for the conveyance of ownership was needed. The directors of the VOC were aware of this and therefore included a rule that regulated how investors could ascertain and convey share ownership in the subscription book of 1602. Shareholders owned those shares registered under their account in the capital books that were kept by the company book-keeper. Title to a share could be transferred by means of official registration.[31]

This procedure was similar to the procedure for transferring unmovable goods such as real estate. Hence, the law also classified shares as unmovable goods.[32]

Van Balck vs *Rotgans* (1622) marks an important step in clarifying the rules for ownership of a share. This case made clear that a shareholder could be certain that the shares listed on his account in the capital book of the VOC were his full property and that previous holders of the ownership of the share could not lay claims on it. The judges thus confirmed the legal force of the capital books. The plaintiff in this lawsuit, Allert van Balck, believed that he had right of vindication on the share he had transferred to Jan Hendricksz Rotgans. Right of vindication means that the transferor of a good could reclaim ownership if the good had not been fully paid for or if he could prove that the purchaser had practised fraud at the time of the transaction – for example by hiding his impending insolvency or fleeing from town without paying.[33] Van Balck had transferred a share, but he never received full payment and therefore claimed the ownership of the share.

Van Balck had sold this particular share to Hans Bouwer on 5 April 1610. Bouwer, for his part, sold a similar share to Rotgans the following day. Rotgans approached Van Balck on the exchange, saying that he wanted to receive his share, but Van Balck replied that he did not know Rotgans and that he had traded with Bouwer. Rotgans then explained the situation and told Van Balck that he should transfer the share to him; he would pay him *f* 1,000 and Bouwer would see to the payment of the remaining sum. Van Balck agreed to transfer the share, but he never received full payment: Bouwer left Amsterdam in the following days to flee from his creditors. Van Balck went to court, where he requested seizure of the share, but the Court of Aldermen refused to adjudicate this; the judges reasoned that Van Balck no longer had title to the share after he had transferred it to Rotgans. Van Balck argued that he still had the right of mortgage of the share, because he had never received full payment. In his view, he still had a claim on Bouwer's share and hence on Rotgans's payment to Bouwer. Van Balck appealed the Aldermen's decision before two higher courts, but both the Court of Holland and the High Council also ruled against him.[34]

The fact that Van Balck and his lawyer appealed the courts' decisions twice indicates that this was not a clear-cut case. This lawsuit was not just about the right of vindication; Bouwer had practised fraud, so there was little doubt that Van Balck had right of vindication. However, the courts had to balance Van Balck's right of vindication and the rights of Rotgans, who gave the impression that he was a sincere buyer who had paid for the transfer, against each other. It so happened that Rotgans was not as sincere as he had the court believe, for in fact he was in league with Bouwer, but Van Balck did not succeed in convincing the court of Rotgans's insincerity.[35] In the end, the courts favoured the interests of the buyer who had purportedly done nothing wrong.

This judgement had far-reaching consequences; with it, the courts safe-guarded the interests of commerce. Share trading could have been severely hampered had Van Balck won this lawsuit, because in that case a buyer of a share would always have to fear that there was still a claim on the share he had bought, which would give the seller the right to claim it back.[36] This particular lawsuit, in other words, took away legal doubts that could have restrained investors from buying shares on the secondary market for VOC shares.

Interestingly, a few years before the High Court pronounced final judgement in this case, the VOC had also recognized the potential problems of transfers of shares that had claims attached to them. The VOC feared that buyers would not only lay a claim on the seller, but also on the company. It therefore changed the share transfer regulation. From 1616 onwards, the buyer of a share had to sign a statement when the bookkeeper added the share to his account that indemnified the company against any future claims. The buyer signed that he had accepted a 'good' share – a real share, in other words, a share that had formed part of the capital stock since 1602 – and that he was satisfied with it.[37]

By extension, the same legal principle that the court applied in *Van Balck* vs *Rotgans* was in force in the forward trade. In a series of judgements, the courts ruled that forward buyers could also expect the underlying asset of their forward contract to be a real share. There was no need to explicitly state in the contract that the share had to be free of any claims; the judges held the opinion that that was a matter of course. The Court of Holland thus clarified the procedure of transfer of ownership in a forward transaction.

The lawsuits that dealt with these matters were to a large extent similar to *Van Balck* vs *Rotgans*, although they look much more complicated at first sight. These court cases all started with Pieter Overlander who found out that the share he had received in settling a forward contract was fraudulent. The seller had transferred a non-existent share to his account, which the company book-keeper had knowingly executed. The complication of this case lies in the fact that many more traders were involved in this transaction; the transfer of a share to Overlander had settled the contracts of a chain of forward traders. The fol-lowing description of the lawsuit shows that these chains of traders could prove problematic if conflicts arose between one pair of traders within the chain.

Pieter Overlander had bought a forward with a ƒ3,000 VOC share as underlying asset from Abraham Abelijn on 13 March 1609, but the share was eventually transferred to him by Hans Bouwer. Abelijn had a similar transaction (a forward with the same nominal value and settlement date) with Dirck Semeij, who for his part had bought a similar forward from Maerten de Meijere. When the contract was due for delivery, Semeij asked De Meijere to transfer the share directly to Abelijn. De Meijere, however, was to receive a share from Jacques van de Geer and Hans Pellicorne and therefore he asked Abelijn if he would be satisfied if they delivered the share to him. Abelijn referred the question to Overlander. But Overlander had just heard a rumour that Van de Geer and Pellicorne were on the verge of going bankrupt, so he refused to accept this deal, unless De Meijere would explicitly indemnify him against any trouble. De Meijere then proposed to let Hans Bouwer, who also owed a share to him, deliver the share instead. Overlander accepted this deal and Abelijn also trusted that this transfer would successfully settle all the above-mentioned transactions: he traded with Bouwer on a daily basis. Overlander had the share transferred to Frans van Cruijsbergen, his brother-in-law, and each pair of traders in the chain came together once more to tear up the contracts and pay possible price differences.

A little later, however, the transferred share was found to be fraudulent, so Overlander started litigation. He summoned Abelijn – the only trader he had a rightful claim on – to appear in court and demanded that Abelijn replace the share with a good one. What makes this lawsuit so interesting is that the Amsterdam Court of Aldermen requested Overlander to give evidence under oath that he had been promised a 'sincere and sound' share on contracting this transaction. His claim would be dismissed if he did not take the oath, which reveals that the lower court did not acknowledge the legal principle that the buyer of a good can always expect this good to be delivered according to the conditions in the contract.

Abelijn's lawyer had made this particular point an important part of the defence, arguing that Overlander had requested to be indemnified against any troubles if Van de Geer and Pellicorne would have transferred the share, but he had not made any such requests when Abelijn proposed to let Bouwer transfer the share. Overlander had thus, according to the defence, accepted the share without reservations.

Overlander did not hesitate to make his declaration under oath and the court consequently sentenced Abelijn to replace the share. Abelijn then summoned his original counterparty Semeij, and the Aldermen pronounced the same judgement. Hence, the chain of share transactions became mirrored in a chain of court cases before the Court of Aldermen. Furthermore, every one of the defendants appealed the Aldermen's sentences to the Court of Holland, resulting in another chain of court cases (this time the other way around: *Abelijn* vs *Overlander*, *Semeij* vs *Abelijn*, etc), but the appeals were disallowed. The judges of the Court of Holland did not require the litigants to make declarations under oath. It was clear for them that the forward traders could expect to be delivered a real share.[38] The Court of Holland thus clarified the procedure of transfer of ownership for forward transactions.

Endorsement

The lawsuits discussed above show that the clearing of multiple forward contracts worked inefficiently in 1609. These pairs of traders first negotiated their transactions individually and then tried to arrange settlement of multiple contracts with a single share transfer. However, to accomplish thus, they constantly had to consult their initial counterparty about whether or not they agreed that a third party would deliver the share. These traders could have spared themselves this trouble had they chosen to resell their original contracts rather than to draft new contracts for each transaction.

It is not surprising, however, that traders were hesitant to assign their forward contract to third parties before maturity; simple assignment of a financial claim to a third party meant that the trader would once again have to make an assessment of counterparty risk. He would have to consider, in other words, whether the new counterparty would live up to his agreements. The risk that the assignor failed to inform the assignee about all the conditions of the contract further complicated assignation – there was always a chance that there was something wrong with the contract. Moreover, the assignee did not get in personal contact with the counterparty of the contract if he bought the claim from someone else and this might hide important information about the counterparty's reputation and creditworthiness. In sum, the assignee might be hesitant to take over the contract under these conditions.

Contract negotiability was the solution to these problems. This concept was introduced in the Netherlands under the reign of Emperor Charles V in 1541 with the intention of enabling merchants to assign letters obligatory more easily. The legal title to a contract could now be assigned to the assignee by way of endorsement, which literally means that the assignee puts his name on the back (*en dos*) of the original contract. If a debtor defaulted, his creditor not only had recourse to the debtor, but also to the previous assignor. This implied that the legal status of the contract improved with every endorsement: the longer the list of endorsers, the more people the ultimate trader in line would have recourse to.[39]

Endorsement also worked in derivatives transactions. The endorser wrote on the contract that he assigned his rights to the endorsee and both men signed the endorsement.[40] The lawsuit *Adriaen van der Heijden and Daniel van Genegen* vs *Abraham Abelijn* (1614) shows the legal force of endorsements and the advantages of endorsements over the chains of traders that figured in the previous example. The conflict between Van der Heijden and Van Genegen and the defendant emerged after the plaintiffs refused to deliver a share. In the original contract, Van der Heijden sold a forward to Van Genegen. Less than a month after the contract date, on 3 April 1610, Van Genegen resold this claim to Abelijn. The resulting transaction was as follows: Abelijn would receive a share from

Van der Heijden on 17 March 1611, the settlement date of the contract, and pay 150 per cent for it. On the settlement date, Abelijn and Van der Heijden disagreed over how to settle the contract: Van der Heijden preferred a monetary settlement, whereas Abelijn requested that the share be delivered. They were unable to come to an amicable settlement and Abelijn started litigation. He summoned both Van der Heijden and Van Genegen to appear in court, arguing that they were both contractually obliged to deliver the share. Van Genegen replied that there was no ground to summon him, because Van der Heijden was sufficiently solvent to comply with the contractual obligations. The judges disagreed with him, however; they ruled that both Van der Heijden and Van Genegen were individually responsible to deliver the share.[41]

To summarize, Abelijn had a legal claim on the holder of the contract, but also on the original counterparty who had resold his claim. It made no difference to the judges that there were no bankruptcies or insolvencies involved in this case. The Amsterdam merchants were probably already familiar with the advantages of endorsements before the Court of Holland pronounced this judgement, but it would nonetheless have made potential share traders aware of the advantages of endorsements. Abelijn's position was similar to that of Overlander and other unwary buyers on the share market, but his legal position was much better. Furthermore, Abelijn did not have to make an assessment of the reputation and creditworthiness of his contractual counterparty Van der Heijden, because he also had recourse to Van Genegen. This judgement spread knowledge about the benefits of endorsements on the share market and might very well have persuaded traders to participate in the forward market rather than in the spot market, because endorsed forward contracts were stronger than spot contracts; it was a significant advantage to have recourse to several counterparties.

With this legal concept clearly defined, the legal framework was in place. From the 1630s onwards, traders knew the legal force of the various transactions that they could choose among. Also, property rights were now clearly defined. Finally, and most importantly, participants in the secondary market for VOC shares could predict how the courts would judge in certain types of conflict. This legal certainty reduced the chance of becoming involved in a court case and thus reduced transaction costs.

Terms of Settlement

The outcome of share trade-related court cases was not always to the benefit of the development of trade. Court judgements of the early seventeenth century confirmed that it was possible to delay the settlement of a forward contract for a seemingly indefinite period of time. Buyers simply delayed requesting delivery of the share until it became profitable for them to do so. Until that moment, they had postponed settlement, for instance under the pretext that they needed more time to gather the money needed for the settlement. The seller, meanwhile, could urge the buyer to accept the share, but he could not legally force him to do so. When the buyer finally requested delivery of the share, the seller could try to object to this claim by arguing that it was unreasonable to suddenly request delivery months after the original settlement date, but the buyer's case stood stronger in court: the judges would decide on the basis of the original forward contract, which stated that a share should be delivered at a certain price after a certain term, without a limitation to the contract's validity. Hence, they would enforce the contract.[42]

It is not hard to see how this hampered the development of trade: it was a rather uninviting prospect for forward sellers that their counterparties could simply linger over settlement until the deal would become profitable to them. The market itself found a solution for this problem. From the 1630s onwards, it became customary to settle a forward contract within three weeks after the original settlement date. Forward buyers could use this period to gather the money needed for the share transfer or to try to find a counterparty willing to roll over the contract. This market custom did not have the status of a legal rule, however. In the early 1640s, for instance, traders already referred to it in their plea before court, but the judges took no notice of it.[43] The market itself, however, did regard it as an official rule; stockbrokers Sebastiaen da Cunha and Hendrick van Meijert attested before a notary in 1659 that a buyer lost title to the forward contract after the customary settlement term had expired.[44] This was thus an example of self-regulation: the trading community expected its members to settle their contracts within three weeks' after expiry of the contract. The absence of conflicts over contract settlement that came before a higher court after 1641 suggests that the traders complied to a large extent with this informal rule.

In the mid-1680s, share trader Samuel Cotinho decided to test this rule's legal status once again. His lawsuit against Vincent van Bronckhorst is especially interesting, because its case file, containing various attestations, survived. This case shows how the judges in the Dutch Republic took statements of market practitioners into consideration. The case went as follows: on 25 June 1683, Van Bronckhorst sold a forward with a *f* 12,000 VOC share as underlying asset to Cotinho. Three days after the settlement date (1 September 1683), Van Bronckhorst notified Cotinho that he wanted to deliver the share, but Cotinho answered that he was unable to receive it. Van Bronckhorst then asked a notary to serve an *insinuatie* containing a request to deliver the share to Cotinho. Cotinho was not at home, though his maid listened to the *insinuatie*. Since no subsequent action was taken on the side of Cotinho, Van Bronckhorst asked permission of the Court of Aldermen to sell the share on the market instead, which the Aldermen granted. A little later, however, Cotinho started litigation; he argued that it was unreasonable that Van Bronckhorst had sold the share to a third party before the customary term for settling forwards had expired. Cotinho held a strict view of the market custom. In his opinion, forward buyers held title to an unsettled contract until the customary term had expired whatever happened in the meantime. He thus regarded it as an extension to the contract's term and wanted to see whether the court would approve of this view.

Both litigants adduced attestations to support their case. A group of regular traders attested on 4 October 1683, only days after the *insinuatie*, that it was customary to settle contracts after two or three weeks, but traders should immediately settle once the counterparty had requested settlement through an *insinuatie*. The attestation used by Cotinho's solicitor was dated 27 October 1684: a number of brokers stated before a notary that the customary settlement term was three or four weeks. In the end, the court ruled in favour of Van Bronckhorst: it had not been unreasonable that he had sold the share before the customary term for delivery had expired.[45]

The market custom regarding the term for contract settlement did thus not have legal status. A contract neither lost its validity after the term had expired,[46] nor were traders able to claim title to a contract on the basis of the market custom. But the courts' judgements did not stop the market from using its customary practices for the settlement of contracts. To be sure, from the end of the 1680s onwards, the market custom was explicitly mentioned on the printed forward contracts used in the forward trade. And, what is more, this extra clause imposed a fine on non-compliance with the market custom. A trader who settled his contract with a *f* 3,000 share as underlying asset too late was fined *f* 7.50 per day. I have found no evidence of traders actually paying this fine, but the fact that this stipulation was included on the printed contracts suggests that it was widely accepted by the trading community. Interestingly, moreover, the clause also stipulated that a contract would lose its validity should its holders refrain from settling it within three months.[47] The trading community thus imposed its own rules where legal enforcement proved to be inadequate. In the case of terms of settlement, self-regulation facilitated the settlement procedure. Without it, however, the market would still have functioned. The next section will address a self-regulatory mechanism that was a *sine qua non* for the scale of forward trading of the second half of the seventeenth century.

Private Enforcement Mechanism

The ban on short selling of February 1610 severely constrained forward trading. Traders were allowed to sell forward contracts only with shares they legally owned as underlying asset, but share traders continued short-selling and the authorities felt compelled to repeat the ban several times. In these reissues, the first of which appeared in 1621, they explicitly stated that brokers were not allowed to negotiate contracts that contained a renunciation clause. Moreover, any contract containing such a clause, which explicitly renounced the ban on short-selling, would be declared null and void.[48]

The use of contracts containing a renunciation clause was nevertheless widespread. All examples of printed contracts that I have found, dating from different periods throughout the seventeenth century, contain such a clause. To be sure, even Vincent van Bronckhorst, himself a councillor of the High Council, did not hesitate to use them.[49] The judges understood that they could not pronounce the entire forward share trade illegal, so they approved the use of the contracts containing a renunciation clause, which shows once more that the courts were disposed to supporting the development of the share trade.

At the same time, however, the Dutch legal system did not enforce short sales. So if a litigant could convincingly prove that his counterparty had not owned the share that was subject of a forward sale at the contract date and during the contract's term, the court would declare the contract null and void. In his case against Andries Polster in 1633, Severijn Haeck convinced the judges of the Court of Holland that Polster had not owned the underlying asset of the forward he had sold him during the contract's term. The court declared the contract null and void, even though Polster had immediately made good tender of the stock after Haeck announced that he was about to start litigation.[50]

A lawsuit that came before court thirty-four years later indicates that traders were fully aware of the fact that the courts would never enforce short-sale contracts. The defendants in the case started by Sebastiaen da Cunha did not even bother to appear in court. Just like Haeck, Da Cunha wanted to be relieved from his contractual obligations. In 1665, he had bought a number of forward contracts with VOC shares with a nominal value of several thousands of guilders as underlying assets from a total of nine counterparties. During the terms of these contracts the Second Anglo-Dutch War (1665–7) broke out, leading to a price decrease of 35 per cent (from around 490 per cent[51] in 1664 to 315 per cent[52] in September/October 1665). Da Cunha realized that he was about to lose a lot of money were he to comply with the contracts and he therefore tried to be relieved from his contractual obligations by taking these contracts to court. The report of the court's session does not state the details of Da Cunha's contracts, but assuming that he traded one forward contract with each of the nine defendants in this lawsuit, that all shares had a nominal value of *f* 3,000 and that the price dropped by 175 points[53] after he bought the forwards, he could have lost up to *f* 50,000 on these forwards. The defendants probably knew that Da Cunha could produce convincing evidence and therefore they realized that they had nothing to win by going to the courtroom in The Hague. They were sentenced by default after the fourth no-show; the court declared the contracts null and void.[54]

Da Cunha's strategy could have posed a big threat to the growth of the forward market: many forward traders owned only a small amount of or zero shares in the capital books of the VOC. Hence, if they sold forwards, these were likely to be short sales, which gave their counterparties the opportunity to legally renege on their purchases. Consequently, forward short sellers would always lose on their transactions: on expiry of the contract, buyers, whose behaviour was solely influenced by economic considerations, would comply with their contracts only if this would be profitable to them. Such was not the case, however. Very few forward buyers – only two examples can be found in the archives of the Court of Holland – employed this strategy to avert losses. It could be possible that these cases were seldom brought before the provincial court, for this was no complicated juridical matter. Hence there could have been little ground to lodge an appeal against the local court's judgement.[55] The archives of the Court of Aldermen cannot be consulted to check this, but there are no signs whatsoever that these cases ever existed: a logical first step for litigation on the basis of the bans on short-selling was to request *aanwijzinge* in the VOC capital books (a buyer could ask a seller to show his ledger in the capital books to verify whether he was the legal owner of a share) via a notarial *insinuatie*. Such *insinuaties* appear frequently in the protocols of the notaries of Amsterdam around 1610,[56] but they are largely absent thereafter. The conclusion must thus be that forward buyers rarely reneged on their contracts.

The explanation for this observation is that a private enforcement mechanism, based on honour, reputation and peer pressure, was in place on the secondary market for VOC shares. This mechanism prevented forward buyers from reneging. Only in cases where the amount of money at stake was too high (as in Da Cunha's case) did this private enforcement mechanism fail.

The strongest form of the private enforcement mechanism was in place in trading clubs like the Collegie vande Actionisten and a somewhat weaker form in the *rescontre* meetings. It should be stressed, moreover, that honour and reputation were very important personal assets in early modern societies in general, so some form of a reputational regulatory mechanism was always in place in early modern trade.[57] The contracts used in the forward trade emphasized the importance of a trader's honour: the names of the parties to the contract were preceded by the word 'honourable' and the traders were called *luyden met eere* (men of honour) in the penalty clause at the bottom of the contracts. The personages in Josseph de la Vega's famous treatise on the stock-exchange business *Confusión de confusiones* (1688) also repeatedly stress the importance of honour and reputation in the share trade.[58]

This was all very well, but the participants of the high-risk forward market, where deals were made that were unenforceable by law, wanted to be sure that their counterparties not only said they were honourable men, but that they also acted accordingly. The correspondence between Lord Londonderry (born Thomas Pitt, Jr) and his cousin George Morton Pitt, dating from 1723, shows that there were indeed a large number of disreputable traders on the Amsterdam exchange who preferably bought forwards and received option premiums. If it turned out that they would suffer a loss on these contracts, they simply reneged. George Morton Pitt added to this that merchants of Amsterdam did not trade with these particular traders; only traders who were unaware of their bad reputations (e.g. foreigners) would enter into a transaction with them.[59] But how could a trader have information about the creditworthiness and reputation of all possible counterparties?

First of all, brokers gathered information about as many traders' reputations as possible, but the regular meetings of the *rescontre* and the trading clubs provided an even better solution to the reputation problem. The strength of these meetings was that a large number of traders were regularly present at the same location. Information about the reputations of the participants of the trading sessions spread quickly among the traders present and a trader with a bad name would find it hard to find counterparties for his transactions. Moreover, traders learnt to know each other very well during the sessions, all the more so since reciprocal transactions occurred frequently.

The private enforcement mechanism of the trading clubs went one step further. These clubs were private meetings and participants could be expelled.[60] Once a share trader was allowed in – it is very well possible that new members were admitted only after the intercession of one of the members – he had the possibility to perform a large number of possibly profitable transactions. If a trader failed to live up to the standards of the club, however, he would be excluded from the trading sessions and his chances of participating in the trading sessions were gone.[61] It was thus in the interest of all parties involved to live up to their agreements.[62] An attestation by four frequent participants stresses the force of honour and reputation within the community that traded in the clubs: they attested how the traders in the clubs rarely used written contracts for their transactions. Oral agreements sufficed for transactions between honourable traders.[63]

I suggest that it is moreover likely that the trading sessions in the clubs were chaired by some kind of committee that could also adjudicate in conflicts that arose from dealings in the meetings. The committee received its authority from the community of participants – a trader who entered the trading clubs also subordinated himself to the adjudicating board. I would argue that this committee-hypothesis is suggested by the fact that the main trading club was called 'Collegie vande Actionisten'. The word 'collegie' implies that there was some sort of governing body that supervised the meetings. Moreover, the name of this club was similar to that of a typical tulip-trading club that regularly met during the Tulipmania of 1636–7: Collegie vande Blommisten. Anne Goldgar has shown that during that winter, most of the trade in tulip bulbs took place in inns, where *collegien* (e.g. Collegie vande Blommisten) presided over the trading sessions. The *collegien* acted as committees of tulip experts who made the rules for the trade that took place in the inns, organized continuous auctions and also adjudicated in conflicts between bulb traders. Peer pressure, which weighed heavily in the small community of bulb traders, gave the *collegie* its power.[64]

Interestingly, a known regulation of the eighteenth-century *rescontre* meetings explicitly mentions the presence of a secretary, an official who could impose fines and a board of 'deciseurs' that adjudicated in conflicts.[65] Presumably, the *rescontre* participants had recognized the advantages of an adjudicating board for the settlement sessions. So, although direct evidence of regulatory and adjudicating bodies is lacking for the trading clubs of the second half of the seventeenth century, the presence of such bodies in similar trading clubs in the 1630s and the eighteenth century makes a reasonable case for their presence in the share-trading clubs.

The trading club ledgers of the Portuguese Jewish merchants Jacob Athias and Manuel Levy Duarte[66] give proof of the effectiveness of these clubs. They show the immense turnovers of Athias and Levy Duarte during each session, but equally interesting is the fact that they regularly traded forwards with Christian participants of these sessions, whereas I have found few examples of high-risk (i.e. forward) transactions between members of different religious communities on the market outside the trading clubs. The peer pressure and the reputational mechanism in the trading clubs persuaded traders to enter into a transaction with traders they did not know very well. But for reasons mentioned before, the large turnover in the trading clubs did not lead to an increase in traders trying to legally renege by suing their counterparties for short selling. What is more, even insolvent traders rarely tried to become relieved of their forward deals by asking the courts to declare their forward purchases null and void.[67] They chose the lesser of two evils: an honourable bankruptcy was apparently better than a dishonourable reneging. And perhaps they hoped to be able to return to the exchange shortly after their bankruptcy had been dealt with.

Sebastiaen da Cunha was probably not indifferent about his reputation either, but the losses he was about to incur on the forward contracts that were subject of the 1667 lawsuit were simply too high. And that was exactly the weakness of the private enforcement mechanism based on traders' reputations: there was a limit to the extent to which the participants of the trading clubs valued their reputations. If the share price fell very steeply, traders had to make a difficult assessment: they could choose to renege and lose their carefully accumulated reputation, or they could comply with their contracts and lose a large amount of money. In Da Cunha's case, the scale tipped toward reneging. And indeed, the price fall during the term of his forwards was clearly exceptional: the years 1664–5 witnessed the largest decline in share price in the history up until that time of the VOC.

Only seven years later, however, the share price experienced an even greater fall. In 1672, the share price fell to 280 per cent in June/July, whereas shares had been sold for 560 per cent in July 1671. For a number of traders, this price fall was so large as to outweigh an unblemished reputation. Unsurprisingly, then, all instances of *insinuaties* explicitly mentioning the intention to renege on the basis of the States of Holland bans date from this year. Antonio Lopes de Castro Gago, alias Jacob Lopes de Castro Gago, for example, answered to two *insinuaties* served upon him that the sellers had sold him nothing but 'air' and that he would obey the official bans. He had bought two forwards in January 1672 with a nominal value of *f*3,000 each at 485 ⅔ per cent and 487 per cent. In early May 1672, the settlement date for both contracts, the share price stood at 325 per cent. He would thus have lost almost *f*10,000 on these forwards.[68]

The price crash of 1688, when the VOC shares subsequently lost 18 per cent of their market value in late August and another 9.5 per cent in October,[69] did not lead to a similar pattern of reneging forward traders. The most plausible explanation is that this price fall was not large enough for the traders to give up their good reputations on the market; the 1688 price decrease was only half as large as its 1672 counterpart. Another, related, explanation is that there was no reneging trader in 1688 who gave the initial impetus for a chain of non-compliances. The participants of the clubs all traded with each other and all tried to keep their portfolios balanced. The individual forwards were risky transactions, but the traders reduced their portfolio risk by netting out their transactions with opposite transactions. This system worked well until one of the traders pulled out. The portfolios of all of his counterparties would then no longer be balanced, which increased their incentive to also renege on one or more of their liabilities, thus possibly starting a chain of unfulfilled transactions. The 1672 price crash thus highlighted the weak spot of the trading clubs with their private enforcement mechanism: it was founded on the honour and reputation of its participants, but consequently, when one of the participants chose to pull out, the system became unbalanced and there were no formal institutions to fall back on.

Conclusions

Together, the legal framework and the private enforcement system of seventeenth-century Holland provided a high level of certainty that the market would consummate all transactions. The two systems may seem to have been in place on fully separate markets; one where the rule of law was indispensable for the development of the market and the other where the rule of law was redundant because informal institutions replaced it. Yet they were strongly connected to each other.

The private sub-market could never have developed into an effective trading arena without a clear legal framework being in place and hence the two parts are inextricably intertwined. I have already mentioned the direct connection between the two: the coming into place of a clear legal framework contributed to the entry of new groups of participants on the share market and thus necessitated the emergence of sub-markets where there were no restrictions as to the amount of shares that could be traded – the market simply grew too large for its legal boundaries. But the sub-markets were in yet another way connected to the principal share market.

It was important that the traders in the trading clubs knew that they participated in a sub-market where other rules applied than on the principal market. This is a marked difference from the trade in tulip bulbs during the Tulipmania. This trade also took place in clubs, the so-called *collegies*, but there did not exist a principal market for bulbs with the same level of development as the market for VOC shares. This became problematic when the bulb price collapsed in early 1637. Many tulip traders went to court to extort payment from their counterparties, but the courts refused to pronounce judgement in tulip-trade-related lawsuits.[70] Thus emerged a situation where traders believed that the transactions they had entered into would be enforced, but as it turned out, their trades were not considered to be legally valid. Consequently, traders lost confidence in the institutions of the tulip trade.

In the case of the share trade, however, participants knew that the courts would not enforce the transactions they performed within the trading clubs. They were aware of this situation because the legal framework of the share trade had been clearly defined in the first decades of the seventeenth century. Hence, traders were well aware that there was a chance that their counterparties in these clubs would renege, and they implicitly accepted this as soon as they started participating themselves. They did not lose confidence in the system in the event that one trader reneged. However, the reneging traders of 1672 did make the trading community realize how risky the forward trade was.

Short Summary of Court Cases

Table 2.1: Court of Holland, extended sentences.

Inv. nr.	Year – nr.	Plaintiff	Defendant	Legal concept	Short summary
626	1612–6	De Meijere	Van Duynen	Transfer of ownership	Buyers may expect shares transferred to them to be genuine and freed from any claims.
632	1614–50	Abelijn	Overlander	Transfer of ownership	Idem. Additionally, there is no need to explicitly ask for indemnification against any future troubles.
632	1614–73	Semeij	Abelijn	Transfer of ownership	Idem.
632	1614–76	De Meijere	Semeij	Transfer of ownership	Idem.
633	1614–118	Van der Heijden and Van Genegen	Abelijn	Endorsement	All endorsers are individually responsible for compliance with a contract, even if the endorsee is solvent.
633	1614–134	Le Maire	Del Beecke	Terms of settlement	A contract does not lose its validity over time.
664	1624–64	Le Maire	Del Beecke	Terms of settlement	A contract does not lose its validity over time.
703	1633–36–1	Haeck	Polster	Upholding of the ban on short-selling	Short-sale contracts are null and void.
703	1633–36–2	Haeck	Van der Perre	Upholding of the ban on short-selling	Idem.
784	1667–60	Da Cunha	Rodrigues Mendes c.s.	Upholding of the ban on short-selling	Idem.

Table 2.2: Court of Holland, case files.

Inv. nr.	Year	Plaintiff	Defendant	Legal concept	Short summary
IIK98	1689	Cotinho	Van Bronckhorst	Terms of settlement	There are limits to a contract's validity: a buyer cannot reverse his decision after the seller has made good tender of stock, but he has refused to receive it.

Table 2.3: High Council, extended sentences.

Inv. nr.	Year	Plaintiff	Defendant	Legal concept	Short summary
708	1616	Abelijn	Overlander	Transfer of ownership	Buyers may expect shares transferred to them to be genuine and freed from any claims. There is no need to explicitly ask for indemnification against any future troubles.
708	1616	Semeij	Abelijn	Transfer of ownership	Idem.
708	1616	De Meijere	Semeij	Transfer of ownership	Idem.
715	1622	Van Balck	Rotgans	Ownership	Seller has no right of vindication on a share that has been transferred in the capital books, but which had only partly been paid for. Recognition of the legal force of the capital books.

3 CO-OPERATIVE BANKING IN THE NETHERLANDS IN PRE-SECOND WORLD WAR CRISES

Joke Mooij

Introduction

Over the years much has been published about banking during times of crisis, yet little is known about the performance of co-operative banks during past crises. In the Netherlands, the early co-operative agricultural credit banks (*boerenleenbanken*) were a response to the agricultural crisis of the late nineteenth century. These banks were founded to provide credit to farmers who had no access to credit facilities from the traditional banking sector. The Dutch *boerenleenbanken* were based on the German Raiffeisen model, which proved to be popular among the rural population. They provide a good example of an institutional innovation that arose in response to a particular economic context. This chapter argues that in the Netherlands the co-operative agricultural credit banks performed better than other Dutch banks during the crisis of the 1920s and 1930s, and that their better performance can be attributed to their innovative legal structure, corporate governance, banking policy, internal control mechanisms and market conditions. The information and arguments presented here are based both on literature and archival research.

To provide some general background, the first section outlines the Dutch economy in the period 1890–1939, highlighting the developments that were most significant to co-operative agricultural credit. The chapter then addresses the development of the agricultural co-operative banks in the first half of the twentieth century, with a focus on the crisis periods. The subsequent sections examine the developments of the banking sector in these crises in more detail, and are followed by a brief assessment of the banks' performance in the years of recovery. Finally, some concluding remarks and observations are offered.

Agricultural Credit and Economic Development up to 1939

In the Netherlands, the rise of co-operative agricultural credit is linked to the process of transformation in the agricultural sector at the end of the nineteenth century. After decades of economic prosperity, the Dutch countryside entered an extended period of agricultural depression (1882–96). Imports of cheap agricultural products from overseas drove prices down, cutting into farmers' profits. Business-economic factors pushed farmers towards streamlining and modernization, but the vast number of small farms, in particular, lacked the capital required to adapt. This was also the era of new agricultural techniques and the introduction of industrial processing of agricultural products. The latter resulted in dairy and sugar factories and the like. These were initially in private hands. Gradually they also started as co-operatives.

Farmers in the Netherlands were not unfamiliar with the co-operative model. From 1876 onwards, gentry and priests supported the setting up of co-operatives for the purchase, processing and sale of agricultural raw materials and products in an effort to improve the farmer's economic conditions. Within a few decades, there were thousands of local co-operative purchasing associations, hundreds of dairy co-operatives, dozens of co-operative auctions, a number of sales co-operatives and a few co-operative slaughterhouses.[1] But even as the need for capital in rural areas grew, there was no adequate financial infrastructure to provide it, leaving small farmers with nowhere to turn but to external credit providers such as civil-law notaries, distributors or shopkeepers, often paying exorbitant interest rates.[2] The State Commission on Agriculture (instituted in 1886), as well as the later agricultural commissions, concluded that a permanent solution for the underdeveloped agricultural sector would involve improvement of agricultural credit by setting up co-operative banks along the lines of the German Raiffeisen model.[3]

Co-operative agricultural credit as an element of the growing co-operative movement was an important innovation in response to the Dutch financial services sector's one-sided focus. The urban-based banks were mainly financing trade and engaged in the security business.[4] The universal bank never developed in the Netherlands, even as it arose in neighbouring countries. Initially, retailers, small businesses and craftsmen could turn to auxiliary banks or loan banks for help, but in the 1910s, most of these small financial institutions were absorbed by the expanding commercial banks. It was partly for this reason that a small-business credit sector along the lines of the Schulze-Delitzsch model, which was more suited to the needs of urban craftsmen and the working class, developed in the Netherlands after 1905.[5] Although some small banks for small- and medium-sized enterprises (*middenstandsbanken*) did provide agricultural credit, the small-business credit system lies outside the scope of this chapter.

The First World War (1914–18) shook the economic foundations of the neutral Netherlands; economic conditions deteriorated and hard times hit the financial sector. After a short-lived post-war boom, a new economic crisis struck in the 1920s, along with a crisis in both the banking and insurance sectors. The banking situation was so grim that the Dutch government and De Nederlandsche Bank (DNB; Dutch central bank) took action to shore up the sector with a number of rescue packages. According to DNB's historiographer Johan de Vries it was in part this banking crisis that drove DNB towards a rapid transition from a bank of issue into a central bank.[6] The crisis in the insurance world led to increased legislation and regulations and the creation of the first supervisory body in the Dutch financial sector, in 1922.[7]

The Wall Street crash of October 1929 did not immediately make front page news in the Netherlands.[8] By the end of the 1920s the country's economy had enjoyed several robust years, although there were signs of looming problems in the agricultural and shipping sectors. It was only in the second half of 1930 that economic conditions truly deteriorated across the board.[9] In the autumn of 1931, the Dutch economy was hit by the financial crisis in Germany and the following restriction of cross-border capital movements. This, coupled with the British government's decision to abandon the Gold Standard (September 1931), caused serious disruptions in the international financial markets and a complete breakdown of world trade. The Netherlands' international competitive position was severely affected. In particular, the country's still relatively large agricultural sector was hit by increased competition on the domestic market on the one hand, and problems in international payment transactions, the loss of the major export markets and protectionist measures elsewhere on the other.[10] The economic effects were so dramatic that in 1933 the Dutch government was finally forced to enact a broad package of protective measures and support geared principally towards the agricultural sector (*Landbouwcrisiswet*).

By the time international economic conditions began to show initial signs of recovery, in 1933, Dutch economy had sunk into a deep malaise. The economic tide only turned after the Netherlands – as one of the last countries – left the Gold Standard in 1936.

Co-operative Agricultural Banks

With support from the newly-formed agricultural unions and the clergy – taking inspiration from the Papal Encyclical Rerum Novarum (1891) – hundreds of agricultural co-operative banks emerged across the Dutch countryside after 1895. Driven by local initiatives, these banks were modelled along the ideas of Friedrich Wilhelm Raiffeisen (1818–88), a socially aware German mayor from the Rhineland. Raiffeisen saw co-operative banking as an effective means of empowering rural populations. His fundamentals for the co-operative credit union were adopted virtually unchanged when Dutch agricultural credit organized itself: unlimited liability of its members; a geographically limited area of operations; unsalaried management and allocation of profits to the reserves; local autonomy.

The legal basis for Dutch agricultural co-operative banks was derived from either the Dutch Freedom of Association and Assembly Act of 1855 or the Dutch Co-operative Associations Act of 1876 (revised in 1925).[11] In either case, the governance of co-operative agricultural banks was structured around three bodies: the management board, the supervisory board and the general meeting. Clerical work and bookkeeping were done by the cashier. Being a cashier was a modestly paid, part-time task. The cashier's home often served as the bank's office.

In 1898, a number of local co-operative agricultural banks, following Raiffeisen's fundamentals, established an umbrella organization. Although there was agreement on the main points, personal differences of opinion, along with differing views regarding the most appropriate legal form as well as on religious issues, ultimately led to the creation of two separate co-operative central (umbrella) banks in 1898: Coöperatieve Centrale Raiffeisen-Bank (CCRB) in Utrecht and Coöperatieve Centrale Boerenleenbank (CCB) in Eindhoven, hereinafter also referred to as the central co-operatives. Governance of these two central co-operatives was similar to local governance, but with the difference that the members of the central co-operatives were the local banks. Both central co-operatives added a strong impetus to the rise of agricultural credit in the Netherlands.

These central co-operatives emerged in a period in which Dutch society was compartmentalizing itself along ideological lines at an ever-increasing pace. This process is referred to as *verzuiling* (pillarisation). This pillarisation also marked both organizations. CCB bore the hallmarks of a Roman Catholic organization, while CCRB abandoned its original ideological orientation in 1901, from then on profiling itself as a neutral organization. In 1903, the unlimited liability of CCRB member banks changed to a limited liability. This important decision drove a few banks away. These banks ultimately joined with the Coöperatieve Centrale Christelijke Boerenleenbank (CCCB) in Alkmaar, a third (Catholic) umbrella organization formed in 1904 by three young, non-member banks in the province of Noord-Holland.[12] This third organization, however, remained too small to survive and ended in a voluntary winding up in the mid-1920s, as explained in more detail below. Whether the compartmentalization was ultimately a decisive factor in the development of co-operative agricultural credit is hard to say.[13] Among others, the geographic centres of the two organizations were different (see Table 3.1). For the smaller CCB, that centre was the southern provinces, while CCRB had most of its member banks in the western and northern parts of the Netherlands. Different soil characteristics in these areas resulted of course in different agricultural activities. And those activities and their seasonal nature dictated local credit needs and operating results of the banks.

All co-operative agricultural banks shared a common objective: to provide cheap credit to their members. The combination of good access to local information, the absence of profit maximization as a prime motivator and low management costs made providing that cheap credit possible, and also allowed paying interest on savings balances that was 0.5 to 1.5 per cent higher than with either the traditional savings banks or the Netherlands Post Office Savings Bank (RPS). Of course, the volume of savings, to a large degree, dictated the capacity to meet the credit demand.

Historically, the agricultural sector had three types of credit needs: short-term (for financing the harvest), medium-term (for purchasing livestock or tools) and long-term (for purchasing land or buildings). The co-operative agricultural banks provided their members (the individual agricultural and horticultural businesses) with advances of a fixed term (initially, a maximum of one year, which in time was extended to ten years), and later, with current account credit. These banks also served as banker to the local purchasing and sales associations, dairies, auctions, etc. that likewise worked on a collective or co-operative basis.[14] Financing the larger co-operatives exceeded the capacity of the local banks, and so this became the task of the central co-operatives. In order to be able to provide long-term mortgage loans, CCB founded a subsidiary, De Boerenhypotheekbank NV (1908). This mortgage bank was a joint stock company. CCB member banks were its shareholders. The separation was designed to give the co-operative banks and their modest reserves more financial breathing room, by opening up the option to divest the fixed (long-term) credit, which had to be financed virtually entirely from deposits, current accounts and savings.

Both CCB and CCRB considered sufficient liquidity of the organization as a whole to be of absolutely vital importance for the continuity of agricultural credit in the Netherlands. Particularly in times of crisis, the central co-operatives devoted extra attention to liquidity and solvency (which will be discussed in greater detail below). Looking back at the first hundred years, Sluyterman et al. conclude that the most significant innovation that agricultural credit brought to the Dutch financial system was connecting a large regional spread and access to central management and support without creating a single, integrated organization.[15]

Between 1900 and 1920, over a thousand local co-operative agricultural banks (*boerenleenbanken*) were created, and by 1930 they could be found all over the Netherlands. Despite the saturation of the market, the number of banks would actually continue to increase slightly into the 1930s (Figure 3.1). On the eve of the Second World War, there were 1,297 co-operative agricultural member banks, along with twenty-five independent co-operative agricultural banks.[16]

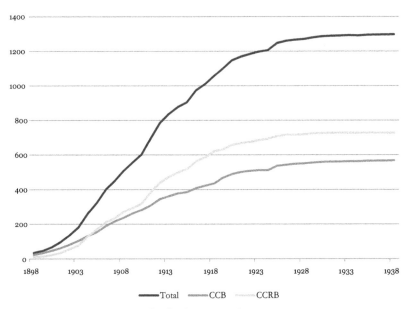

Figure 3.1: Member banks CCB and CCRB, 1899–1939.

Source: CCB and CCRB, Annual reports.

The First World War had far-reaching consequences for both the agricultural sector itself and the co-operative banking sector. Although the Netherlands were not at war the co-operative banking sector had to deal with the economic consequences of the international turbulence. As a result of shrinking investments and a lack of good investment opportunities the volume of deposits increased at the local banks, while at the same time the central co-operatives had problems finding investments for these resources that were both safe and offered adequate returns. In the initial post-war years, the agricultural credit sector struggled with huge fluctuations in deposits. In addition, the credit lending volume also varied dramatically.[17] On the whole, however, the sector grew in this period, as Table 3.1 illustrates.

Table 3.1: Development of member banks of CCB and CCRB, 1899–1936.

Year	Total member banks	Total members	Total savings (x NLG. 1000)	Total loans (x NLG. 1000)	Current account Debit balances	Credit balances
1899*	33	1,128	199	44	–	–
1909	557	44,441	24,858	12,869	2,893	635
1919	1,101	128,712	214,336	73,467	47,449	16,854
1929	1,280	215,663	446,792	206,851	134,121	39,033
1936	1,295	227,077	421,949	203,255	111,819	41,072

* 1899 = CCB only. This also includes the co-operative dairy banks in Leeuwarden and Alk-
    maar as well as the co-operative agricultural bank-trade associations.
–: no data
Source: CBS, *Omvang*, table 5, p. 12.

Banking Crisis

During the early 1920s, the Dutch financial sector was in the grip of a banking crisis. A total of thirty-three small-business banks as well as four commercial banks, twenty-six provincial banks and two overseas banks faced serious financial difficulties, and this led to bankruptcy for nineteen of these sixty-five institutions. Of course, their financial problems had their roots in business-economic factors, but in many cases they were aggravated by a lack of knowledge, experience and integrity. Some banks suffered from mismanagement and fraud. In this period, in an effort to 'cut the losses' by granting liquidity support to individual banks, DNB developed into a 'lender of last resort'.[18] This crisis, however, did not result in any form of institutionalized supervision of the banking sector.

Thanks in part to the vast reserves that had been accrued in the agricultural sector in previous years, the agricultural credit sector weathered the banking crisis largely unscathed.[19] Nevertheless some banks disappeared. In 1924 two CCB member banks were wound up.[20] Other casualties were Centerbank in Leiden and CCCB. Of the former, little is known. After a difficult start, CCCB was further weakened by the economic malaise of 1916. Ultimately, its financial reserves proved insufficient to cover its lasting negative operating results, and at the end of 1924 CCCB went into liquidation. Too few members, and consequently, insufficient financial capacity, became its undoing.[21] Its former member banks joined with one of the other two central co-operatives.

Earlier that same year, DNB had revoked CCB's discount facility, as DNB considered that, because of the interest rate policy pursued by the agricultural co-operative banks, they could not accrue sufficient reserves. Although CCB never had to appeal to DNB's resources, in DNB's view the lack of sufficient equity capital was a risk to the solvency of the agricultural co-operative banks, since their assets consisted of the incrementally retained earnings, backed by guarantees and members' liability. DNB's critical attitude was no doubt dictated in part by the turbulence in the financial sector, and particularly CCCB's liquidity and solvency problems, and in part by the failures in the small-business credit sector and CCB's direct financial involvement in the failed Hanzebank in 's-Hertogenbosch (1923), a major local bank at the time. In addition to revoking CCB's discount facility, DNB also criticized the agricultural credit system in general in its 1925–6 annual report.[22] Among economists and bankers, there was also criticism on the high interest rates paid and low interest rates charged by the agricultural co-operative banks. In 1929, a leading banker opined that co-operative agricultural banks had managed to avoid major losses so far thanks to the good state of the Dutch agricultural sector, but would be in for a rude awakening in a protracted depression unless they reformed themselves into general banks.[23] Until early 1929, DNB maintained its criticism on the interest rate policy pursued by the agricultural co-operative banks. Following a comprehensive audit it had instituted, DNB would grudgingly relax its critical attitude and offer both central co-operatives access to its discount facilities once more, but with a maximum of only NLG 5 million. But in the end both organizations made little or no use of it.

Crisis in the 1930s

Between 1929 and 1939, 101 commercial banks disappeared, most in the period from 1931 to 1934.[24] Correcting for the forty-three new commercial banks that emerged in this period, this meant a net loss of fifty-eight, so that in 1939 the total number of commercial banks in the country had fallen to 340. By comparison, in that same year there were over 1,300 co-operative agricultural banks in the Netherlands, and in the 1930s, the sector lost only two banks to financial problems (in 1934 and 1937). As their independent existence was jeopardized these two were, in keeping with the co-operative philosophy, taken over by neighbouring banks belonging to the same organization rather than declaring bankruptcy. A further two co-operative agricultural banks had their memberships revoked by their central co-operative (one in 1930 and the other in 1931) due to their failure to comply with the rules of membership. But this slight drop in numbers was more than compensated for by the seventeen new, young local member banks joining the co-operatives in the same period, primarily in the provinces of Noord-Brabant and Limburg (historically the base of the smaller CCB organization, as illustrated in Table 3.2).

At the local level, too, the membership increased as time went on. At the end of 1929, CCB banks had 72,486 members, and the CCRB banks a total of 143,195. Earlier that year, CCB had decided to provide financial support to member banks that had recently joined the co-operative, so as to give them a healthy foundation for further expansion of the membership.[25] Membership would increase every year save one (1934), albeit less than had been hoped for owing to the relatively high member attrition during the crisis. Still, it should be noted that this membership growth was largely the result of seven new member banks. In the case of CCRB the crisis was reflected in the local bank membership numbers as early as 1932. In the years 1932–4, total membership declined by 1,446. After a year of recovery (1934), membership dropped again slightly in 1935. The fact that CCRB banks were established in areas where the farmers were vulnerable to international developments may explain this short-term downward trend in membership.

Table 3.2: Distribution of local member banks by province, 1929 and 1939.

Province	1929		1939	
	CCRB	CCB	CCRB	CCB
Groningen	70	–	70	–
Friesland	104	6	103	7
Drenthe	53	8	56	8
Overijssel	46	44	46	45
Gelderland	105	70	104	72
Utrecht	40	8	39	8
Noord-Holland	116	27	119	28
Zuid-Holland	114	30	115	31
Noord-Brabant	18	198	18	202
Zeeland	58	11	58	11
Limburg	1	153	1	156
Total	725	555	729	568

Source: ARN, CCRB and CCB, Annual reports.

As Table 3.2 shows, in the pre-Second Word War period the average number of members per bank rose faster for CCRB banks than for CCB banks, presumably due to the fact that some CCRB banks developed into urban banks, and their membership also included an unknown number of small business enterprises.[26]

Table 3.3: Average number of members per co-operative agricultural bank, 1905–40.

	1900	1905	1910	1915	1920	1925	1930	1935	1940
CCB	46	77	87	101	115	124	132	133	133
CCRB	–	62	84	103	134	175	212	215	227

–: no data
Source: ARN, CCRB and CCB, Annual reports.

Interestingly, Dutch co-operative agricultural banks would reinforce their market position during this crisis. A comparison of the balance sheet totals of some major financial institutions for the years 1928, 1933 and 1938 shows that the position of the agricultural banks improved, both in absolute and relative terms. Incidentally, the general savings banks, the RPS (Post Office Savings bank) and the giro services improved their positions even more. The big losers were the commercial banks and the mortgage banks.[27]

Co-operative Banking during a Crisis

As a rule, the evaluation of a credit application was a matter for the local management. Local board members were familiar with local conditions and the borrower's personal circumstances. Working together, bank and member would endeavour to arrive at an affordable and effective credit with an appropriate term of repayment, in consideration of the nature of the borrower's operations.[28] There were, however, also central guidelines for credit lending by local member banks. Some forms of local credit were subject to approval by the central organization. There were also central guidelines for interest rates on savings balances.

In the early 1920s, the Dutch agricultural sector struggled with falling export revenues, and the impact of this could soon be seen on the co-operative agricultural banks' ledgers. In 1923, turnover fell for the first time in many years. CCB attributed this to the general public's loss of confidence in banks in the wake of the serious problems in the small-business sector.[29] In view of the malaise in the agricultural sector, CCB chose to further shore up its financial basis to be prepared for any eventuality. Unlike CCB, CCRB had had no direct financial involvement in the small-business banking sector. For both central co-operatives, the firestorm of publicity on the causes of bank failures was reason enough to hammer home to their member banks the importance of effective control and close monitoring of liquidity and solvency.[30] In addition, the central organization intensified inspection (which will be discussed in greater detail below).

When the new agricultural crisis hit, the initial effect was an increase in the demand for credit. At the same time, economic conditions were still good and so there was an increase in savings. The impact of the events of October 1929 was first felt in the securities portfolios. The results remained positive, but as the agricultural crisis wore on, the economic outlook became more clouded. This ultimately prompted both central co-operatives to introduce changes in their internal controls. A more intensive monitoring was intended to protect the co-operative banks and their modest reserves from unexpected financial setbacks. If nothing else, these measures served to reassure the members, who, it should be remembered, were bound to unlimited liability. Furthermore, this early form of internal prudential supervision gave the central co-operatives an insight in the trends at work in nearly 1,300 individual banks across the country.

Intensification of Control and Supervision

For the co-operative banks, internal control and supervision were regulated from the outset. To a large degree, this had to do with their decentralized structure. Every *boerenleenbank* was an independent co-operative. It had its own governance and management, kept its own books and was responsible for its own balance sheet. Banking supervision within the co-operative system was also institutional innovation in the banking sector in the Netherlands.

The rise of organized agricultural credit brought with it central rules and regulations to which the member banks had to comply. Member banks were, for example, obliged by their (internally approved) articles of association to subject themselves to central inspection and maintain their bookkeeping as prescribed by the central co-operatives. Over time, the articles of association were gradually adjusted in keeping with the organizations' growth and changes in national legislation and regulations.

At the local co-operative agricultural banks control consisted principally of a monthly squaring of the cash work by the local board members. In addition, they also were to conduct a detailed annual audit of all savings, advances and current account ledgers. This included a comparison of the number of ledger credits issued against the number registered in the general ledger. They also had to check all balances. Finally, this was followed by an item-by-item audit of each ledger to verify whether the entry and date matched the bank's bookkeeping. These periodic inspections were designed to prevent fraud, but also allowed the central co-operatives to ascertain whether the local member bank's administration and bookkeeping remained in compliance with the directives as set out in CCB and CCRB membership bylaws. Member banks obtained the forms and ledgers needed from their central co-operative. This form of standardization made local work easier as well as simplified central inspection. The central co-operatives also endeavoured to expand local banking knowledge and expertise by providing information and training for cashiers and local management.[31] Taking a cue from co-operatives in Germany and Belgium, CCB began offering courses on administration and bookkeeping for agricultural co-operative banks in a number of different locations in 1910. In 1925, a separate course was organized for the former Alkmaar member banks.[32]

Both central co-operatives maintained a small inspection division. The inspectors visited each local member bank one or more times a year (sometimes unannounced), subjecting the bank's administration and management to an extensive audit and verifying compliance with the articles of association, internal rules and applicable law. Afterwards, the inspector would discuss his findings with the management of the local member bank and, where applicable, give recommendations for improvement. The central inspectorate also had the task of sounding the alarm if a local member bank's liquidity was ever at risk from potential repayment arrears or overextended credit resources. During the crisis years, the co-operatives had an even greater interest in limiting risks. As a result, along with solidity, the local member banks' liquidity position became an additional point of attention. When a bank applied for membership with one of the central co-operatives, that co-operative's inspection department would first audit the bank. The outcome of the audit was an important element in the decision whether membership would be granted or not. The central co-operative's accounting was itself subject to an external audit.

In 1930, CCB underscored the importance of compliance with banking standards by creating an internal list of member banks at which CCB inspectors had identified problems. The banks on the list would be subjected to intensive monitoring (unannounced cash desk checks and extraordinary audits), until the administration and management was brought back into compliance with all requirements. In the period 1930–3, the number of banks on this list of problem banks would nearly double from its initial size (see Table 3.4). This increase was most likely the result of more intensive management monitoring, which, in turn, was a response to the fact that in these crisis years, the local member banks demonstrated their true co-operative values by making allowance for the problems their borrowers were facing whenever possible. But arrears in interest payments and insufficiently solid guarantees were risks, and the central co-operatives did everything in their power to limit risks.

Table 3.4: CCB's problem banks, 1930–7.

Year	Number	Percentage of total
1930	37	6.6
1931	48	8.6
1932	62	11.0
1933	85	15.1
1934	–	–
1935	49	8.7
1936	46	8.1
1937	23	4.1

– : data unavailable
Source: ARN, CCB, minutes of board meeting 14 August 1933 and 10 May 1937.

In the late 1930s, the number of banks on CCB's list dropped. This is an indicator of improving conditions in the Dutch agricultural sector (which can in part be attributed to the financial support at the national level in response to the crisis), as well as of the effects of more stringent supervision. Intensification of the inspections, both local and central, revealed irregularities at an earlier stage, which meant that appropriate steps could be taken sooner and the potential financial impact on the bank and its members (with unlimited liability) could be avoided or kept to a minimum. And this, in turn, also limited the potential consequential loss for the other banks, something that should not be understated in reference to the crisis years, when unexpected and large financial repercussions of fraud and the like could be a significant blow to the reserves and liquidity of co-operative banks.

The increase in the number of members of local banks facing financial difficulties is confirmed by the expansion of legal work being carried out at the central co-operatives. In addition to providing legal advice to the local member banks, these activities included offering assistance with collections and making arrangements with debtors.

The crisis also exposed something else: many agricultural co-operative associations (those not in the financial arena) struggled with management issues. Because this had its impact on the agricultural co-operative banks, in 1936 CCRB resolved that its member banks would henceforth require the approval of the central co-operative for the granting of new credit and the continuation of existing credit. It was not long before supplementary provisions effectively placed all credit lending activities of the agricultural co-operative associations under central control.[33]

Figures and Trends

A by-product of the intensified inspections was that CCB and CCRB built up a set of hard data on the trends in local credit lending and savings. Their central reporting was a source of facts and figures for all member banks. The centrally collected figures were also published in the annual report of the central co-operative. Until late into the twentieth century, there were no legal requirements on the format for this reporting. Unlike other annual reports, such as those of the commercial banks or of DNB, the annual reports of CCB and CCRB received little to no attention in the financial media of the time.[34]

Having a set of financial data of all member banks proved to be a major advantage in the pre-war period, when banking statistics were still done by hand and risk modelling did not yet exist. Coupled with the option of using the interest rate as a control mechanism for the central co-operatives' advances to the member banks and the member banks' deposits to the central co-operatives, these data offered a powerful means for adjustment to be used when locally undesirable tendencies were observed. The interest rate instrument was indeed used, for example in 1931 and 1937 when large flows of 'hot money' into savings accounts were observed (see below).

The financial turbulence of the 1930s would lead to the first tentative calls for 'state supervision' of the banking industry.[35] At that time, there was no deposit guarantee scheme, nor was there any form of institutionalized banking supervision; this would only begin to take shape with the Credit System Supervision Act of 1952. The implementation of a deposit guarantee scheme in the Netherlands was only completed in 1978. Without the latter, the bank's customers stood to lose their entire savings in the event of a bank failure. The chances of failure of an agricultural co-operative bank were, however, small, thanks to the double co-operative organizational structure, the internal safeguards, a high degree of mutual solidarity and, last but not least, the group discipline.

The history of the 1930s shows that not one agricultural co-operative member bank failed during this crisis, and that two banks in financial difficulties were taken over by neighbouring banks of the same co-operative, while member banks that did not follow the rules were expelled from the organization. How the non-member agricultural co-operative banks fared in the 1930s crisis is less clear. We do know that one bank was refused membership in 1932 after an audit revealed it was experiencing financial difficulties.

Conservative Banking Policy

In their annual general members meetings of 1930, the chairmen of both central co-operatives stressed the need for a conservative banking policy in view of prevailing conditions. This meant 'restraint in credit provision' and close monitoring of the collateral of both new and existing loans. The central co-operatives urged their member banks to increase their local reserves, which, they said, should total at least ⅓ (CCB) or ¼ (CCRB) of the amount of all liabilities. Meanwhile, it was the central organizations' task, in turn, to monitor the overall liquidity position. This did entail (in part) that member banks could not lock savings into loans with longer periods to maturity. The specific rules that each central co-operative enforced in terms of duration and conditions, however, were different.[36] In consultation with their members, the central co-operatives would tighten the rules and the supervision of the member banks as time went on. One effect of this was that the number of transactions subject to prior approval of the central co-operatives increased. But despite this cautious credit policy, the banks still had on occasion to seize collateral in subsequent years, when as a result of the crisis members proved to be no longer capable of repaying their loans on time. In a few isolated cases, the central co-operative had to cover the loss.

In 1931, the impact of the agricultural crisis in the Netherlands was clearly being felt in mixed farming, which up until then had been less affected than other businesses such as the single farming operations (a segment that had been suffering from price declines since 1928). Exporting agricultural sectors, including horticulture and bulb growing, were impacted by international monetary developments. Falling exports as a result of a wide body of international trading and payment restrictions had an indirect effect on the operations of the agricultural co-operative banks: the credit segment shrank, both in terms of advances and debit balances in current accounts. Although cash flows were still strong, in 1931 they were largely the result of a temporary glut of extra savings into the agricultural co-operative banks. In addition, these banks could not escape the effects of the crisis on the money and capital markets.

After October 1929, investments of all types had lost their appeal, and affluent individuals and businesses were seeking safe havens for their cash. As a result, the agricultural co-operative banks (as well as the traditional savings banks) were suddenly awash with savings. The policy of both CCB and CCRB was designed to discourage the unexpected flood of this 'hot money', so called in view of the presumed temporary nature of these deposits. But the flow dried up on its own after England abandoned the Gold Standard in 1931.

As a result of the turbulence on the financial markets, the two central co-operatives and their member banks suffered considerable losses in their securities portfolios in 1931. Nearly half of the CCB's losses of over NLG 4.2 million could be covered by the special reserves accrued in previous years. The CCRB's reserves were decidedly smaller, as a result of which this co-operative could only cover from its reserves NLG 0.5 million of its NLG 3.5 million losses incurred on securities holdings of NLG 17 million (as per the end of 1930). The board was not inclined to charge the remaining NLG 3 million loss against the ordinary reserves, because that would effectively wipe out those reserves, and would consequently send the wrong message to the market. In addition, the board expected that to some degree, the losses on securities would be temporary in nature and disappear on their own as the economy recovered. In the two years thereafter, some of these losses were compensated by a slight rise in share prices, and another portion was written off against the profit and the ordinary reserves.[37]

For the co-operative agricultural banks, 1932 and 1933 were defined by the crisis. In 1932, extra cash needs forced CCRB to call on DNB's discount facility, albeit only for the modest amount of NLG 200,000. Beginning in 1932, the central co-operatives fully halted all independent credit activities of their member banks. Any form of credit lending was made subject to centralized decision making. Furthermore, credit lending was restricted to purely short-term business credit, in order to maintain the full liquidity of the organization for potential emergencies. Under the new guidelines, only purely productive (short-term) credit could be extended, and only to fully creditworthy members. For long-term loans and land credit, farmers were referred to the banks that had previously been set up specifically for those objects. In that same year, the volume of savings held by the co-operative agricultural banks began to decrease, a trend that would continue at CBB until 1936. The decreasing results were another reason to tighten the management controls on the member banks.

The drop in savings at the local member banks affected the amount of funds these banks were able to deposit with the central co-operatives. This development was attributed internally to the decline in local credit demand as a result of shrinking exports in agricultural and horticultural products, only partially offset by the positive effect of governmental support. Nonetheless, a certain degree of impoverishment was taking hold across the countryside, and the local member banks' clientele were tightening their belts accordingly.

The central co-operatives continued to impress the importance of sufficient liquidity on their members, because 'many of the loans from our banks, which if not loaned would remain fully liquid, have the tendency to be at least partially converted to fixed assets and to be frozen. And as that happens it is possible that this will gradually necessitate a greater dependence on savings, so that on the one hand the regular repayment of the advances may not proceed as smoothly as before, and on the other the normal growth of savings becomes a decrease', board chairman A. N. Fleskens (1874–1946) commented during CCB's June 1933 general meeting.[38]

Earlier that same month, both central co-operatives had been invited for discussions with the board of DNB. The agenda included the central co-operatives' liquidity position, the tight interest rate margins and the insufficient (in DNB's view) reserve and capital formation. After the discussions, the board of CCRB observed that the co-operatives had apparently acquitted themselves quite well in the eyes of the DNB board, because no follow-up meeting was planned,[39] although DNB had stipulated that it should be regularly kept informed of the two co-operatives' banking activities.

In retrospect, one can see that through discussions like these, DNB was attempting to gain more insight into the trends in the Dutch banking system. The roots of this 'prudential supervision', which was concentrated on the commercial banks, date from the period after the fall of the British pound, and were based entirely on voluntary co-operation on the part of the banks.[40]

A Comparison

As described above, the rapid rise in the loan capital of the central co-operatives came to a halt in the early 1930s. The figures published by the four largest commercial banks of the time (Amsterdamsche Bank, Twentsche Bank, Incasso Bank and Robaver) present a similar picture, and they also show that thereafter the loan capital of all these banks save one (Twentsche Bank) likewise fell.

After several hard years, the figures of both central co-operatives exhibited a slight turnaround in 1933, while the downward trend continued at the commercial banks. In these years, the agricultural co-operative banks were able to access external funding in the form of deposits, while the commercial banks had to turn to other, usually more expensive, forms of funding (unlike before the 1930s when they were able to draw on savings from the market).

Recovery

Good harvests and state support brought some relief to the Dutch agricultural sector. It was almost a given that the national support payments to the farmers went through the co-operative banks. But this came at the cost of a heavier administrative burden on the central co-operatives and the local banks. These payments, often in cash, represented a virtual doubling of the workload for the smaller agricultural co-operative banks. In its 1933 annual report CCRB announced that the various agricultural organizations, which normally would have been drawing on credit, had maintained a significant positive balance as of 31 December of that year.

Generally speaking, by the second half of the 1930s most agricultural businesses were investing again, and this led to a pickup in the demand for credit. As mentioned before, the co-operative banks were able to strengthen their position in the face of the crisis. Despite the deteriorating economic conditions and the more conservative banking policy, their credit lending was never fully stopped. In addition, they maintained a lower debit interest, and they would not participate in the severe interest rate hike that the commercial banks implemented in the second half of 1935 in response to DNB's discount increases. While the commercial banks were charging 7–8 per cent interest, the agricultural co-operative banks were charging 4–4.5 per cent.

In 1936, after the depreciation of the guilder, the co-operative agricultural banks saw savings returning. That year, the funds entrusted to CCB banks rose by a total of NLG 600,000. In the year thereafter, that amount reached nearly NLG 15.5 million. Savings held by CCRB banks rose by NLG 25 million. Once again, these were primarily 'floating savings'. As before (in 1931), CCRB and CCB tried to discourage the flow of this 'hot money' in a number of ways, including by lowering interest rates.[41] Nonetheless, the savings interest rate of the co-operative agricultural banks was still higher than the percentage offered by the RPS and the ordinary savings banks, and this did not change after a new interest rate cut in 1938. Once again, the primary reason for 'floating savings' was the lack of good investment opportunities elsewhere. Interest rates on government bonds and other negotiable instruments continued to fall due to conversion, and interest on advances against collateral, bills of exchange, treasury bonds and cash loans to municipalities had fallen to unprecedented levels. It should be noted that the co-operative banks were also gradually lowering the interest rates on advances. The rock-bottom interest rates and the threat of war (from September 1938 on) took their toll. The flow of new savings to CCRB banks plummeted to a meagre NLG 3 million in 1938, while CCB banks received less than NLG 0.5 million. In 1939, the international political tensions put even more pressure on the agricultural co-operative banks' savings activities, and balances fell even further, although the demand for credit increased.

Looking back, CCB executive G. W. M. Huysmans (1902–48) concluded in 1941 that the crisis of the 1930s was, in many ways, the litmus test for the efficacy of agricultural credit in the Netherlands.[42]

Conclusion

After a review of the period before the Second World War, it is clear that the rise of the co-operative banking system in the Netherlands answered to a real demand (access to credit for small-scale farmers). As such it represented an important institutional innovation in the Dutch financial sector. Within two decades, the co-operative agricultural banks acquired a solid position, and then succeeded in reinforcing that position and shoring themselves up against the disastrous conditions of the early 1920s and into the 1930s. And this was by no means a given, in view of the fact that the target market of the co-operative agricultural banks, the agricultural sector, was struggling with a severe agricultural and economic crisis, exacerbated by financial and international political unrest. Despite the turbulent times, the co-operative agricultural banking sector was able to hold its own and consolidate its market share, where the commercial banking sector was not. No doubt one contributing factor was that not a single member bank of CCB or CCRB went bankrupt during the crisis of the 1920s or the 1930s.

Supervision of compliance with rules and regulations tended to increase during times of crisis. In view of previous experiences and the consequences of the recent agricultural crisis, the central co-operatives had already moved towards adjustments in internal control and external orientation in 1930 (with the consent of their members). These adjustments were designed to reduce the risks and maintain sufficient liquidity of the member banks as well as of each co-operative organization as a whole. Of course, unlike the listed commercial and general banks, the co-operative agricultural banks could not attract extra capital quickly when unexpectedly faced with significant financial setbacks. But the chance of failure of a bank member of CCB or CCRB was quite small. The features of the co-operative organization included not only internal safeguards and a high degree of mutual solidarity, but also, from the beginning, dedicated supervision by the central co-operatives, which was actually built into the fabric of the business model of the Dutch co-operative agricultural banks and their apex co-operation. This supervision was reinforced, partly in response to the falling results during the crisis of the 1930s, and developed into a sort of forerunner of present prudential supervision. In addition, each central organization had extensive data and figures on all its member banks. Coupled with the option of using the interest rate as a control mechanism for the central co-operatives' advances to the member banks and of the member banks' deposits to the central co-operatives, this provided the means to adjust whenever locally undesired tendencies were observed. Even in economically turbulent times, the agricultural co-operative banks proved to be solid banking institutions.[43]

Acknowledgements

The author thanks colleagues, friends and the participants of the EABH conference at Brussels (2010) for their useful suggestions and comments. This chapter presents work in progress.

4 THE DISCREET CHARM OF HIDDEN RESERVES: HOW SWISS RE SURVIVED THE GREAT DEPRESSION

Tobias Straumann

The recent Great Recession was surely one of the most severe economic crises since the end of the Second World War, but the Great Depression of the 1930s still stands out as the greatest economic catastrophe of the last hundred years.[1] However, seen from the Zurich headquarters of Swiss Re (SR), one of the leading global reinsurance companies, the exact opposite is true. The Great Depression was certainly a severe test, but it was in 2008 that SR had to report the first annual net loss in 140 years. In search for new capital, SR had to raise equity and to turn to Warren Buffet, a major competitor in the market, in order to replenish its capital. Furthermore, in February and May 2009 the chief executive and the chairman of the board of directors respectively resigned.[2] The Great Recession, not the Great Depression, proved to be the most severe crisis in the company's history.

This chapter tries to show why and how SR was able to maintain its position in the midst of a collapsing global economy during the 1930s. My conclusions are based on the minutes of the board and the internal figures that were available to directors and senior managers at the time. The main result of this investigation is that SR's survival can be explained neither by short-term actions nor by strategic decisions taken by the board in the course of the crisis. The effects of short-term actions were too limited to make a difference, and there were practically no strategic decisions aimed at reorienting the business model in order to mitigate the losses. It was rather the high level of hidden reserves accumulated prior to the crisis which saved SR. Without them, the company would have become insolvent in 1931. Conversely, if during the recent Great Recession SR had disposed of the same amount of hidden reserves, the net gains would have been quite high, and the chairman and the chief executive would still be in office.

This insight is not entirely new, of course. We know from other studies in insurance history that hidden reserves repeatedly played a crucial role in cushioning financial and economic shocks. Clive Trebilcock, for example, mentions in his seminal study of *Phoenix Assurance* that '[s]trong expansion of the "hidden reserve" in the 1920s held the line against the worst the markets could throw at it [*Phoenix Assurance*] during the crash years'.[3] But there is no doubt that our knowledge of how macroeconomic shocks were absorbed by the financial sector is not developed well enough. In this context, the chapter tries to make two contributions. First, it is the first article providing and interpreting internal figures of a leading global reinsurance company during the Great Depression. While there has been at least some research on the history of the reinsurance industry – though still too little given its crucial role for the insurance business and globalization – there has been no research at all regarding the reinsurance industry during the Great Depression.[4] Second, this study adds another piece of evidence to the growing literature on the interaction between macroeconomic shocks and the financial sector.[5] In particular, it confirms the view that the course of a financial crisis cannot be understood without archival research and a detailed analysis of the balanced sheets of financial intermediaries. Evidently, published figures are worthless in the context of short-term economic fluctuations.

The remainder of this chapter consists of four parts. Part one provides an overview of SR's history from its foundation in 1863 to the late 1920s. Part two reports the gains and losses during the Great Depression. Part three discusses SR's policy during the 1930s. Part four closes the chapter with a short conclusion.

A Brief History of Swiss Re (SR)

SR was founded in late 1863 by a transport insurance company and two commercial banks: the Allgemeine Versicherungs-Gesellschaft Helvetia in St Gallen, the Basler Handelsbank and the Schweizerische Kreditanstalt in Zürich. The driving force was Moritz Grossmann (1830–1910), director of Helvetia and one of the leading insurance experts in Continental Europe at the time. He was born into a converted Jewish family in Mischlenitz (Galicia, Austria-Hungary) and made an impressive career in Vienna and Trieste where he was employed by Nuova Società Commerciale di Assicurazioni, a subsidiary of Generali and a major pillar of Jewish insurance in the Mediterranean. In 1858 Grossmann immigrated to St Gallen to become Helvetia's first director when called by a group of Swiss merchants.

The rationale behind the foundation of SR was straightforward. Switzerland, though by the mid-nineteenth century one of the most industrialized regions on the European Continent, lacked a reinsurance company providing the emerging insurance industry with sufficient cover against fire catastrophes. The creation of SR was strongly motivated by economic nationalism that had also been a major factor behind the foundation in 1856 of the Schweizerische Kreditanstalt (today's Credit Suisse), Switzerland's first commercial bank. When Grossmann came up with the idea of founding a reinsurance company in Switzerland, he was inspired by developments in the German states. Since the 1850s, so-called professional reinsurance companies had been operating in this new field, most notably the Kölnische Rückversicherungs-Gesellschaft. These new German

reinsurers specialized in providing cover for insurance companies while tradi-
tionally insurance companies had reinsured each other. In July 1863, Grossmann
submitted a memorandum to the board of Helvetia, calling for the creation of a
professional reinsurance company in Switzerland and predicting a bright future
for this new kind of business.[6] Grossmann's arguments convinced leading figures
of the Swiss banking and insurance establishment, among them Alfred Escher,
the president of the Schweizerische Kreditanstalt. A few days before Christmas,
SR was founded in Zurich.

SR's history until the eve of the Great Depression can be divided into three
phases. The first few years were dominated by the struggle for survival.[7] Shortly
after the foundation a series of losses threatened to bring a fast end to the Swiss
experiment in reinsurance. The company could only survive thanks to the actions
taken by Grossmann and the managing director Giuseppe Besso who also had
worked for the Nuova Società in Trieste and was recruited by Grossmann after
the sudden death of SR's first managing director. By the end of the 1870s when
Besso left in order to take a leading position at Generali under his brother Marco
Besso, the business was stabilized.[8] SR remained a small company, but was quite
profitable.[9] From this perspective, SR was not only founded, but also brought up
by insurance managers from Trieste.

The second phase began in the 1890s when a rapid geographic expansion
set in. Increasingly, SR underwrote US business, especially in the states on the
Pacific Coast. Accordingly, the great San Francisco earthquake in April 1906
proved a major setback for SR's US business. In the medium run, however, the
earthquake accelerated SR's overseas expansion as it served as a catalyst for the
founding of the first US subsidiary in New York in 1910. The architect of the
expansion was Charles Simon from Strasbourg who, recommended by SR's
founder Grossmann, had entered the firm in the mid-1890s and served as its
director since 1900. He represented the typical insurance manager in its ideal
form. He spoke several languages, commanded a vast knowledge in the humani-
ties, and knew how to use his charm in order to get the best conditions. He also
never backed away in the face of mounting difficulties. His contemporary biog-
rapher cited a professional musician observing that when playing difficult pieces
on his piano Simon would rather decelerate the time than give in by skipping the
passage altogether.[10]

With the outbreak of the First World War, a third phase began. SR continued
to expand, but the character of this expansion changed radically. While before
1914 the reinsurance market as a whole was prospering, SR was now growing
thanks to the decline of its competitors. The main German rivals, in particular
Munich Re, were banned from the US market after President Wilson brought
his country into the war in April 1917. The Russian insurance companies, which
before the First World War had acquired an even larger market share in the US
than the German reinsurers, withdrew after the Russian Revolution in November 1917. Almost overnight, SR became the leading professional reinsurer in the

US market. Its position in the US was further strengthened in 1923 when SR began to offer reinsurance in life insurance business. As inflation and hyperinflation after the war further weakened European competitors, SR also took over other reinsurance companies and – for the first time in its history – acquired stakes in direct insurers in France and Germany. The architect of the rapid rise to the top was Erwin Hürlimann, the first Swiss manager in SR's history to climb to the top position. He was a former banker, trained in London, and fascinated by financial markets. He loved the Anglo-Saxon way of doing business, married a British woman, and had himself built an English rural house in Central Switzerland. In the 1920s, Hürlimann increased SR's share of stocks, especially in the US, in order to optimize the financial result. In 1928, he initiated the foundation of an investment company, dubbed Intercontinentale Anlage-Gesellschaft (IAG), which was to manage a large part of SR's stakes in other insurance and reinsurance companies in Europe.[11] This shift towards more risky assets was always supported by the board, in particular by Charles Simon who had become its chairman in 1919.

Summarizing, at the end of the 1920s SR was in a very strong position. It offered every branch of business and was present in all major countries, especially in the US which was by far the most dynamic market of the time. As for the asset side, SR had a high exposure in US shares. SR's evolution since the turn of the century had been spectacular. In 1900, it had been a minor player in the international market, employing only little more than 100 staff and doing business almost exclusively with Austrian, German and Swiss insurance companies. At the end of the 1920s, SR employed 400 staff and was one of the most globalized companies of the world, with two of the most respected and experienced reinsurance specialists being at the helm, Charles Simon and Erwin Hürlimann.

Gains and Losses during the Great Depression

Since SR as a global company was exposed to the fluctuations of all major markets, the US downturn starting in late 1929 was immediately felt in Zurich. It took some time, however, until the full impact of the global slump began to be taken seriously by the board. The stock market crash on Wall Street in October 1929 and the beginning of a global recession in 1930 were not seen as particularly unsettling events. In the annual report for the year 1930 the board did not sound alarmed.[12] One reason it remained cautiously optimistic was that the technical results had been good and were expected to withstand the storm. In general, the reinsurance business had been independent of the business cycle because of its long-term outlook. The fluctuation of profits and losses was related to the premium cycles and the irregular frequency of major natural or man-made catastrophes. Only the asset side was directly linked to the business cycle.[13] But, so far, the losses were not worrying.

Not even the collapse of the Austrian Credit-Anstalt in May 1931 and the German banking and currency crisis two months later were seen as turning points.[14] Only when the British pound fell in September, the SR board began to realize that this slump was more than a severe, though normal recession. Investors were frightened and desperately searching for liquidity. Switzerland, closely linked to the British market, was one of the main targets of speculators. A few Swiss banks were also beginning to show signs of weakness. SR's share price plunged from 3,025 Swiss francs to 2,600 Swiss francs within a few days. On 26 September, the board scheduled a special meeting although chairman Simon and chief executive Hürlimann were absent.[15] The SR was now fully affected by the depression, and the struggle for survival began. In his report to the shareholders of May 1932, Simon used biblical terminology to describe the situation: 'Since the devaluation of the British pound occurred and the economic crisis further deepened, we live in constant fear and trepidation.'[16] In the annual report for the year 1931, the board spoke of a 'catastrophic development'.[17]

The downturn in fact proved to be disastrous. Figure 4.1 plots SR's financial and technical results, showing a dramatic deterioration of the situation in 1931. The financial result brought a loss of almost forty million Swiss francs. The figure also reveals that the recovery did not set in before the Second World War. Further losses resulted in 1933, when the dollar was devalued, as well as in 1935, 1937 and 1938. Only in 1934 and 1936 the financial result was satisfactory. In 1936, the devaluation of the Swiss franc by 30 per cent explains part of the positive financial result.

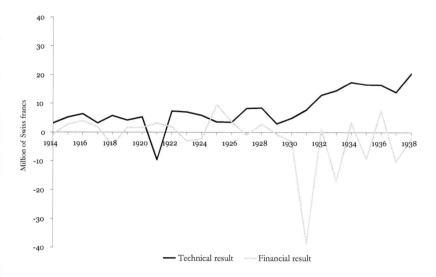

Figure 4.1: Technical and financial results of Swiss Re.

Source: SR Archives Zurich (Switzerland): P. Guggenbühl, *Hausstatistik der Schweizer Rück* (Zurich, 1939).

Further statistical data reveal that the financial losses resulted from a plunge of share prices on the asset side (Table 4.1). Hürlimann's decision to increase the weight of US stocks during the 1920s proved fatal. From 1930 to 1938, total write-downs in the United States amounted to nearly twenty-six million Swiss francs, in France to more than nine million Swiss francs, and in Germany to 2.3 million Swiss francs. To be sure, some of the losses were due to the fact that for regulatory reasons SR had to invest a large share of its US premiums in the US market. But SR's main losses resulted from the collapse of share prices between 1929 and 1933 when first-rate corporate and government bonds remained largely untouched by the crisis. Shifting from bonds to stocks was the main source of the losses, not the investments in the US market as such.

Table 4.1: Composition of Swiss Re's assets.

	Total Assets	Securities	Bonds	Stocks
1920	267,971	79,887	49,077	3,157
1921	230,316	74,648	51,166	3,808
1922	208,699	78,756	59,268	4,374
1923	239,536	89,558	61,259	14,033
1924	263,625	105,793	67,984	22,802
1925	286,751	111,999	60,103	26,796
1926	325,178	129,949	71,514	34,026
1927	380,142	151,077	82,229	39,052
1928	435,368	188,136	83,316	71,911
1929	478,397	181,943	77,751	74,926
1930	499,812	179,639	78,306	74,568
1931	482,023	140,796	68,518	46,011
1932	514,394	151,013	77,847	45,522
1933	501,455	137,841	72,479	39,221
1934	546,957	181,296	113,471	39,346
1935	577,566	181,081	120,788	34,506
1936	716,772	231,330	166,060	39,549
1937	738,188	231,534	168,749	36,584
1938	780,375	244,203	184,030	33,931

Source: SR Archives Zurich (Switzerland): P. Guggenbühl, *Hausstatistik der Schweizer Rück* (Zurich, 1939), pp. 325, 329.

Swiss Re Policies during the 1930s

Despite the tremendous losses on the asset side, SR survived the Great Depression quite well, at least officially. The reported gains were always positive, the dividends remained stable, and neither the chairman nor the chief executive had to step down. At the end of the decade, SR was still the world's largest reinsurer and proved strong enough to survive the Second World War without major setbacks, even though the international insurance networks collapsed.

So, was it luck or strategy that allowed SR to overcome the Great Depression? Given that both Simon and Hürlimann enjoyed great esteem in the word of reinsurance, it is obvious to assume that there must have been a clever strategy behind the good performance. The historical evidence, however, suggests the exact opposite. Management was more or less helpless in the face of the large macroeconomic shock following the European banking and currency crises in 1931. There was hardly any need for strategic discussions because nobody was able to look far ahead. Surely, the SR board did all it could to contain the effects of the crisis. Yet, what ultimately saved the company from bankruptcy was the accumulation of hidden reserves prior to the crisis (Table 4.2). In 1931, nearly thirty million Swiss francs were taken out of this reserve pool in order to cover the record loss. In one stroke, this payment wiped out nearly the whole amount of hidden reserves the board had built up in the aftermath of the San Francisco earthquake of 1906. By the end of 1931, the amount of hidden reserves had shrunk to 4.4 million Swiss francs. In an internal report commissioned by chairman Simon at the end of the 1930s, SR concluded that 'only thanks to its prudent reserve policy the company was able to overcome the shocks ... without taking permanent damage'.[18]

In view of this extraordinary reduction of hidden reserves, other actions taken by the SR board were clearly secondary. One measure consisted in supporting the share price. As mentioned, its sudden decline following the fall of sterling in September 1931 prompted the board to schedule a special meeting even though the chairman and the chief executive were not in Zurich at the time.[19] A few days later, after a failed attempt to support the share price by intervening in the market, chairman Simon, back from his vacation in Nizza, issued a press release that made an end to rumours about SR's imminent collapse. In the first week of October 1931, the share price climbed back to 2,800 Swiss francs, near the old level. Furthermore, the board decided to intervene in the market in case the share price was to fall again, but the decision had no practical consequences because the Swiss stock markets remained calm for a while.[20]

Table 4.2: Real gain, reported gain, hidden reserves and dividends (in Tsd. of CHF).

	Real gain/loss	Reported gain/loss	Hidden reserves	Dividends
1920	6,878	2,240	35,681	1,500
1921	−6,433	2,226	27,022	1,500
1922	9,140	3,048	31,614	1,500
1923	4,063	3,406	31,271	1,785
1924	3,600	3,864	30,007	2,250
1925	13,107	3,994	38,120	2,250
1926	7,065	4,072	40,113	2,320
1927	7,374	5,660	39,827	2,320
1928	11,168	6,167	43,828	2,321
1929	2,203	6,755	39,876	4,330
1930	1,697	7,873	33,700	6,186
1931	−30,865	8,435	4,400	6,186
1932	14,112	8,112	10,400	6,186
1933	−2,503	5,297	2,600	6,283
1934	20,654	8,654	14,675	7,288
1935	7,276	8,076	13,875	7,405
1936	23,882	10,382	25,875	7,404
1937	3,696	8,146	22,725	7,404
1938	18,082	10,207	29,300	7,404

Source: SR Archives Zurich (Switzerland): P. Guggenbühl, *Hausstatistik der Schweizer Rück* (Zurich, 1939), pp. 369, 371–2.

Another measure was the replacement of dollar assets by gold. The decision was taken in mid-October 1931, although not unanimously. While the board in Zurich was determined to reduce the exposure in the US market, Hürlimann who had been sent to the United States to get a picture of the economic conditions remained very confident. On 11 November he sent a telegram, and on 18 December he was back in Zurich to give an account of his impressions. He was still convinced that the recession was near its end and that SR should continue to expand in the United States, especially in casualty reinsurance, which entailed further investments in US dollars. The board was not convinced, however, and continued to sell its dollar assets. By the end of 1931, the investment was reduced from 70.9 million Swiss francs to 42.5 million Swiss francs.[21]

After the dramatic events in the fall of 1931, the SR board remained unable to address strategic issues, although the economy began to show signs of recovery in 1933 after the Roosevelt administration had devalued the US dollar and cleaned up the banking system. The reason for SR's paralysis was that the investment situation remained extremely difficult. Since 1931, Germany and a number of Central and Eastern European countries had imposed various restrictions on foreign investments, transfer payments and capital mobility. The so-called gold bloc, formed in 1933 and consisting of France, Italy as well as Belgium, the Netherlands, Switzerland and Poland, was expected to fall apart any time soon. In 1934 Italy introduced capital controls, in 1935 Belgium abandoned its parity, and in September 1936, almost exactly five years after the fall of the British pound, France decided to devalue, followed by the Netherlands and Switzerland. Additionally, the exchange rates of the sterling bloc against the Swiss franc were not yet stabilized.[22]

Only the US dollar seemed to be a stable currency after its devaluation in April 1933. Accordingly, SR began to increase its investments in the US securities markets as soon as conditions would allow. This moment came when the devaluation of the Swiss franc in September 1936 brought a considerable short-term gain because SR had transformed its franc assets into gold several months before the devaluation occurred. The new cash holdings were invested in dollar securities. The board expected that the US had overcome the depression and that the stock market would bring stable profits again. Yet, the newly gained confidence was deeply shattered when the US economy plunged into another recession in the second half of 1937. SR had to write down several million US dollars. The weight of shares was reduced dramatically.[23]

After 1933, the SR board took only one far-reaching decision when resolving in May 1934 to merge with its subsidiary Prudentia.[24] Prudentia had been founded in 1875 as an in-house *retrocessionaire* (i.e. reinsurer of a reinsurer) in the transport business and had acquired a concession in New York in 1918 in order to capture the orphaned German business in the US market. The New York branch of SR, founded in 1910, was not allowed to take over these German treaties because it was bound by its close cooperation with the British insurance company Phoenix. Accordingly, when SR merged with Prudentia in 1934, it had to sever its ties with Phoenix which proved to be surprisingly unproblematic. By the end of the year the merger was complete.[25] Yet, although the merger had more far-reaching consequences than all other measures taken during the 1930s, the motivation behind this measure was mainly short-term in its nature. SR was confronted with the problem that the dramatic decrease of hidden reserves in 1931 threatened to reduce the level of dividend payments. Fearing that a likely protest of shareholders would provoke negative market reactions, the SR was in search of new funds. By merging with Prudentia, it obtained new capital without making the shareholders suspicious. The dividend payments could be upheld at the old level (30 per cent of nominal value of share).

Besides the decision to merge with Prudentia, the board also tried to reorganize its holdings. During the Great Depression, the companies in France and Germany acquired after the First World War had suffered from considerable losses to be covered by SR. In September 1933, it was decided to sell the Austrian insurance company Anker to Generali. Yet, the deal did not materialize.[26]

Another opportunity in 1934 also failed after serious negotiations began.[27] At least, the board could go forward with the liquidation of the investment company AIG, but the decision was not taken before December 1937, since the board had been divided on this issue for several years. The liquidation represented the last step in the process of readjusting SR's investment policy towards safe and liquid assets. Strategically, it was of no relevance.

Conclusions

The question of how SR survived the Great Depression has a surprisingly simple answer. It was due to the high amount of hidden reserves accumulated after the San Francisco earthquake of 1906. They allowed the SR board to report a positive result although the real financial results were catastrophic in some years, especially in 1931. Thus, neither specific short-term actions nor strategic decisions made a crucial difference. Moreover, the role of strategic decisions did not increase once the worst was over. On the contrary, the SR board remained cautious and continued to focus on tactical changes in the short run.

This finding may be relevant for the ongoing discussion on how to regulate the financial sector. Surely, there are many similarities between the Great Recession and the Great Depression. Then and now, the slump was severe and extraordinary, causing huge losses across the insurance and reinsurance sector. Furthermore, the technical results remained stable in both episodes. And most important, the weakness in both periods was SR's investment strategy prior to the crisis: the increase of US shares in the portfolio during the 1920s, and the investment in the US subprime market in the 2000s. The crucial difference between then and now seems to be only the lack of hidden reserves. In the final decades of the twentieth century, shareholders may have had good reasons to become increasingly suspicious of how management used various tricks and means to hide part of the annual earnings. From a historical perspective, however, the trend towards more transparency has come at some cost.

The main result of this case study may also be relevant for a future research agenda in financial history. Quantifying the importance of hidden reserves for the absorption of the macroeconomic shocks in the past could shed new light on the interaction between the economy and the financial sector. The recent financial crisis has clearly taught us that the analysis of aggregate figures is not sufficient to understand the linkages between the banks and the so-called real economy. We have to study and better understand the balance sheets of financial intermediaries. Financial historians appear to be in a particularly good position to find new data and come up with surprising insights. Important steps have already been taken, but there is still a long way to go.[28]

5 THE REDESIGN OF THE BANK–INDUSTRY–FINANCIAL MARKET TIES IN THE US GLASS–STEAGALL AND THE 1936 ITALIAN BANKING ACTS

Federico Barbiellini Amidei and Claire Giordano

Introduction

The 1930s banking crises triggered a sweeping legislative response in many countries, where each regulatory action tended to be crafted in order to address what was considered as the main cause of the recently occurred domestic banking crisis, so as to prevent the break-out of similar ones in the future. Hence, notwithstanding some similarities, each act was country-specific and aimed at eradicating different types of 'evils': thus, the usefulness of cross-country analyses. This chapter provides a historical comparison between the 1933 and 1935 US Banking Acts and the 1936 Italian Banking Act, in their parts relative to the redefinition of the links between banks, industry and financial markets.

Our main claim is that the Italian Banking Act differed in this respect more than the – surprisingly scanty – existing comparative literature seems to suggest, particularly because little attention has been given to the second of the mentioned US Banking Acts. We challenge the commonplace conclusion that in Italy, as in the US, the 1930s banking legislation aimed primarily at splitting commercial from investment banking. As well as contributing to historical knowledge, this research question appears to be quite timely as economists, regulators and politicians worldwide are redesigning the new regulatory architecture after the 2007–8 crisis. An in-depth analysis of the historical precursors of the current proposals, and the 'evils' they aimed to address, may be useful to gain a better understanding of the current debate and of its policy implications.

To achieve the two-fold aim of this chapter, we have analysed the US Congressional Record and the Italian Parliamentary Acts. In the Italian case, the 1936 Banking Act was designed within the walls of the Istituto per la Ricostruzione Industriale (IRI); we have thus analysed contemporary documents of IRI, as well as of the main banks of the time and of the Bank of Italy.[1] This archival research was supplemented by the analysis of papers published by contemporary economists and commentators in scientific journals in the two countries, as well as of relevant press articles of the time.

The following section briefly retraces the evolution of the US and Italian banking sectors and their relations with the financial markets in the decades prior to the 1930s. After a recapitulation of the banking crises in the two countries, and of the rescue measures undertaken, the chapter focuses on the letter of the two sets of legislation, with respect to the bank–industry–financial markets linkages, in order to highlight analogies and differences. Conclusions are presented in the final section.

The Italian and the US Banking Sectors in the Decades Prior to the 1930s

Since the nineteenth century, the banking systems in the two countries had developed along a different track. In Italy, after the 1893–4 financial crisis, 'mixed banks' (*banche miste*) came to play a leading role in corporate finance. They advised and assisted IPOs, frequently underwriting large amounts of shares. Trustees of the banks routinely sat on the boards of the main client firms, becoming actual 'inside directors'.[2] Furthermore, banks, acting as safe-keepers of stocks for their clients, were generally able to exercise the relative voting rights without being disclosed as official stock-holders.[3] Compared with Germany, in Italy, where legal institutions were weaker, the banks resorted to more intense relationships with the stock exchange and used contango loans on stocks (*riporti su azioni*). As a result, banks acquired relevant market-maker positions in the three main stock exchanges (Milan, Turin and Genoa). Italian commercial banks on the one hand freely underwrote and traded securities – mainly stocks – in-house; on the other they lent long-term, accepting securities and real estate as collateral. Investment trusts and investment banks did not appear in Italy, since the mixed banks engaged, unconstrained, in the entire array of financial services.

The 1907 stock market crash thwarted the development of Italy's security markets. The traders in the Genoa stock market were identified as the main culprits of the crisis and this led to the enactment of new restrictive financial regulations in 1913.[4] In particular, the law reserved outcry trading on the stock market exclusively to exchange and securities brokers, thus cutting out all other financial intermediaries, such as mixed banks. However, according to the 'single capacity' principle,[5] brokers could only act for account of their clients and not for their own account.[6] Furthermore, brokers could not engage in banking activities or become stakeholders of private banks.[7] They also could not obtain monopolistic control over listed securities' tradings. Banks thus traded securities among their customers and took only the net transaction to the market. A 'shadow system' dominated by the mixed banks became a forum of exchanges, thereby subtracting liquidity from the official market and reducing the significance of the prices determined there. In conclusion, the 1913 law actually reined in the role of brokers in financial intermediation, leaving the stage clear for an unprecedented financial market-impairing expansion of (unregulated) mixed banks.

Conversely, in the US, according to the 1864 National Banking Act, national banks could not underwrite, trade or hold equities for their own or for their customers' account. The Act also set restrictions on their real estate loans. As a result of these regulations, commercial banks had no significant role in the expanding equity markets. Due to their restrictions in security dealings until World War I, national banks also suffered from competition coming from investment trusts, which operated under looser state laws. Trust companies first appeared in the US in the 1820s and were initially engaged in personal asset administration. From the 1850s onwards they could receive deposits of money in trust and purchase corporate securities. From the 1880s, they also began to lend on collateral of securities and buy paper in the market, thus moving into the more traditional banking business.[8] Forbidden from engaging in trust operations, national banks organized state-chartered trust affiliates. Similarly, to evade the restriction on securities dealings and underwritings, they formed dedicated state-chartered affiliates. The 1913 Federal Reserve Act later allowed national banks to exercise trust powers directly and loosened the restrictions on their loans on real estate.

Investment banks too began to develop in the US in the second half of the nineteenth century, often joining together in syndicates, which were managed by originating houses, such as J. P. Morgan and Kuhn Loeb, as well as Lehman Brothers and Goldman Sachs after 1906.[9] These (unregulated and unsupervised) houses negotiated directly with issuing corporations, advising them and defining the type and terms of the security and the details of the offering. Corporate debt was the main security transacted. Representation of investment banks on boards of directors became common. Investment houses could take the entire issue themselves or organize a 'purchase syndicate' in which institutional investors (i.e. state-chartered commercial banks, security affiliates, investment trusts) and wealthy individuals were invited to participate by the originator, and contractually agreed to sell the securities at a uniform price at specified times and places. In the case of large flotations, the originating houses could ask several commercial banks to form a 'banking syndicate' to lend the purchasers the necessary funds. The process was slow: syndicate agreements often lasted one year and the distribution several months.

World War I was a turning point in both countries, in that it changed the structure of their financial systems. In the US, commercial banks began dealing in securities on a large scale; in Italy the mixed banks evolved into actual holding companies of industrial firms.

In the US, both commercial and investment banks alike had participated heavily in distributing government bonds to finance the war effort. This nation-wide sales drive had two important effects: (a) it enabled the banks to develop an efficient distribution network for securities; and (b) it made the public more receptive to purchasing securities.[10] Furthermore, in the bull securities market of the 1920s, corporations began approaching the equity and bond markets directly in order to raise funds. New securities offered by corporations increased fourfold in that decade, from $2.788 million in 1921 to $9.377 million in 1929.[11] The flip side of this growth was a decline in commercial bank borrowing on corporate balance sheets, a 'technical revolution in debt financing'.[12] The downsizing of commercial banks' traditional lending business was also due to an increase in competition from other financial institutions, such as investment, finance or insurance companies;[13] commercial banks thus had to seek employment for their funds elsewhere. Hence 'banks' new financial services were not begun as part of a speculative lark ... [but] represented a move by these firms to offset the decline of their traditional business and meet the challenges presented by trust companies and investment banks'.[14] As a result, in the 1920s, US commercial banks were heavily involved in credit extension, security distribution and in the exercise of fiduciary and trust functions. Their earnings from fees in fact doubled between 1920 and 1930, passing from 6.3 per cent to 11.9 per cent.[15]

Investment banks' activities also changed in these years. A new *stratum* was added below underwriting syndicates, known as '"selling groups"',[16] whose members committed to purchasing securities only to the extent that they could find buyers. It was still the originating house, however, who decided the terms of distribution. The distribution process was speeded up to a matter of days. Also due to a general improvement in the quality of available information on corporate profits, investors moved into equity purchases. The number of share-owners thus passed from half a million in 1900 to two million of investors in 1920.[17] By 1929 established investment bankers were complaining that their business was decreasing in profitability due to a general hike in competition. The entry of commercial banks especially posed a threat because of: (a) the greater capital they could devote to underwriting; (b) the larger sales staff they employed; and (c) the large pool of potential clients they had among their depositors. Rather than lending funds for short periods to investment banking syndicates, as they had previously done, commercial banks began to use those funds in direct competition.[18]

Commercial banks engaged in security businesses in two ways. They could operate via state-chartered securities affiliates, which were often tiny and operated from the same premises of the parent banks, whilst benefiting from their parents' name and reputation.[19] Alternatively, national banks could directly deal in investment securities via their internal 'captive' bond departments, as this was unofficially approved of by the Office of the Comptroller of the Currency (OCC). They could not, however, deal in equity nor offer residential mortgages internally. The number of national banks engaged in securities activities went from seventy-two to 178 between 1922 and 1933.[20] By 1929 commercial banks and their security affiliates had equalled investment banks in terms of volume of securities underwritten.[21]

Many small investors might still have shied away from buying securities, not having sufficient capital to buy a diversified portfolio of stocks. This need was satisfied by the lightly regulated investment trusts, whose numbers increased (from forty before 1921 to 265 in 1929[22]), or by public utility holding companies in the case of utilities. Many trusts dealt in securities, participated in underwriting and made short-term loans;[23] some even bought shares in other trusts, 'a definite pathology'.[24] Investment banks soon began sponsoring them, succumbing 'to the investment trust mania that swept American finance in the late 1920s':[25] by 1929 over 60 per cent of trusts were sponsored by investment banks, brokers or dealers.[26] The latter profited from the distribution of the trusts' securities and received management fees for operating the trust, which in turn could lend money to its sponsoring investment bank, deposit funds in it and could be used to purchase securities that the investment bank underwrote.

In Italy, during and immediately after World War I, a new type of financial institution appeared. On the industry side, big corporations made intensive use of financial holdings (and, after 1923, of shares with multiple voting rights), in order to guarantee control, while at the same time minimizing the capital. On the banking side, the Italian mixed banks increasingly resorted to more intricate financial relationships with industry, through 'under the line' operations, with the recourse to front agents funded by contango loans to buy and sell stocks on behalf and in the interest of the banks, as well as through the institution of holding companies and of controlling syndicates.[27] The contemporary Italian economist Piero Sraffa's words were prophetic: 'The greatest danger entailed in the financing of industry by banks is to be found in the consequent close relations between banks and industry', in the general tendency towards 'the formation of large "groups" of companies of the most varied kinds concentrated around one or more banks, mutually related by the exchange of shares and by the appointment of Directors common to them'.[28] The danger arising in this picture from 'the contrast between the shortness' of Italian banks' debts and 'the non-liquidity of their credits' was heightened by the significance of their big debtors' *conti di corrispondenza* amongst their deposits ('by far the more important').

> Most of the deposits of each bank thus belong to the same group of persons and concerns to which the bank makes loans ... Thus, in substance, a large part of the deposits constitute the common capital of a group of industrial concerns ... In such

conditions, should a bank refuse its industrial clients the loans they require, it would also lose their deposits.[29]

As the CEO of Banca Commerciale Italiana (hereafter Comit), one of the three main mixed banks, would later say:

> The physiological symbiosis had turned into a monstrous Siamese twinning. The banks were still 'mixed' banks formally, but substantially they had become *banques d'affaire* ... Nor was this all: to protect themselves ... the banks had bought back practically all their capital: they owned themselves via the ownership of the financial holdings created and financed by them to guarantee 'the control' over their capital ... The Siamese twinning led to *catoblepismo*.[30]

Both the US and Italy went through an unprecedented stock market boom in the 1920s.[31] In Italy, the 1922–5 boom was fuelled by the mixed banks' purchases, motivated by the huge profit opportunities. In the US 1922–9 boom, where 'the universal bank format, in which banks own equity and households own liabilities of banks, was not the practice',[32] the banks were nevertheless involved in the financing of equity positions, as securities were used for collateralized borrowing, and also through their involvement in the securities underwriting, dealing and distributing process.

In Italy, when the stock market weakened already in 1925, the banks stepped in to stem the falling value of equities. They tried to recover liquidity through the strategy of fictitious sales and transfers of securities to new captive holding companies.[33] Unable to reverse the bear market on their own, they jointly created the Società Finanziamento Titoli (Softit) in order to 'purchase and sell securities, receive and extend contango loans, offer and collect funds on listed securities and engage in any correlated financial operation'[34] so as to support the market price of securities. Softit received heavy financial support from the Bank of Italy and the Treasury. Since this attempt too failed, the banks had no alternative but to hold on to their equity portfolios, to limit their losses. The other side of the story is that industrial enterprises became even more dependent on bank lending as a source of funding.

As a delayed response to the 1920s banking crisis in Italy, which saw the collapse of a large mixed bank and the bailout of another (Banco di Roma), the first commercial banking regulation was enacted in 1926.[35] The law introduced restrictions on lending to any single borrower, but admitted exceptions which were successfully exploited by the main banks; thus it did not effectively deal with the dangerous bank–industry interconnections. In the US the McFadden Act was passed one year later (in 1927) in an opposite attempt to lift existing restrictions. The law, in fact, further encouraged nonfarm real estate loans by national banks and it made internal bond – but not stock – operations officially permissible for national banks on a par with the state-chartered ones.[36]

The 1930s Banking Crises and Regulatory Responses

The 1930s Banking Crisis and Crisis-Management Measures in Italy and the US

The October 1929 stock market crash is commonly considered as the starting date of the Great Depression. The first banking panic began to develop in late 1930, the first of four.[37] The failure of the large New York-based commercial Bank of United States in December 1930, the largest in US history up to that time, had a particularly adverse effect on depositor confidence.[38] Security dealings, conducted by its affiliates, were pinpointed as the main cause of the bank's failure.[39] No action was taken.

The crisis also marked the beginning of a 'new era in commercial bank lending' in the US.[40] Some of the large city banks began to provide borrowers – mainly utility and manufacturing firms – with one- to three-year loans, as the sharp decline in corporate profits, followed by the collapse of the bond market in late 1930, left many corporations with no alternative but to resort to bank loans to finance their operations. Some extended short-term loans were converted into long-term loans.

The initial banking crisis did not last long, as bank failures declined in early 1931. In their scramble for liquidity, however, banks dumped their low-grade corporate bonds, whose prices fell and thus increased the pressure on the bond market.[41] By reducing the market value of banks' bond portfolios, declines in bond prices in turn reduced capital margins, and in this way contributed to subsequent bank failures.[42] The onset of the second banking crisis is dated March 1931 and was aggravated by the repercussions from the banking panic in Central Europe in the summer and by Great Britain's departure from the gold standard in September.[43] President Hoover promoted the creation of the Reconstruction Finance Corporation (RFC) in January 1932 to make one-year loans to banks and to railroads owned by them, which were on the verge of default, but on 'full and adequate security'.[44] After the creation of the RFC, the banking panic subsided.[45]

A month later, the first Glass–Steagall Act was enacted on 27 February 1932; it was an emergency measure, which mainly broadened the collateral the Federal Reserve System could hold against loans to individual banks. Glass was then 'prepared to go ahead with the permanent legislation which we have in mind'.[46] A new peak in bank failures was attained in March 1932 and only in April, under heavy Congressional pressure, did the Federal Reserve System embark on large-scale open market purchases. Bank failures again subsided. By the end of 1932, however, a new banking panic ensued.[47]

The assets of US commercial banks shrank by almost one third between 1929 and 1932, and almost 40 per cent of these banks actually failed.[48] Furthermore, by 1932 an estimated 2,000 investment banks and brokerage firms had also gone out of business. J. P. Morgan's deposits fell by nearly a half, from $504 million in 1929 to $319 million in 1932, whilst Kuhn Loeb's reduced six-fold, from $88.5 million to $15.2 million.[49] Many investment trusts failed too, and their total assets shrank by around 60 per cent between 1930 and 1933.[50]

On 6 March 1933 the new President Roosevelt declared a nationwide banking holiday until 9 March, the day on which Congress enacted an Emergency Banking Act, authorizing emergency issues of Federal Reserve Bank notes and allowing the RFC to invest in the preferred stock, capital notes and debentures of commercial banks. Insolvent banks were closed in an attempt to lessen the uncertainty driving the panic. This was followed by the US leaving the gold standard in April 1933.

Italy did not stand aloof from comparable contractions. Industrial output declined by one fourth between 1929 and 1932. Confronted with deflation and falling demand, industrial firms could hardly rely on financing out of retained profits, while at the same time they saw the real value of their debts increase. They could thus only turn to banks for further loans. Banks were forced to 'hold, if not increase, the credit extended to industry, which otherwise would have found itself in a situation of ... financial imbalance'. On the other hand, it was impossible to float industrial shares on the internal markets:

> financial markets practically stopped working: they did not absorb new issues anymore to demobilize banks' industrial credits, but instead demanded long and continuous interventions by the banks to avoid sharp drops in prices, that would have discouraged the already few investors[51]

The withdrawal of foreign lines of credit made banks ever more dependent on credit from the Bank of Italy. By the beginning of 1931, Comit and Credito Italiano (hereafter Credit) had no alternative but to turn to the government which secretly mandated loans to them, via the Liquidation Institute, ultimately financed by the Bank of Italy.[52] In turn, the banks accepted a restriction of their activities to 'ordinary' credit operations, including a ban on holding any new stake in industrial or real estate firms.

As Italy's industrial enterprises saw their long-term credit lines cut off by these agreements, a State-owned long-term credit institution was created in the same year.[53] The Istituto Mobiliare Italiano (IMI) was to finance itself on the market through the issuance of ten-year bonds with State guarantees, as it was banned from collecting deposits.[54] IMI's bonds were listed on the stock exchange, could be taken to the Bank of Italy to be discounted and could be accepted by public entities as cautionary deposits. Funded in this way, IMI was supposed to extend loans to industrial firms on the collateral of securities or real estate, as well as to hold equity stakes in the firms and to engage in trust activities. Hence IMI, in its first years, potentially was not only a medium-term credit institution (extending mortgages and funds fuelled by bond issues), but also: a financial holding (buying financial assets and extending credit on the security of stock); an investment bank (issuing, underwriting and managing bonds and equity); and an investment trust (able to manage savings of private and institutional investors, i.e. a sort of forerunner of mutual funds). In short, all functions which defined the *credito mobiliare* activity.[55] The idea was that of creating 'a credit institution at the centre if not an actor of the industrial development programmes',[56] which would fill the void left by the imminent demise of mixed banking. Industrial firms with sound collateral could thus obtain loans from IMI and then use such funds to pay back their bank loans. To close the circle, banks could then free themselves from their long-term credits to these clients and hence limit themselves to 'ordinary' credit thereafter. The final outcome should thus have been a conversion, in the firms' balance sheets, of long-term bank debt into long-term debt towards IMI. Also, the control over industry would have been transferred from banks, representing private interests, to the State-owned IMI, which represented the public interest.

In practice, however, few loans were extended, due to the under-funding of the institution and to the strictly conservative outlook of its first managers.[57] Fiduciary activities were not undertaken.[58] As a result, the alleviation of the mixed banks' balance sheets was minimal and IMI was not able to solve the intricate proprietary relationships between these banks and industry.

Italy's banking crisis was finally settled in March 1934 by three deals (*Convenzioni*) between the State and each of the main mixed banks (Comit, Credit, Banco di Roma). The latter committed themselves to maintaining the nature of commercial credit banks, devoid of shares and credit stakes in industrial firms. In return, they were freed both from their excessive debt burden towards the Bank of Italy and from their excessive credit exposure towards firms. All industrial securities in the banks were transferred to the Sezione Smobilizzi of the Industrial Reconstruction Institution (IRI), created the previous year, which absorbed the existing Liquidation Institute.[59] IRI also had a Financing Section, which was similar to IMI, in that it aimed at making loans to businesses, but for a twenty-year period (vs ten years for IMI). To finance its activities, IRI issued long-term bonds bearing a fixed interest rate, guaranteed by the State. IRI thus not only was able to offer much needed fresh capital to Italy's industrial world, but also set up a plan to (partially) repay what the Bank of Italy had previously injected into the mixed banks. It became a permanent institution in 1937.

The Banking Acts in the Two Countries

In Italy the 1934 *Convenzioni* set the foundations of the 1936 Banking Act which was finalized after a parliamentary *iter* of nearly two years. The legislative history of the second Glass–Steagall Act was much shorter, extending from its introduction as a bill in March 1933 to its enactment into law in June of that same year.

The US Act's explicit aims were manifold, in particular: (a) provision for a safer and more effective use of the assets of banks; (b) regulation of interbank control; (c) prevention of the undue diversion of funds into speculative operations. In Henry Steagall's words:

> [t]he purpose of the regulatory provisions of this bill is to call back to the service of agriculture and commerce and industry the bank credit and the bank services designed by the framers of the Federal Reserve Act. The purpose is to strengthen the banking structure, to establish adequate credit requirements, to provide more effective regulation and supervision, to eliminate dangerous and unsound practices, and to confine banks of deposit to legitimate functions and to separate them from affiliates or other organizations which have brought discredit and loss of public confidence.[60]

In particular, Sections 3, 7 and 11 of the Act restricted the activities of member banks. Federal Reserve Banks could refuse loans to banks who were using credit for the speculative holding of or trading in securities (Sec. 3). Restrictions were set on loans collateralized by securities (Sec. 7). Banks were forbidden to act as a medium or agent of any non-banking corporation in making securitized loans or loans to brokers/dealers (Sec. 11).

However, it is the Sections 16, 20, 21 and 32 which are commonly known as the Glass–Steagall Act. Section 16 forbade national commercial banks from underwriting any issue of securities, as well as imposing severe restrictions on purchasing investment securities for their own account, with a complete veto for stocks. Section 20 instead forced member banks to divest themselves of their security affiliate relationships. Hence, the two sections together mandated the separation between commercial banking and investment banking. Investment banks thus gained a monopoly over the securities markets activities.[61] A further step in setting a barrier between commercial and investment banking was taken by prohibiting director and employee interlocking within the banking sector (Sec. 32).[62] Also, Section 19 required banking holding companies (BHCs) to divest themselves of investment banking affiliates within five years to avoid the commercial–investment banking separation being circumvented in this manner. However, in general, '[t]he bill does not ... prohibit member banks from lending to investment banks and thus assisting in flotations'.[63] It did raise the question though about the legality of long-term loans which had developed as a reaction to the financial market crises. The issue was clarified by the later 1935 Banking Act.

After having restricted the activities of commercial banks on the one hand, the Banking Act then proceeded to protect them. Section 21, in fact, forbade investment banks from collecting any type of deposits, which became an exclusive source of funds, covered by mandatory insurance, for commercial banks.

Also in 1933, another 'reformatory and far-reaching piece of legislation' was passed: the Securities Act.[64] In President Roosevelt's words, the Act was designed 'to correct some of the *evils* which have been so glaringly revealed in the private exploitation of the public's money'.[65] It raised the cost of underwriting, by imposing mandatory disclosure of information concerning security sales and a twenty-day waiting period between the filing of the registration statement and the beginning of retail selling. The 1933 Securities Act, concerned chiefly with supervising IPOs, was soon after supplemented by the Securities and Exchange Act of 1934, which extended federal controls over trading on the national exchanges. It imposed regular information disclosure for the whole period in which the securities were exchanged on the market.

What emerges clearly from an analysis of the US Congress Record is that once the divorce between commercial and investment banking had been successfully attained, a new issue came up: how to finance industry. Corporations were in fact dissuaded from issuing new securities by the additional costs imposed on IPOs by the Securities Act, and by the fact that commercial banks were prohibited by the Banking Act to underwrite them. The Industrial Advances Act of 19 June 1934 was a first step towards solving the problem. Federal Reserve banks were thus authorized to make direct loans to or purchase obligations from any established business, unable to obtain assistance through customary credit channels. The maturity of such obligations could not exceed five years. Furthermore, the RFC's authority was enlarged by permitting direct loans, of maximum five years, to non-bank institutions 'on adequate security'.[66] On 31 January 1935, the law was further liberalized: loans by the RFC could be extended 'upon such security as in the judgement of the board would reasonably assure payment of the loans'[67] and the maturity of loans was extended to ten years.

However, these were emergency measures; permanent legislation was again called for. The result was the 1935 Banking Act, passed on 23 August. First, national banks were permitted to grant loans on real estate with fewer restrictions than before. Second, corporate notes that matured in over one year were explicitly allowed to be taken to re-discount. Third, regulations were changed to induce commercial banks to move into long-term lending to households and business. So as well as revising the powers of banks to extend real estate loans, examination practices were altered. While previously the standard acceptable maximum maturity for a loan had been six months, after which examiners had usually classified loans exceeding this term as 'slow', and banks were pressured to liquidate them, bank examiners were now instructed not to question a loan's viability merely because its maturity period was more than six months.[68] Fourth, express permission to national banks to buy and sell stocks for the account of customers, but in no case for their own account, was stated in the new Act. Brokerage by commercial banks was hence explicitly allowed. Finally, the 1935 Banking Act also liberalized the provision on directorate interlocking introduced only two years earlier: bankers henceforth could serve simultaneously as directors, officers or employees of 'not more than two banks'.

Another relevant piece of New Deal legislation is noteworthy. The Investment Company Act was passed in 1940, and regulated investment companies, i.e. publicly held corporations or trusts 'engaged ... in the business of investing, reinvesting, owning, holding, or trading in securities', in other words the former investment trusts. They were thus different from 'investment bankers', who were 'engaged in the business of underwriting securities issued by other persons'. Investment companies were required to disclose considerable information on their objectives and financial and investment policies. The Act also limited the number of underwriters, bankers, brokers and investment advisers who could serve as directors of these companies. The legislator thus hoped to prevent the abuses and conflicts of interest that had occurred in investment trusts in the 1920s, by reducing the influence of investment houses and banks.[69] The Act thus 'created' a third main actor on the securities market, additional to investment banks and corporations, which replaced the former investment trusts.

Let us now move on to the Italian legislation. The 1936 Banking Act took two years to be passed in Parliament.[70] However, its roots can be traced back another two years at least to the 1934 *Convenzioni*. Furthermore, the law matured mainly in the IRI environment, therefore externally to Parliament, largely ignored by the press and the general public.[71] The Act created a new regulatory and supervisory authority, the Inspectorate for the Safeguard of Savings and for Credit Activity, subordinated to a Committee of Ministers, led by the Prime Minister. The Head of the Inspectorate was, however, the Governor of the Bank of Italy and, *de facto*, the Inspectorate never operated separately from the central bank.[72]

The tight inter-relations between banks and industry were pinpointed as the main cause of the 1930s banking crisis, as the 'root of all *evil*'.[73] To avoid the recurrence of a similar crisis, the solution adopted was the division of the banking system into two different sectors, insulated from one another so that a crisis of one part would not necessarily extend to the other.[74] The new perimeter of regulation included two separate categories of institutions, distinguished according to the maturity of their liabilities, short-term vs medium/long-term. The former category, which included the three ex-mixed banks (named Banks of National Interest, BINs), public law credit institutions (IDPs), deposit-taking institutions, savings banks, pawn banks and rural banks, was regulated by Title V of the law, a dense collection of requirements and restrictions. The latter category was made up of publicly controlled entities (including IMI) and was subjected to Title VI, which simply transferred to the Inspectorate the existing regulatory and supervisory powers attributed by previous *ad hoc* laws to various regulating entities.[75]

IMI deserves special mention. Due to a different law of 1936, which closed down IRI's Financing Section and assigned IMI's presidency to the Governor of the Bank of Italy, the latter institution was officially defined as the central *credito mobiliare* institution.[76] However, IMI's new position was defined within the IRI environment; thus IRI's control over industrial stakes in firms and trust activities remained unchallenged. A new, more limited notion of *credito mobiliare* was assigned to IMI, as compared to its founding law of 1931: its restricted purpose was to intermediate between the collection of funds on the financial markets via the issuance of bonds and the financing of industrial and commercial firms via mortgages which covered their medium- and long-term needs, not covered by retained profits, newly collected capital and credit from the large deposit-taking banks.[77] IMI was *de facto* excluded from any transaction of firms' risk and debt capital on the financial market.

Going back to the 1936 Banking Act, the idea was that of a 'functional specialization according to maturity':[78] short-term liability credit institutions were to extend short-term loans, whereas medium and long-term liability ones were to extend medium and long-term loans. 'Since a clear-cut distinction between the two types of credit is not possible, the inescapable needs of clarity in laws led to fixing the discriminating criterion, not from the point of view of the credit activity but of the necessarily complementary one of the collection of savings'.[79] Whilst the 1934 *Convenzioni* explicitly forced the BINs to respect this separation, the 1936 law was more subtle in stating that certain types of investments required the regulator's authorization (Art. 32, 33 and 35). The aim was not only to align the timespan of banks' assets and liabilities, but also to prohibit deposit-taking banks from holding equity stakes in industry.

The 1936 Banking Act, and its underlying principles, survived the Second World War and the demise of the Fascist regime.

> Deposit banks must ... keep well away from undertakings that involve them in the risks of the productive process, and must engage only in those necessary to cover cash outflows which emerge in the period between cost registration and revenue collection in the short term, and must prefer, as a means of extending credit, the discounting of short-term commercial paper or the opening of credit lines guaranteed by self-liquidating securities, retaining in any case the right to call back their loans at their discretion.[80]

Since in some sectors long-term institutions were not able to satisfy the industrial demand, short-term liability institutions requested and attained the authorization to lend medium-term, drawing on funds with similar maturities. Hence the

Special Credit Sections of the Banco di Napoli and of the Banco di Sicilia were established, as well as Mediobanca on the initiative of the three BINs. Finally,

> [r]elative to the issue of *credito mobiliare* institutions holding shares, the prevailing opinion ... is that a restriction cannot be introduced, both because the contribution to the capital of a firm is a form of industrial financing typical of *credito mobiliare* institutions and because the acquisition of shares by the institutions must very often, for technical reasons, be combined with extension of credit.[81]

The Bank of Italy too clarified certain aspects of the Banking Act, also to better distinguish between short-term and medium-term credit institutions. In 1949 the Bank of Italy specified that medium-term credit institutions could only collect funds by issuing bonds, notes with a maturity between eighteen and sixty months, and twelve- to sixty-month deposit certificates (which had to be called 'deposit certificates for long-term credit' to avoid any ambiguity).[82] The main issue was to 'regulate the nature of deposits and of the securities representing deposits, in order to avoid the collection of funds whose name could deceive the saver'.[83] In general, therefore, short-term credit institutions could extend credit and collect savings up to one year; medium-term credit institutions could do so from one to five years.[84] Another noteworthy point is that medium and long-term liability institutions could not collect funds from short-term liability banks, and hence could not circumvent the maturity separation in this manner.[85]

The 1936 legislation also disciplined the ownership of short-term liability banks, which were required to be public limited companies or limited partnerships based on capital. Their shares had to be registered, so as to hinder speculative manoeuvres by identifying the agents responsible.[86] However, the control industrial firms could have over banks was not explicitly regulated. Again, this had been forbidden in 1934 for the BINs. It was however not *de facto* allowed for the other banks too, in that: (a) they were mainly State-owned – private banks' assets dropped from 56 per cent of the total in 1927 to only 17 per cent in 1936;[87] and (b) moral suasion exercised by the Bank of Italy in the following years helped avoid such interlinkages. Finally, limits were introduced on interlocking directorates: bank directors were prohibited from sitting not only on the boards of other banks, but also of industrial firms, unless duly authorized.[88]

Thus far we have referred to the bank–industry relationship, but what about the bank–financial market ties? The only two articles concerning securities in the 1936 Italian Act are Articles 2 and 45: deposit-taking institutions in Italy were allowed to underwrite and deal in all kinds of securities, bonds but also stocks, only with prior authorization of the issue by the Inspectorate (later the Bank of Italy).

A Systematic Comparison

We now move on to draw more systematic comparisons between the two sets of legislation. Relative to their actual content, the two regulatory responses aimed at eradicating different 'evils'. In Italy the main concern was to prevent banks and firms from being owned simultaneously by each other, with the subsequent negative consequences on bank's risk-taking behaviour and the firms' investment policy, as well as from immobilizing unwitting depositors' short-term savings in long-term assets. In the US the emphasis was on the questionable trading practices of commercial banks in the financial markets and hence on the speculative use of deposits, as well as on banks' biased relationship towards their private clients, to which they offered low-quality securities due to the existing conflicts of interest as underwriters and distributors. As a result, in Italy the priority was that of placing a barrier between the banking and the industrial sector; in the US the priority was to limit commercial banks' activities in the financial markets. To own or to be owned by non-financial companies was one major issue underlying Italian mixed banking; the simultaneous engagement in banking and securities activities was the problem underlying American broad banking. Both a debt stake (via long-term loans) and an equity stake (via ownership or control of stock) in industrial firms were to be banned in Italy; commercial and investment activities taking place in the same bank, in-house or via affiliates, were to be prohibited in the US. Let us now articulate these differences across five key issues of banking activity.

(1) The Use of Deposits

It is clear that a main preoccupation in both countries was to impede the banks from employing deposits in risky undertakings: in Italy the new legislation aimed at preventing them being tied up in long-term loans and in equity stakes; in the US it stopped deposits being used in speculative transactions on the stock markets. There are some subtle differences: in Italy deposits had been used to invest directly in industrial enterprises; in the US the deposits were believed to have been 'gambled' on the financial markets. In the former country, deposits had been used to support specific industrial firms, which were often, as well as being the banks' main borrowers, also their main depositors. Not only was concentration of risk extremely high, but Italian bankers ended up being involved in the entrepreneurship of firms, with all the connected risks. In the US, by contrast, deposits were invested in more diversified securities activities, in order to benefit from the numerous profit opportunities offered by a bull market; as a result US bankers had become professional stock market players, with all the risks linked to that activity. This different use of deposits in the two countries was due to the dissimilar set of incentives and/or conflicts of interest commercial bankers were faced with, but it was also due to the different degree of development of financial markets in the two countries. As we have seen, in Italy the capital and bond markets were underdeveloped and bank lending was the industrial firms' priority channel of funding. Hence the new regulation acted directly on the bank–industry channel in Italy, and not on the bank–financial market–industry channel as it did in the US.

Furthermore, while the Italian legislation focused on the use of short-term deposits (that is, with a maturity of less than one year), the US legislation excluded investment banks from receiving any type of deposit whatsoever, short-term or long-term. '[T]he result was to make investment banks dependent on commercial banks for credit'.[89] The veto for investment banks to collect deposits also resulted from the fact that the 1933 US Banking Act introduced deposit insurance. Investment banks, which were not subject to the regulation and supervision imposed on commercial banks, were thus to be excluded from the newly introduced government safety net. In Italy, no deposit insurance scheme was introduced, mainly because most banks passed under the control of the State; hence an implicit guarantee was already present.

In conclusion, the aim of regulation in Italy was to protect the unwitting short-term depositors, in the US it was to protect the savers and the private investors alike. Both sets of legislation thus aimed at defending the public interest, but via two different channels: in the US, via a safe and efficient market for securities, as well as via deposit insurance; in Italy via the limit on bank exposure to entrepreneurial risk and via the State owning a 'golden share' in the banking system.

(2) Commercial vs Investment Banking

The US Glass–Steagall Act, as we have seen, led to a (quasi) complete divorce between commercial and investment banking. Whilst some exceptions were allowed for trading bonds and other 'investment securities' (i.e. trading upon the order and for account of customers; trading for their own account if authorized by the OCC and respecting certain quantitative ratios), underwriting securities, as well as trading in stocks, were banned *in toto*. The desire to avoid the 'speculative orgy' of the 1920s, presumably fuelled by commercial banks, was evident. It is true that in Italy too mixed banks had contributed to the boom and bust of the stock market in the 1920s, but this aspect was not perceived as the main problem, also because many transactions were undertaken outside the official markets and the stock market was not at the epicentre of corporate finance. Hence, in Italy, banks could participate in placement syndicates of stocks and bonds, if the issue was authorized by the Inspectorate. The Inspectorate's authorization was, in general, granted, as the activities of banks in the following decades show. Italian banks in the 1950s, and in particular the two main BINs, had in fact a 'bridge function' between their client firms and the stock exchange and had a great placing power of the former's shares and bonds.[90] Yet the credits the banks extended were never transformed into equity stakes.

It is noteworthy that in the US the Securities Act and the Securities Exchange Act were introduced to regulate the securities markets, whilst in Italy new financial market regulation was introduced only in 1974. Again, a significant sign that stock market activities were not considered the main 'root of all *evil*' in Italy. So, while in the US the aim was to restore confidence in the financial markets as a whole, in Italy the focus was on rebuilding trust in the banking system, which anyhow was dominant. We may even push the argument further by stating that the 1936 Italian Banking Act crystallized the bank-orientation of the financial sector, whilst the US banking and other financial New Deal Acts opened the way to a new evolutionary path for the financial markets, with different weights and roles assigned to both commercial and investment banks, including in the face of the development of the other, old and new, financial institutions (for example, insurance companies and mutual/pension funds, respectively). The importance of financial markets in the US was in the end actually increased. The 1933 Banking Act ensured that banks were more restricted than markets. It is true that the latter were set under the control of the SEC; however, this Commission was not only a regulator, but became a guarantor of the integrity and vitality of the country's securities markets.[91]

(3) Maturity Mismatches

The 1936 Italian Banking Act – as is confirmed by later documents produced by the Bank of Italy – aimed at minimizing maturity mismatches between banks' assets and liabilities, by introducing temporal specialization. The maturity of assets had to be symmetrical to that of the credit institutions' liabilities, as prescribed by law. In the US on the contrary, 'separation of commercial banking from savings banking' was defined an 'academic question', not feasible in practice.[92] Thus, the issue was debated, and known to the US contemporaries, but regulation in that direction was not deemed a priority. Furthermore, the industrial world was suffering from a scarcity of funds, hence commercial banks were actually urged to use their deposits in long-term loans and investments. As we have seen, the development of long-term lending by commercial banks in the US was primarily a response to the deepening depression, whilst in Italy it was primarily perceived as one of the causes of the banking crisis. Subsequently, direct term loans to businesses were further encouraged by the 1935 US Banking Act, which loosened pre-existing restrictions.

Another significant difference is that while in the US investment banks could rely – and had to rely, after the ban on deposits – on funding from commercial banks, in Italy the medium and long-term liability institutions could not receive loans from the short-term ones, to eliminate the possibility of a circumvention of the temporal separation in this sense.[93]

(4) Bank Specialization and Competition

An interesting analogy in both sets of regulation is the introduction of bank specialization, albeit of different forms, and hence of a limitation of competition in each defined sector. In the US, commercial banks obtained a monopoly over the deposit business, and traditional banking business in general, whilst the investment banks obtained one over securities markets activities. Similarly, in Italy, short-term liability banks controlled short-term lending and special credit institutions long-term lending.

(5) Bank vs Industry

With regard to the bank–industry link, Italian banks could not hold equity stakes in industrial firms anymore (via the *Convenzioni* and via denials of authorization by the regulating entity). Conversely, industrial firms could not own or control banks (again via the *Convenzioni* and moral suasion by the Bank of Italy). In the US such veto was not introduced;[94] yet to vote their banks' stock, the owning firms for instance had to shed their investment bank affiliates. Again, the Americans' concern was not that of severing the bank–industry link, but that of stopping banking holding companies from getting around the commercial–investment banking separation. The 1933 US Banking Act thus only eliminated the control commercial banks had over non-financial firms via securities affiliates. So if this Act did set some restrictions on the bank–industry link, it did so only indirectly, as a result of regulation aimed at other purposes.[95]

US commercial banks actually expanded the control they had over industrial enterprises via an increase in long-term lending,[96] further encouraged after 1935. This form of control was obviously lost by Italian deposit banks. Another form of control was that of interlocking directorates. Bank directors could sit on the boards of non-financial corporations in the US; in Italy they were not allowed to do so, unless authorized by the regulator.

Conclusions

This chapter has attempted a comparison between the 1930s banking legislation in Italy and the US – introduced in response to the severe domestic banking crisis in both countries – with regard to the redefinition of the links between banks, industry and financial markets.

The study first described the (different) evolution of the banking systems in the two countries since the nineteenth century, with particular emphasis on the last decade in the run-up to the Great Depression. The 1930s banking crisis was severe in both countries, as was the recession in the real economy. In response, sweeping banking legislation was passed, quickly and under the spotlight of the public opinion in the US in 1933, and, with a significant lag, 'secretively' in Italy in 1936. Curiously enough, these laws turned out to be long-lasting in both countries: the 1933 US Banking Act was repealed only in 1999; the Italian Banking Act lasted until 1993.

With regard to the contents of the 1930s legislation, the different position and weight of banks, industry and the stock exchange in Italy and in the US, as well as the different *evils* perceived to be at the roots of the 1930s banking crisis, resulted in two differently focused regulatory responses, each attempting to constrain different, albeit connected, aspects of banking activity. The US regulators were much more concerned with the commercial banks' direct and active role in the stock exchange market, the key mediator in savers and firms' exchanges; Italian regulators instead dreaded direct equity and long-term debt stakes between industrial firms and banks, which were not usually mediated by the stock exchange. As a result, in the US a rigid barrier between the traditional banking business (i.e. collecting deposits and extending loans) and investment banking was erected, whereas the close ties that existed between commercial banks and industrial firms through long-term loans, equity stakes and interlocking directors were not directly tackled. In Italy on the other hand, strict limitations were imposed on the links between short-term liability institutions and industrial firms. These new banking institutions could only be short-term and non-proprietary in nature, whilst underwriting and trading in securities continued to be allowed. In other words, while the 1930s US regulation led to a divorce between commercial and investment banking, the contemporary Italian legislation brought about a rigid separation between banking and industry (i.e. non-financial activities): two divides that were not perfectly overlapping.

Acknowledgements

The opinions expressed in this chapter are those of the authors and not necessarily of Banca d'Italia.

We are extremely grateful to Chiara de Vecchis, Renata Giannella and all the staff of the Biblioteca della Minerva for their assistance and hospitality in our research at the Italian Senate Library. We also thank Roberta Pilo and the other colleagues from the Bank of Italy's Law Library for the same reasons. We thank Enrico Galanti, Alfredo Gigliobianco, Robert Hetzel, Elisabetta Loche, Ivo Maes and Alessandro Roselli for suggestions, comments on previous versions of the chapter and/or help in various forms. Finally, we are grateful to Stefano Battilossi, Eugene White and to all the participants of the Conferences organized by SEEMHN at the Central Bank of Turkey, Istanbul (April 2010) and by EABH at the National Bank of Belgium, Brussels (May 2010), where earlier drafts of this chapter were presented. However, any error is entirely our own.

6 REGULATION AND DEREGULATION IN A TIME OF STAGFLATION: SIEGMUND WARBURG AND THE CITY OF LONDON IN THE 1970s

Niall Ferguson

Introduction

If journalism is the first draft of history, then the first draft of the history of the 2007–10 financial crisis offers a trenchant verdict. According to commentators such as Paul Krugman, the crisis was primarily the result of a policy of financial deregulation dating back to the 1980s. 'Reagan-era legislative changes essentially ended New Deal restrictions on mortgage lending', Krugman has written:

> It was only after the Reagan deregulation that thrift gradually disappeared from the American way of life ... It was the explosion of debt over the previous quarter-century that made the U.S. economy so vulnerable. Overstretched borrowers were bound to start defaulting in large numbers once the housing bubble burst and unemployment began to rise. These defaults in turn wreaked havoc with a financial system that – also mainly thanks to Reagan-era deregulation – took on too much risk with too little capital.[1]

In another column, Krugman looked back fondly to a

> long period of stability after World War II, based on a combination of deposit insurance, which eliminated the threat of bank runs, and strict regulation of bank balance sheets, including both limits on risky lending and limits on leverage, the extent to which banks were allowed to finance investments with borrowed funds.[2]

This pre-lapsarian age was indeed an Eden: the 'era of boring banking was also an era of spectacular economic progress'.[3] Krugman is by no means a lone voice. Even Richard Posner has recently joined the chorus calling for a restoration of the Glass–Steagall Act, which separated investment banking from commercial banking in the United States.[4] It is a truth almost universally acknowledged that this and other measures of deregulation were fervently wished for by bankers, pursued by their lobbyists and enacted by corrupt politicians.[5]

To a British reader, if not to an American, there is something implausible about this story. British banking was also tightly regulated prior to the 1980s. Yet there was anything but 'spectacular economic progress'. Nor was the pre-1980 period characterized by a lack of financial crises. On the contrary, the 1970s were arguably the country's most financially disastrous decade since the 1820s, witnessing not only a major banking crisis, but also a stock market crash, a real estate bubble and double-digit inflation. The experience of the City of London in the 1970s casts serious doubt on the simplistic proposition that tight regulation of banks is good and deregulation bad. It should also make us pause before incorporating the Krugman thesis into the second draft of the history of the most recent financial crisis. Surely more important in the crises of both the regulated Seventies and the deregulated Noughties was monetary policy, as well as fiscal policy. In each case, it was the errors of central bankers and finance ministers that caused the bubbles and busts.

Another widely cited scapegoat in the current crisis has been financial innovation. Figures as respected as Paul Volcker and Adair Turner have cast doubt on the economic and social utility of most, if not all, recent theoretical and technical advances in finance.[6] I take a somewhat less negative view of financial innovation. Focusing on the most innovative of all post-war British banks, S. G. Warburg & Co., this chapter shows how its numerous contributions to the revival of the City of London as a financial centre were essentially set at nought by crass errors perpetrated by government. Nor is there much evidence of a sustained campaign for financial deregulation on the part of the bankers. Many of the key decisions of the 1970s appear to have been taken by the mandarins of the Bank and the Treasury, with startlingly little consultation with the private sector. The Warburg's director Bernard Kelly regarded it as a great innovation when he and a few other City executives began to dine occasionally with a few Treasury officials in what he called 'seven-a-side ... City–Treasury dinners'. The aim of these dinners (on both sides) was 'getting to know each other and no doubt becoming known if either side has to find candidates for interesting jobs'. Contrary to the widely held belief that there was a close, even symbiotic relationship between the City and the Treasury, the encounters tended to expose a considerable gulf in terms of intellectual assumptions and material aspirations, which was not easily bridged.[7]

Warburg: Successful Banking in a Regulated Market

The City of London in 1970 was anything but a free financial market. It was regulated by an elaborate web of traditional guild-like restrictions. The merchant banks – members of the august Accepting Houses Committee – concerned themselves, at least notionally, with accepting commercial bills and issuing bonds and shares. Commercial or retail banking was controlled by a cartel of big 'high street' banks, which set deposit and lending rates. Within the Stock Exchange autonomous brokers sold, while jobbers bought. Over all these gentlemanly capitalists the Governor of the Bank of England watched with a benign but sometimes stern headmasterly eye, checking ungentlemanly conduct with a mere movement of his celebrated eyebrows, afforced by the head prefect in the form of the Principal of the Discount Office. This was still a world in which bankers were by convention forbidden to visit stockbrokers in their offices; the latter, no matter how venerable, were obliged to call on the former, no matter how lowly. In the same way, bankers were not allowed to communicate directly with the Treasury; all such communications had to go through the Governor of the Bank of England. Direct communication between other actors and the Bank – journalists in particular – were frowned upon. Bankers, brokers, jobbers and an army of clerks went about their business much as they had before the war. Many of the bankers even dressed as their fathers had, complete with bowler hats and black umbrellas. This world remained largely intact until the 'Big Bang' of 1986.[8]

On top of these guild-like practices, a bewildering range of regulations had been imposed before, during and after the Second World War. The 1947 Exchange Control Act strictly limited transactions in currencies other than sterling, controls that remained in place until 1979. Even after the breakdown of the system of fixed exchange rates established at Bretton Woods, the Bank of England routinely intervened to influence the sterling exchange rate. Banks were regulated under the 1948 Companies Act, the 1958 Prevention of Fraud (Investments) Act and the 1967 Companies Act. The 1963 Protection of Depositors Act created an additional tier of regulation for deposit-taking institutions that were not classified as banks under the arcane rules known as 'Schedule 8' and 'Section 127'.[9] Following the report of the 1959 Radcliffe Committee, which argued that the traditional tools of monetary policy were insufficient, a fresh layer of controls was added in the form of ceilings on bank lending.[10] Consumer credit (which mainly took the form of 'hire purchase' or instalment plans) was also tightly regulated. Although it had been nationalized in 1945, it is true that the Bank of England retained a high degree of autonomy in its own sphere. Successive post-war governors did what they could to revive London as an international financial centre, encouraging foreign banks to open establishments in the City.[11] Yet the Bank officials of the 1950s and 1960s believed in keeping their home-grown charges on a relatively tight leash. Banks recognized as such by the Old Lady of Threadneedle Street were required to maintain a 28 per cent liquidity ratio, which in practice meant holding large amounts of British government bonds (known as gilt-edged securities or 'gilts' for short).

In this stuffy, less than efficient and occasionally downright sclerotic setting, Siegmund Warburg stood out as an impatient and creative financial innovator.[12]

A refugee from Nazi Germany, Warburg had essentially started his firm from scratch, having arrived in London with very little capital aside from the cachet of the family name and the City connections that went with it. Having lived through both hyperinflation and deep deflation, and having seen the family firm of M. M. Warburg & Co. all but wiped out, first by illiquidity in 1931 and then by 'Aryanization' in 1938, Warburg devised a highly risk-averse business model. As he made clear shortly after the firm adopted his name, the primary object of S. G. Warburg & Co. should be 'giving service to British industrial firms'.[13] The firm, he explained to his father-in-law in early 1946:

> does not do acceptance or deposit business but acts in the first place as a service house giving advice to its industrial and merchant clients, and in the second place as a placing and issuing house. In addition to the usual sort of general clients we have now around us a group of, say, 20 to 30 industrial and trading firms, for all of which we act as general advisers and some of which we control on behalf of syndicates led by us and consisting of firms like Prudential, Fleming's, Benson's, Rothschild's and ourselves. For those 20 to 30 firms we not only arrange the financial facilities that they require both in the way of long-term and short-term money, but we [also] advise them on problems of costing, marketing and management in general. We have made it a rule that the financial risks which we take never represent in any case more than a certain very limited percentage of the capital of the firm. Our chief risk lies in our overhead expenses which have to be relatively heavy considering that the sort of work we are doing depends on the highest possible quality of management.[14]

In some accounts, Warburg has been portrayed as the custodian of a tradition of relationship banking very different from the transactions banking that came to dominate London in the decades that followed his death in 1982.[15] This was certainly a part of his carefully cultivated self-image. 'The important elements of a first-class private banking business', he wrote in 1953, were:

1. Moral standing
2. Reputation for efficiency and high quality brain work
3. Connections
4. Capital funds
5. Personnel and organization.[16]

In the eyes of at least one director of his bank, Warburg was 'a banking snob', who 'wanted Warburgs to be elitist, to be *haute banque*, to give well-thought-out objective financial advice to top-class companies and governments'.[17]

Yet this was to overestimate Warburg's conservatism. A modern-day *Hofjude* he was not. Under his leadership, Warburg & Co. very rapidly evolved from being little more than a high-end financial consultancy to being the most dynamic of all the City's merchant banks – a category in which the firm only nominally belonged. In the words of one Bank of England official writing in 1951:

> They like to be described as merchant bankers but we prefer to look upon them as a finance or investment house. They are interested in various industrial and merchanting [*sic*] enterprises who no doubt keep deposits with them. They do a certain amount of placing and re-organizing and also do some Stock Exchange business on behalf of clients.[18]

Two years later, another senior Bank official voiced concern about 'the ever and rapidly expanding field of Warburg's interests'.[19] When, in 1947, Warburgs secured a place on the Accepting Houses Committee by taking over the small house of Seligman Bros, the *Economist* marvelled at the new bank's 'record-making progress'.[20]

The financial performance of S. G. Warburg in the 1950s was indeed impressive. In 1949 its paid-up capital had been just £2.75 million. Thirteen years later its market capitalization was £20 million (around £1 billion in 2008 terms). As the *Sunday Times* pointed out in 1961, someone who seven years before had bought 100 shares in Mercury Securities, the Warburg parent company, would have invested just over £237:

> For that money he would now have 274 shares at £18, and his investment would be worth £4,930, 20 times the cost ... In this period the company's earnings have multiplied six times, and the dividend nine and a half times. This means that the original holder would now have a dividend yield of 42½ per cent on the original cost of his investment, and an earnings yield of no less than 145 per cent on the same basis.[21]

Retail prices in the same period had risen by 24 per cent, for a real return of 121 per cent. The average real return on UK equities in the same period was 91 per cent.[22] It was not quite the 'phenomenal rate of growth' applauded by the *Sunday Times*, but it was a strong performance for a relative newcomer to the City.

Warburgs owed its success to a series of innovations that can be summarized only briefly here. It was responsible for the first hostile takeover in post-war City history (of British Aluminium by Tube Investments in 1959), dominating the UK mergers and acquisitions business for the better part of the next thirty years. The bank's core advisory business – which covered the full spectrum of British industry from automobiles through newspapers to textiles – entitled Warburg to regard himself as Britain's 'financial physician'. The bank's investment department (little though Warburg himself liked it) was also a leader in the field of asset management. In 1969 it became a distinct subsidiary as Warburg Investment Management (later Mercury Asset Management).[23] Less well known, but equally important, were Warburg's path-breaking methods of management. At a time when most City firms were still stiffly hierarchical, the partners hidden away from the clerks in dark, oak-panelled rooms, the Warburg offices were modern, the doors wide open, and decision-making had at least the appearance of being democratic, with old and young directors alike taking turns to chair the crucial Monday morning meeting. In-coming and out-going correspondence was copied and circulated. Every meeting generated a memorandum, which was then also circulated. Each afternoon a daily summary was sent around of every important communication received or sent, including telephone calls and internal memoranda. When directors left the office at night, they were given 'a cyclostyled twelve-page summary of all the day's letters and memoranda, just in case we had missed something'. Recruitment methods were novel, too. In place of the Old Boy Network, Warburg looked for brains, relying on literary questions and graphology to identify talent.

Although initially focused on the needs of British industry, S. G. Warburg & Co. quickly took on the character of an international bank, with a complex network of continental affiliates and subsidiaries in Hamburg, Frankfurt, Paris and Zurich. Outside Europe, the firm built up considerable business in Canada, Japan and the United States, where Warburg tried (in vain) to resuscitate the moribund Wall Street giant Kuhn, Loeb & Co. Warburg himself has a legitimate claim to be regarded as the founder of the offshore Eurobond market, launching the first Eurobond issue for the Italian company Autostrade in 1963. This was only one part of Warburg's sustained campaign to bring more international business to London. In 1965, for example, his firm joined forces with Hambros and Rothschilds to lobby the Bank of England to exempt foreign bonds issued in London from stamp duty; at the same time, the banks pressed the Treasury to lift the requirement that income tax be deducted from the interest on bonds issued by UK-domiciled companies.[24] In a letter to *The Times*, Warburg and Jocelyn Hambro deplored:

> the quite ludicrous situation that on the one hand the City of London is arranging long-term borrowing in Continental Europe for American oil companies, Italian nationalized industries and various Scandinavian quarters and on the other hand any attempt to perform the same service, even for British borrowers of the highest quality, is being frustrated by certain fiscal requirements which are without any practical substance and which could easily be eliminated.[25]

Yet such explicit requests for changes to government policy were remarkably rare. Warburg was not, as we shall see, averse to a relatively high degree of government intervention in the financial system. So long as the Eurobond market, like the Eurodollar market that preceded it, was tolerated as an offshore phenomenon, Warburg was content with the status quo in the City. In any case, important as its international business was, it was UK corporate finance that came first. As Warburg reminded his executive directors in October 1967:

> [O]ur chief interest should be to look after our important industrial clients in this country, in the United States, and on the Continent of Europe. One fee which we earn from giving good service to one of our large industrial clients can be far in excess of what we earn in a whole year in connection with Euro bond issues.[26]

In an uncontested takeover, the bank could expect one half of one per cent of the amount paid for the acquisition; in the case of a successful contested bid, one per cent.[27] As the total value of mergers rose to £2,313 million in 1968 compared with £800 million the previous year, the rewards of corporate finance grew commensurately.[28] Between 1959 and 1969 Mercury net profits rose six-fold after allowing for inflation. The 1960s were the group's golden decade, with the share price surging to a high of £213 in January 1969, twenty times the price of a decade before. The market as a whole was up by a factor of less than 1.5. That truly was phenomenal.

Britain's Economic Malaise

The paradox of Warburg's success as a banker was that it unfolded in the very unpromising context of Britain's abject failure as an economy. Warburg was by nature a pessimist. About nothing was his pessimism more justified than Britain's post-war economic performance. With an average annual per capita GDP growth rate of 2.4 per cent between 1950 and 1973, the United Kingdom was the weakest of all the West European economies; growth in Germany was twice as rapid.[29] The 30 per cent devaluation of sterling in September 1949 (which lowered the dollar–sterling exchange rate to $2.80) did not impress Warburg because in his view, 'the opportunity for using devaluation as a starting point for a new policy of harder work, decrease in Government expenditure, and liberalizing trading within Western Europe' had been 'entirely missed'. Despite the stimulus provided to British exports by devaluation, he could 'well foresee that by the end of the year sterling will be ... again at a discount and futile talk about devaluation will start again'.[30] This proved prescient. Conservative and Labour Chancellors alike, as Warburg foresaw, would struggle to achieve internal and external balance throughout the post-war period.

'Is Britain becoming an underdeveloped country?', Warburg asked himself in 1956.[31] His fear (as he made clear a year later) was that the economy of his adopted homeland was heading for that combination of low growth and rising prices which would indeed bring the United Kingdom to the edge of 'the abyss' in the mid-1970s.[32] When the short-lived Tory Chancellor of the Exchequer, Peter Thorneycroft, raised the possibility that Britain might need a loan from the International Monetary Fund, Warburg expressed the view that it was 'a gamble which would not come off and that we were in for a 1931 crisis, but this time with rising unemployment and rising prices simultaneously'.[33] This was certainly an exaggerated fear at a time when the unemployment rate was below 2 per cent and the consumer price inflation rate was below 5 per cent and falling (it briefly turned negative in 1959). It was nevertheless an intimation of the trouble that lay ahead.

By twenty-first-century standards, to be sure, the United Kingdom did not run excessively large current account deficits in the 1960s (the largest, in 1964, was equivalent to just 1 per cent of gross domestic product, compared with 4.9 per cent in 1989). Nor were net outflows on the capital account especially large in relation to GDP (they totalled just £174 million between 1960 and 1969). But because of the relatively limited amount of international capital available at that time, compared with the rapidly growing volume of international trade, these modest imbalances could easily give rise to serious economic difficulties – particularly for a country like the United Kingdom, with expensive naval and military commitments overseas and large foreign holdings of sterling. Long before 1967, the possibility of another devaluation was already in the air; there were speculative attacks on sterling in July 1961, November 1964, July 1965 and July 1966.[34] The advent of a Labour government under Harold Wilson in 1964 intensified the pressure on the British currency.

Far from solving Britain's financial problems, another devaluation in 1967 – just as Warburg had predicted – offered only a temporary respite. Though the government tightened its fiscal policy, raising taxes and cutting defence spending, restoring the Bank of England's much depleted reserves took time and it was not long before speculation against sterling resumed. In 1961 the previous government had secured a credit of £2 billion from the IMF. It was a facility Wilson had already had to use to defend the pound in 1965 and he had to seek yet more help from foreign monetary authorities after the devaluation. The trouble was that the IMF now insisted on tough deflationary policies, including a balanced budget and limits on domestic credit expansion – conditions that drove James Callaghan to resign the Chancellorship. Was there any alternative? Warburg bluntly told Wilson 'that we should borrow more from Germany, particularly for the nationalized industries'.[35] One idea canvassed by Warburg was that public sector bodies like British Steel or the Gas Council should raise money abroad by means of deutschmark-denominated Eurobond issues. The Gas Council did in fact raise around £31 million by this route in 1969.[36] By October 1971 British public sector agencies had raised a total of $122 million (£51 million) through such loans.[37] The trouble, as the Treasury was not slow to point out, was the serious currency risk embedded in such loans. In the event of further devaluation of sterling, or a unilateral appreciation of the deutschmark, the sterling value of the debt would increase overnight. And that was highly likely. In four successive quarters from mid-1967 to mid-1968, the authorities had to spend £2.2 billion on defending the pound's new lower rate – much more than the Bank of England's total reserves, and vastly more than could be raised by the government on the Eurobond market. Only the IMF and other central banks were keeping sterling from yet another devaluation.

By the end of the 1960s, with sterling still under pressure and unemployment and inflation both significantly higher than they had been when Wilson entered

10 Downing Street, the government's grip on power was crumbling. The title of the government White Paper *In Place of Strife*, published in 1969, said it all: heady visions of 'dynamic, exciting, thrilling change' had given way to a hungover reality of chronic industrial unrest. It was by now painfully obvious that Britain's economic malaise went much, much deeper than the rate of exchange of (in Wilson's famously hollow phrase) 'the pound in your pocket'. The Labour government had come into office intent on modernizing the British economy with a National Plan. It had created new Ministries for Technology and Economic Affairs. It had increased public sector investment by a massive 29 per cent. And yet the results were distinctly underwhelming.[38] To be sure, between 1960 and 1970 there was a 34 per cent increase in GDP and a 42 per cent increase in productivity. There were current account surpluses between 1969 and 1972. But performance in every other major industrial country was superior, including even Italy, where productivity grew more than twice as fast. Britain led the world in only one respect: nowhere did unit labour costs rise faster. And partly for that reason, nothing could stop the inexorable retreat of British manufacturing from world markets: Britain's share in world trade in manufactures fell by more than a third.[39] Symbols of Britain's proud past, ranging from Rolls Royce to *The Times* newspaper, teetered on the verge of insolvency. Could a new Conservative government under Edward Heath, who defeated Wilson in the June 1970 general election, turn Britain around?

Stagflation, Policy Failures and the Banking Crisis of 1973–5

The Heath government was, in theory at least, committed to financial deregulation. Its first step in this direction was to follow the lead of the United States and a number of European countries by allowing the currency to float. It might have been expected that a banker like Warburg would welcome this. He had repeatedly expressed his hostility to the 'gold fetishism' of the Bretton Woods system. As early as 1940 he had facetiously suggested that the best use of the vast US gold reserve after the war would be to manufacture ashtrays to sell to tourists.[40] Already in 1961 Warburg was looking ahead – ten years ahead, as it proved – to a world of managed but flexible exchange rates, unfettered by the dollar's 'ridiculous tie to those various lumps of gold stored at Fort Knox'.[41] He was dismissive of the 'perverted gold hallucinations' of 'intellectuals who are more brilliant than sound', and urged the United States to sever the link between the dollar and gold sooner rather than later.[42] The 'gold complex', he argued, was one of 'many kinds of superstition which are highly contagious diseases of the mind'.[43] 'Gold somnambulism' was another of the terms of abuse he reserved for proponents of a return to pre-war ways; he was enraged by the French attempt to undermine the paramountcy of the dollar by 'going for gold'.[44] So Warburg could hardly disapprove of the death of Bretton Woods, which began when President Richard

Nixon finally ended the (vestigial and limited) convertibility of the dollar into gold on 15 August 1971.

However, Warburg had a very low opinion of Tory Chancellor of the Exchequer Anthony Barber, whom he regarded as 'very, very shallow'[45] and 'a sort of half-wit'.[46] Barber's stewardship of the UK economy amply vindicated this assessment. This was not wholly the Chancellor's fault, to be sure. The great 'realignment' of currencies of the early 1970s was indeed more chaotic than most people had anticipated. While two major currencies depreciated relative to the dollar – the British pound and the Italian lira – the rest grew markedly stronger, led by the deutschmark and the Swiss franc. Within Europe the moves were dramatic: in deutschmark terms the pound slid from just above 4.00 in 1969 to 1.72 by the end of 1979, more than doubling the cost of German imports to British consumers. The Bank of England could not quite reconcile itself to this new volatility and so continued to intervene regularly in the currency market in a vain attempt to arrest the downward slide of the pound.[47] Moreover, the leap in inflation from below 6 per cent in the summer of 1972 to above 10 per cent in November 1973 could partly be blamed on the oil shock following the Yom Kippur War. Yet the principal drivers of British inflation were domestic, not external. The problem could be summed up in a single word coined by the Conservative MP and editor of the *Spectator* Iain Macleod as early as 1965: stagflation. For the decade as a whole, the average inflation rate was just under 13 per cent, roughly the same as for Greece, Italy, Portugal and Spain, and twice the OECD average (see Figure 6.1). Yet all these economies were growing much faster than that of the UK.

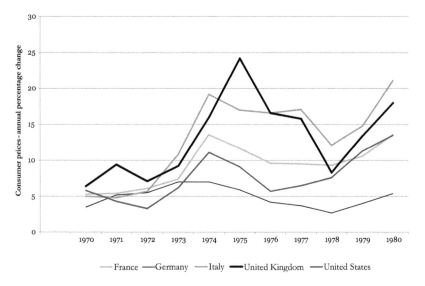

Figure 6.1: Annual inflation rates, selected OECD countries, 1970–9.

Source: OECD.

From the vantage point of 2009, the so-called 'secondary banking crisis' has a distinctly familiar look to it. It had its origins in a combination of ill-judged pro-cyclical fiscal and monetary stimulus. Between 1970 and 1974 the public sector swung sharply from a surplus of 3.4 per cent of gross domestic product to a deficit of −4.1 per cent. At the same time, after minimal consultation with the Treasury, the Bank of England embarked on a relaxation of credit controls. This was the pet project of the Bank officials John Fforde and Andrew Crockett, who had never cared for the crude quantitative restrictions on bank lending introduced in the 1960s. In pursuit of a 'uniform, competitive banking system', they recommended the lifting of ceilings on bank advances, the breakup of the high street banks' cartel and the replacement of the 28 per cent liquidity ratio with a new reserve asset ratio rule requiring banks to hold just 12.5 per cent of their liabilities in specified reserve assets. Henceforth, credit would be regulated through the variation of reserve ratios, the creation and variation of 'special deposits' and more active operations in the gilts market. The new scheme, entitled 'Competition and Credit Control', was published on 14 May 1971, and came into effect four months later.[48] At the same time, the old 'Bank Rate' was replaced by the more technocratic-sounding 'Minimum Lending Rate'.[49]

The results were unintentionally explosive. Quite simply, Fforde, Crockett and their colleagues had underestimated the inflationary potential of their new regime. Bank lending leapt upwards, increasing by 33 per cent in 1973.[50] The annual growth rate for broad money surged from 12 per cent in 1970 to above 20 per cent in 1972 and 1973. This, more than the oil shock, explains Britain's bout of double-digit inflation. Significantly, the Bank's Oxford-trained economists still clung to the vulgar Keynesian illusion that inflation was a result of cost pressures.[51] Even more dramatic was the increase in house price inflation, as the liberalization of banking regulation and cuts in direct taxation fuelled a classic asset bubble, made all the worse by the Heath government's relaxation of controls on property development, including the abolition of the Land Commission. Between February 1971 and February 1974, bank advances to the property sector rose sevenfold, from £362 million to £2,584 million.[52] At their peak in late 1972, existing home prices were rising at an annual rate of more than 40 per cent (see Figure 6.2). On average, the price of British housing doubled in the space of just four years. At the same time, there was a stock market boom. From its low point in March 1971, the *Financial Times* ordinary share index rose by two thirds in the space of just fourteen months.

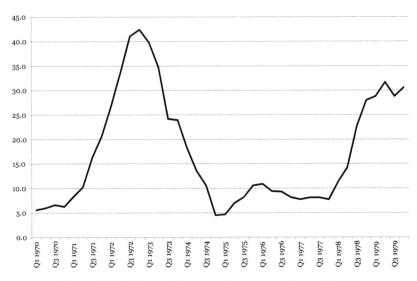

Figure 6.2: UK house prices, annual percentage change, 1970–9.

Source: Nationwide Building Society.

The inevitable switch from 'Go' back to 'Stop' – which took the form of hikes in the Bank of England's new minimum lending rate from 6 per cent to 9 per cent in the last quarter of 1972, and then again from 9 per cent to 13 per cent in the second half of 1973 – failed to tame inflation.[53] Not much more effectual were the 'supplementary special deposits' (the so-called 'corset') introduced in December 1973 to check the growth of interest-bearing bank liabilities. Monetary tightening did succeed in bringing house price inflation back down to single digits. A less obviously intended consequence of all this was a stock market crash. By the end of 1974, the FT All Share index was down a wrenching 69 per cent from its peak. Adjusted for inflation, the losses were even greater – comparable, indeed, with the losses suffered by American investors in the Great Depression (see Figure 6.3).

Figure 6.3: *Financial Times* **All-Share Index, nominal and real.**

Source: Office of National Statistics.

Not for the first time in post-war British history, a politically motivated stimulus led not to higher growth and lower unemployment but to higher consumer
prices, spiralling wage claims, a widening current account deficit and yet more
downward pressure on sterling. What made the currency crisis of the early 1970s
unusual – but distinctly familiar from today's vantage point – was that it was
accompanied by a banking crisis.[54] In the 1970s, as in more recent times, there
was a 'shadow banking system': the so-called 'fringe banks' that had sprung up on
the periphery of the existing regulatory framework – recognized as 'Section 123'
banks by the Bank of England, but ignored on account of their relatively small
size. For these new 'secondary' banks, which had proliferated and expanded their

operations in the heady days of the Barber boom, the effects of higher interest rates and falling asset prices were catastrophic, particularly for those who had lent most enthusiastically to property developers. The first to get into trouble was the Scottish Co-operative Wholesale Society (SCOOP), followed in November 1973 by London and County Securities and Cedar Holdings. At first it seemed that the Bank had averted a full-blown crisis by summoning – rather as it had done in the Barings Crisis of 1890 – representatives of the big banks and persuading them to create a support fund, to which the Bank itself made a modest contribution.[55] But as the City was swept with a 'contagion of fear' (in the words of the Governor, Gordon Richardson), much more was needed. This was the first bank panic in London since 1866 and it posed a direct threat not just to the fringe but to the core of the system: witness the steep declines in the share prices of the big four clearing banks, Barclays, Lloyds, Midland and National Westminster, which ranged between 83 and 89 per cent from peak to trough. The so-called 'Lifeboat' ended up needing more than a billion pounds (£1,189 million) to bail out the so-called fringe banks, of which 10 per cent came from the Bank itself. The amounts committed represented approximately half the clearing banks' shareholders' funds.[56] Far from being 'fringe' institutions, the secondary banks had posed a systemic risk that the Bank of England had wholly overlooked. Indeed, the news of the insolvency of Triumph Investment Trust in November 1974 nearly sparked a run on the National Westminster. In all, twenty-six banks or bank-like entities received funds from the Lifeboat of which only four subsequently emerged intact. In addition, five institutions were supported by the Bank of England alone, of which three were actually bought outright, most famously Slater Walker Limited, the banking arm of the group founded in 1964 by the flashy financier Jim Slater and the Tory MP Peter Walker.[57] Less well known, but almost as large in scale, was the Bank's rescue of the Crown Agents, which had deviated from their colonial roots into hot money and real estate speculation, with disastrous results.

It is usually argued that the Heath government sentenced itself to electoral defeat in November 1972, when it was driven to revive the Labour policy of wage control, or in December 1973, when the three-day working week was introduced in an attempt to reduce energy consumption. By the time Heath called an election on 7 February 1974, the miners were on strike. 'Who Rules Britain?' was the Conservative election slogan. The obvious answer was: Not Heath. Yet it was surely the banking and financial crisis, more than the resurgence of organized labour, that really doomed Heath. For the impact on Conservative voters of a simultaneous bursting of both the bubbles Barber had inflated – in the stock market and in the real estate market – was without question greater than the impact of the miners' strike. Then, as in our own times, Opposition MPs and journalists were not slow to question the justice of bailing out the 'Smart Alecs' of the City at a time of ruinous losses for ordinary investors.[58]

By the time Harold Wilson returned to 10 Downing Street in March 1974, following Heath's failure to form a coalition in the wake of the previous month's inconclusive general election, Britain's economic predicament was dire indeed. With a yawning current account deficit, miners on strike and the entire economy on a three-day working week, to say nothing of the virtual civil war in Northern Ireland, the situation in Britain increasingly resembled that of Argentina. As Warburg put it, Wilson was resuming office 'at a time when the country is facing the most serious economic crisis in its history, a crisis which indeed is not only of a material character but is a crisis of the whole fabric of our society'.[59] Warburg at once recommended a $2–3 billion loan from the International Monetary Fund 'to prevent a further flight from the pound by foreign creditors and to increase the country's foreign exchange reserves with extremely large amounts'.[60] Privately, he could muster only faint praise for the government: 'At least one can say that the Wilson government is not quite as bad as the Heath Government'.[61] When he met Wilson in early June he was dismayed by the premier's 'unbelievably detached attitude regarding his colleagues, regarding the Opposition, regarding the trade unions, and really regarding everyone and everything of importance'.[62]

Warburg's principal worry was that the new government was still underestimating the inflationary danger.[63] It was. Retail price inflation was running at 8 per cent when Labour returned to power; by August 1975 it was 26.9 per cent, the worst inflation the country experienced in the entire twentieth century. When, on 16 March 1976, Wilson unexpectedly announced his intention to resign – claiming that he was exhausted, but perhaps fearing the consequences of early-onset Alzheimer's disease – Warburg shed no tears.[64] Within months, with the public sector borrowing requirement approaching 10 per cent of GDP, Wilson's successor, 'Lucky Jim' Callaghan, had been forced to turn to the International Monetary Fund for a $3.9 billion loan. It came with stringent fiscal and monetary conditions attached. The *Wall Street Journal*'s headline of the previous year summed up the country's plight: 'Goodbye Great Britain'.[65]

Banking in Adverse Conditions

For financial markets, stagflation spelt double trouble. With corporate profits squeezed, returns on stocks turned negative. With inflation surging, bonds offered no protection. Between 1970 and 1979, the average annual return on UK stocks was –1.4 per cent, allowing for inflation; on bonds the return was –4.4 per cent.[66] In inflation-adjusted terms, the FT-Actuaries All Share Index – the broadest London equity index – fell by 78 per cent between the peak May

1972 and the nadir of December 1974. As late as December 1979 it was still at 28 per cent of its 1972 high.

Warburg was only a little better prepared for this storm than the man in the street. In 1966 he had conveyed his fears of inflation to the American journalist Joseph Wechsberg:

> He is convinced that money is becoming worth less all the time. He speaks wistfully about the wise law of Solon in Athens that all debts not paid back within seventy years must be cancelled. People who contract debts pay the interest. But ... the money they pay back [today] is always worth less ... Warburg's 'painful experience' after the First World War, when bondholders lost nearly everything while shareholders who didn't sell eventually came out all right, has formed his basic investment philosophy.[67]

But what exactly did that 'philosophy' mean in practice? Although Warburg was right to expect 'further heavy falls' both on Wall Street and in the City, his advice to Nahum Goldmann in August 1970 to 'be about half invested in equities and half invested in fixed interest securities' – the latter of which promised 'a really worthwhile income ... coupled with maximum security' – was woefully inadequate.[68] Goldmann would have done much better to stick to equities, and better still to buy gold. Even in a quicksilver mind like Warburg's, expectations adapted more slowly than in neoclassical economic theory. His partner Henry Grunfeld admitted many years later how completely he too had been caught out by inflation, and how little he and Warburg had been able to do to protect their bank from its ravages.[69] The only precaution Warburg himself seems to have taken in the face of 'monetary anarchy' was to hold 'as much money as possible in Swiss Francs or German Marks' – something his residence in Switzerland allowed him to do, since it removed him from the UK exchange controls.[70] It was not until June 1974 that he saw the need for a new kind of index-linked bond that would offer investors protection against inflation – an idea he immediately proposed to the British government.[71] (It was finally adopted in 1981.)

The crisis affected not only Warburg himself, but also his family. In 1970, seven years after resigning as a director of S. G. Warburg, his son George went into partnership with his friend Milo Cripps, the nephew of the former Labour Chancellor Stafford Cripps, and also an ex-Warburgs director. Together they set up C. W. Capital Ltd. – an abbreviation doubtless chosen to avoid a clash with his father over the use of the sacrosanct family name. The firm, George Warburg told Henry Grunfeld, was to be a merchant bank, 'active mainly as financial advisers and as investment managers' but perhaps also taking deposits and making loans. With ordinary share capital of £500,000 and thirteen employees, C. W. was conspicuously not backed by S. G. Warburg & Co. Instead, its principal investor was the august banking house of Williams & Glyn.[72] Warburg *père* naturally kept a wary eye on Warburg *fils*, expressing guarded interest in the new firm's agency relationship with New England Merchants National Bank.[73] Dealings with S. G. Warburg were entrusted to a young American, who lost little time in requesting a short-term lending facility of £250,000 from Warburgs. The response from 30 Gresham Street was cool. While it was certainly 'Sir Siegmund's wish ... to develop a relationship with C. W. Capital', nevertheless the upper bound for such credit would be £100,000 'until such time as we obtain a clearer picture of the nature of their lending'.[74] By March 1972, the desired clarity had been attained. With assets of nearly £9 million, C. W. had made – as Warburg Senior was happy to admit – 'fine progress'.[75] In January 1973 he gave his blessing to a fateful name change: C. W. became Cripps Warburg.[76] Shortly afterwards Warburgs invested £225,000 in the form of partly convertible unsecured bonds (equivalent, if they were converted, to around 2.5 per cent of the firm's equity). With the backing of both the family name and the family firm, Cripps Warburg grew by leaps and bounds. By the end of March 1973, its balance sheet had more than quadrupled to £37 million. Unfortunately, as we have seen, Cripps Warburg had acquired its new name on the eve of one of the worst banking crises in modern British history.

Tensions first arose in early 1973 when George Warburg complained to Grunfeld about his 'unforthcoming attitude' in connection with a transaction that was supposed to be handled jointly by Cripps Warburg and S. G. Warburg.[77] On 19 July 1974, Cripps and Warburg called on David Scholey to confess that they had 'manoeuvred themselves into a rather bad situation through having entered into large commitments in financing real estate propositions of various kinds'. To be more precise, their capital had been very nearly wiped out by multiple bad loans to small property companies – a business strategy inspired by Cripps's naive insight that 'in our era of increasingly galloping inflation the business field which deserved more intensive attention and involvement than any other one was real estate'.[78] The elder Warburg seethed. His son and his partners had committed the ultimate sin of 'wishful non-thinking'. They had committed 'grave errors'. They should have admitted to these 'at a much earlier stage'. The fact that the ailing firm bore the Warburg name 'should ... not carry any weight with us'. There could be no question of investing more money; that was the responsibility of Williams & Glyn and the other founding shareholders. The most he would recommend was that 'we might assist them with special facilities on a proper business basis'.[79] Even the explanations now offered for the firm's difficulties were marred by 'sloppiness' and 'ambiguities'.[80] It was simply 'false' to regard Cripps Warburg as being 'closely associated with us', Warburg snapped.[81] His son's abject contrition – 'he blames himself utterly and ruthlessly' – did not change Warburg's mind. He was willing to offer advice, but not to throw good money after bad.[82]

The refusal of S. G. Warburg to support a recapitalization of Cripps Warburg doomed the firm.[83] In the spring of 1975 it went into voluntary liquidation with losses exceeding £4 million.[84]

Regulation Taking its Toll

In January 1981 Siegmund Warburg sent an irascible memorandum to the S. G. Warburg Chairman's Committee:

> An infectious mental disease seems to have taken hold in certain quarters of our group which has paralyzed the ability to visualise negative trends in the future with the result that those suffering from the disease are only able to foresee increases in turnover and furthermore assume that increases in turnover automatically result in proportionate increases in profits. In my view one-sided calculations of this character are not only contrary to experience but are bound to lead to wrongly based deliberations and fallacious decisions.
>
> When we look back on the last ten years or so it is, of course, obvious that turnover and organizational scope have increased enormously but that the trend in profits has been generally much slower and in certain sections of our business rather arrested. If we were to substitute for presentations in sterling figures analytical statistics based on inflation accounting we would be bound to arrive at several gloomy conclusions and would find that the return on net assets in our group leaves much to be desired in comparison with some past periods.[85]

At the time, some younger directors may have been inclined to dismiss these as the grumblings of an old man who long ago should have retired. Yet what Warburg said was perfectly true. Nominally, net profits at Mercury Securities had risen by 79 per cent between 1976 and 1981, to just over £12 million (around £68 million in today's terms). Adjusted for inflation, however, they had fallen by 30 per cent. They did not regain their 1976 level until 1983, a year after Siegmund Warburg's death (see Figure 6.4). Small wonder that the Mercury share price in March 1981 was exactly what it had been in January 1969.

The 1974 stock market crisis and the inexorable slide of sterling had taken their toll on the merchant banks, which were fast becoming (as the *Economist* remarked) the 'genteel poor of the international banking community'. As a direct consequence of regulation, they were nearly all under-capitalized. The Bank of England prevented them from having assets more than twelve times the size of their capital. The Treasury refused to allow them to hold even a part of their capital in foreign currency. And the Inland Revenue insisted on taxing unrealized foreign exchange gains on currency loans, but denied tax relief on corresponding increases in the cost of repaying foreign borrowings.[86] The onset of stagflation was devastating. The value of Hill Samuel's assets, for example, declined by nearly half in real terms between 1973 and 1977.[87] Even the best of the breed was struggling. And Warburgs was the best in terms only of profitability; in terms of its balance sheet, it ranked sixth in the City (see Table 6.1).

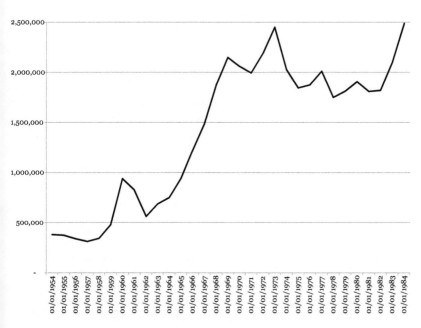

Figure 6.4: Real net profits at Mercury Securities, 1954–94 (pounds of 1954).
Source: Mercury Securities annual reports; figures adjusted using the official consumer price index for the financial year.

Table 6.1: Merchant bank balance sheets, millions of pounds, 1973–7.

	Balance sheet 1977–8	Percentage change adjusted for inflation over past 4 years	Deposits incl. inner reserves and tax provisions	Shareholders' funds	Disclosed net attributable profit
Kleinwort Benson	1,430	-23	1,114	77	7.5
Hambros	1,423	-32	1,048	65	7.1
Hill Samuel Group	1,304	-46	868	63	6.9
Schroders	1,177	-23	944	45	3.5
Morgan Grenfell	863	27	706	31	5.5
Mercury Securities	765	-3	499	66	8.1
Lazard Brothers	569	-17	443	38	3.8
N. M. Rothschild	528	-11	470	20	0.6
Baring Brothers	326	-32	147	20	0.7

Source: *Economist*, 31 March 1979, p. 58.

Thatcherism and Financial Deregulation: A Different Perspective

Though it was strictly a British affair, the financial crisis of 1973–5 had much in common with the crisis of 2007–9. It had its origins in basic errors of monetary and fiscal policy. Deregulation played a role, but it was not something for which innovative banks had been clamouring. What bankers most wanted from government by 1979 was not so much deregulation as time-consistent policy. Britain began 1979 in the grip of the 'Winter of Discontent', the economy paralysed as car workers, truck drivers, ambulance drivers and local authority workers – including refuse collectors and gravediggers – went on strike against the Labour government's 5 per cent cap on pay rises. Yet by the end of 1980 Warburg felt able to make a startling and highly uncharacteristic admission:

> I must confess that, for the first time for more than ten years, I am becoming a *little* bit more optimistic about the political situation in our Western world. It seems likely that the new American President [Reagan] will make fewer mistakes than his predecessor and in Britain Mrs Thatcher ... is as a whole showing great courage in cleaning up a situation which under successive Labour and Conservative governments of the post-War period had continuously deteriorated. The mess which she has inherited is almost unmanageable but she has shown determination to tackle it.[88]

Margaret Thatcher's election victory on 3 May 1979, was without question a turning point in financial history. There was indeed successful financial deregulation, as opposed to the fiasco of the Barber era. Exchange controls were scrapped in October 1979, followed by special deposits and supplementary special deposits at the end of the year. Yet it would be a mistake to caricature the Thatcher government simply as an agent of financial deregulation. For that would be to miss important continuities from the aftermath of the Barber boom, which in fact led in the direction of more – and more effective – regulation, rather than less. Under Richardson, the Bank of England sought to maintain a distinction between banks, which it preferred to manage with the old tools of moral suasion, and other financial institutions, which it did not mind consigning to statutory regulation. This two-tiered system was much less easy to defend after the secondary banking crisis, which had patently arisen somewhere between the two tiers. It also came under pressure from the European Economic Community, which Britain had finally joined under Heath. The 'Draft Directive for the Coordination of the Legal and Administrative Provisions for the Taking Up and Exercise of the "Independent Operator" Activities of Credit Institutions' made it clear that the continentals expected *all* banks to be licensed and regulated in a uniform way.[89] Further pressure for a more consistent regime came from the ten-country Standing Committee of Banking Supervisory Authorities, which first met in Basel in December 1974. The Thatcher government also inherited from its predecessor two further sources of regulatory stricture: the legacy of IMF conditionality – which had the effect of forcing monetary targeting on a sceptical Bank – and the 1979 Banking Act, which introduced deposit insurance some forty-six years after its adoption in the United States. Although the legislation still maintained Richardson's pet distinction between 'recognized' banks and 'licensed' institutions, this did not long survive; the 1987 Banking Act swept it away.[90]

The really important thing about the Thatcher government was that government expenditures were slashed, short-term interest rates cranked up in real rather than only nominal terms, and the over-mighty trade unions confronted head-on, all signalling a decisive regime change and thereby altering public expectations of inflation.[91] The contrast could scarcely have been more complete than with the French Socialists. The election of François Mitterrand as French President in May 1981 proved to be the last gasp of an unreconstructed socialism based on the old policy prescription of state control, increased workers' rights, high direct taxation and reduced working hours. Its implications for the financial sector were especially dire as the government implemented its plan to nationalize the country's biggest banks – including S. G. Warburg's partner Paribas – triggering capital flight and a currency crisis that ultimately forced a *volte face* on the government.

One might therefore have expected the Thatcher government's policies to have enjoyed the wholehearted support of the City of London. It was surely not without significance that on 13 February 1981, Margaret Thatcher herself came to lunch at 30 Gresham Street,[92] or that Warburg himself had a private meeting with her the following May.[93] Yet the affinities between Thatcher and the City were much less close than is often assumed, particularly at the beginning. Many bankers lined up more with the so-called 'Wets' within the government, who felt their leader was acting too aggressively on all fronts. As a man who had throughout his life identified much more with the Left than with the Right – who counted as his political friends Emanuel Shinwell, Stafford Cripps and Harold Wilson, and who had been regarded by Hugh Gaitskell as a 'rather Left-Wing financial man' – Siegmund Warburg was never likely to be an uncritical Thatcherite.[94] Though he was unstinting in his praise of 'the courageous and positive elements in the policy of the Thatcher Government', and the 'valour and fortitude' of the Prime Minister herself, he was frequently critical of her Chancellor Geoffrey Howe's application of monetarist theory. Publicly he defended Howe's anti-inflation budget of 1981.[95] Privately, like many at the Bank of England, he had doubts. 'Fatal mistakes are in my opinion being made by the Treasury', he confided to one Warburgs non-executive director, 'in trying to manipulate with interest rates a situation which has to be tackled by a delicate mixture of economic and financial steps'. Like a majority of British economists, Warburg believed the appreciation of sterling (due in part to the discovery and development of North Sea oil), in combination with the much tighter domestic credit conditions, would drive unemployment up to intolerable heights.[96] Though attracted to Keith Joseph's desire 'to bring private business into this picture' (the policy that became known as 'privatization'),[97] Warburg worried that the government had 'no proper backing either from industry or from the trade unions or even any of the sound groups in the middle of British politics'.[98] As Joseph put it after a meeting in October 1981, Warburg 'underestimated ... the extra burdens we face from nationalized industries and trade unionist attitudes'.[99] To the last, indeed, he retained the German faith in corporatist deals between big business and organized labour. 'Monetary policy is not a sufficiently effective medicine against inflation', he grumbled, 'unless it is accompanied by an incomes policy of some sort'.[100] In Britain, at least, it was the politicians who led the bankers to the free market, not the other way round.

The financial history of the 1970s makes it clear that the recent past cannot be cast as some kind of morality play, in which conservative politicians conspired with rent-seeking bankers to deregulate the world to the point of a near depression. In Britain there was no pre-1979 Eden of regulated finance. The regulations of the 1970s did nothing to prevent financial crisis. And the first steps in the direction of deregulation after 1970, far from helping British bankers, disastrously weakened them.

Then, as in our time, the drivers of economic volatility were not financial innovations, much less the greed of the financiers, but politically driven decisions about monetary and fiscal policy. Imprudently low interest rates and unjustifiably large public borrowing together are always a toxic combination. The responsibility for such policies, then and now, lies more with the political class than with the financial.

7 FINANCIAL MARKET INTEGRATION: AN INSURMOUNTABLE CHALLENGE TO MODERN TRADE POLICY?

Welf Werner

The last sixty years have been an era of rapid globalization. While reduction of transportation and communication costs contributed to the development of trans-border economic activities, the single most significant contribution came from modern trade policy. Eight negotiating rounds under the auspices of the General Agreement on Tariffs and Trade (GATT) proved to be instrumental in rolling back barriers to trade and protecting the trading system against protectionist backlash. Multilateral regulations such as the most favoured nation clause (MFN) helped create a rules-based international level-playing field with high transparency and reliability. Besides the GATT and the World Trade Organization (WTO), regional agreements also contributed to these advances. Although such preferential trade agreements (PTAs) are discriminatory vis-à-vis non-member countries and thus only a second-best solution, they have helped to tackle new and controversial trade policy issues.

While the importance of modern trade policy for the globalization process is well known, it is less clear what role it has played in the last sixty years in the integration of service markets and especially of financial service markets: Have financial services been subject to regional or multilateral trade policy initiatives? If so, how successful have these initiatives been in rolling back barriers and securing liberalization commitments? Have such policy initiatives brought advantages to global financial markets such as improved transparency and reliability? Have rules such as MFN been employed to ensure the same market access conditions to firms of different nationalities? The answers to these questions are especially relevant against the background of current discussions of a new global financial architecture. Since the onset of the global financial crisis in 2007 these discussions have focused on guaranteeing stability of financial markets through better coordination of national prudential regulation in international organizations such as the G20, the Financial Stability Board (FSB) and specifically the Basel Committee of the Bank for International Settlements (BIS). Because guaranteeing stability and securing open markets are the two most important goals of any international financial order, institutional developments to realize these goals have been interwoven in many ways. As we will see, modern trade policy for financial services has not only been concerned with opening borders but with many aspects of guaranteeing stability. One of the key concerns of these initiatives has been on how to cope with the many differences in national prudential regulation, the main instrument of nation states for guaranteeing the stability, safety and soundness of their domestic financial markets and for regulating market access of foreign financial firms. Capital and liquidity standards, for example, are not only important for the stability of financial markets but also for creating a level playing field for domestic and foreign firms.

But which modern trade policy initiatives have been concerned with financial services? And how have these initiatives contributed to an emerging global financial architecture? As three fields of study – trade policy, trade law and finance – have not found common ground for discussing such initiatives, knowledge about them is scattered and a basic picture of their development has not emerged.[1] Earlier research shows that coverage of financial services in regional and multilateral initiatives dates back to as early as the post-war years. The OEEC already included financial services in its attempt to liberalize trade in goods in 1951. While extremely limited in scope by today's standards of rapid financial market globalization, the OECD's *Code of Liberalization of Trade and Invisible Transactions* introduced a set of multilateral rules that was not only applied to goods but also to services and financial services. In later years, initiatives for financial services liberalization were further developed in the EEC's Common Market and the EU's Single Market, establishing a specific European learning process. Finally financial services became subject to multilateral negotiations in the WTO's Uruguay Round (1986–94). In 1997 financial services were belatedly included in the General Agreement on Trade in Services (GATS).[2]

The initiatives by OEEC, EEC, EU and WTO and their contributions to the development of global financial architecture will be analysed by addressing three questions: (1) What is the reach of the initiatives regarding lines of business and modes of trans-border supply? (2) What specific rules and concepts are applied for liberalization and (3) what concepts are employed for guaranteeing stability? The first question highlights issues such as whether initiatives focused on a very few, narrowly defined trans-border activities or whether they established the goal of an all-embracing liberalization programme, covering all major financial services and modes of trans-border supply. The two most important modes of supply considered are 'cross-border supply of services' and 'operations of foreign firms'.[3] Regarding liberalization concepts the main question is whether full reciprocity or first-difference reciprocity is applied. While first-difference reciprocity means that countries are moving towards a common liberalization goal with approximately the same speed, full reciprocity goes an important step further in that it proclaims the goal of reaching the same absolute level of liberalization commitments for all signatories. Finally, regarding concepts for guaranteeing stability three different approaches to coordinating national prudential regulation are considered; (a) harmonization, (b) minimum harmonization, and (c) mutual recognition. While mutual recognition aims at minimizing regulatory gaps and overlap but leaves differences of prudential regulation intact, minimum harmonization and harmonization represent attempts at a partial or complete harmonization.

Finally, factors that have influenced the nature and outcome of the trade policy initiatives of OEEC, EEC, EU and WTO are discussed. Specifically two framework conditions are considered: the predominant international monetary regime and the main trade policy agenda of the international organization in which the trade policy initiative for financial services was undertaken.

Changes in the international monetary system divide the last sixty years into two distinct eras with a transition period in the 1970s. In the 1950s and 1960s the Bretton Woods system of fixed exchange rates set tight limits to what elites deemed possible or desirable regarding liberalization of financial services. The pursuit of two policy goals, fixed exchange rates and independent monetary policies geared towards full employment, meant that short-term capital flows had to be restricted.[4] This restriction was not only a by-product of strong political imperatives for the pursuit of the first two economic policy goals, but was a strong independent goal. The GATT and the IMF, the two major Bretton Woods institutions, were not to promote trans-border economic activities of any kind including those of financial firms but specifically trade in goods: The GATT was to focus on tariffs, the IMF's focus was on current account convertibility, not on capital account convertibility. While the post-war monetary system restricted short-term capital flows and the many financial services that come along with them, its demise in 1973, initiated by a free floating dollar, opened new policy options to financial service liberalization through capital account liberalization which began in OECD countries in the late 1980s.

The other factor of success considered is the main trade policy agenda of the international organization in which the liberalization initiative for financial services is undertaken. Since financial services liberalization has never been the main target, but only one of many topics of a greater trade policy agenda, its progress has been largely dependent on what the main trade policy agenda happened to be. In the immediate post-war decades, multilateral trade policy focused almost exclusively on trade in goods and more particularly on border-specific barriers such as quantitative restrictions and tariffs. Barriers of specific importance to financial firms, such as barriers to establishment and restrictions in the form of domestic regulation, were largely outside the scope of main trade policy agendas. This changed rapidly once barriers to trade in goods had been successfully dismantled. The period of transition for trade policy was, as for the monetary regime, the 1970s. The EEC had successfully completed the customs union in 1968. Six negotiating rounds under the auspices of the GATT had helped to bring down industrial tariffs in sixty-two countries. After the EEC's Common Market and the GATT's Tokyo Round had already made first inroads at widening the trade policy agendas beyond trade in goods, the EU's Single Market programme and the WTO's Uruguay Round firmly installed a wide range of new topics into modern trade policy. Among the topics that proved to be instrumental for the multilateral liberalization of financial services are international trade in services, foreign direct investment (FDI) and domestic regulation.

Post-War Initiatives: The OECD Codes of Liberalization

The OEEC was the first organization that engaged in multilateral liberalization of financial services.[5] In the literature it is well known for other activities: its role in the management of the funds of the European Recovery Programme (ERP) and its engagement in the early liberalization of trade in goods in Western Europe. Regarding its main trade policy focus, the integration of goods markets, the Paris-based organization had two closely connected objectives in the 1950s: the reduction of quantitative restrictions on trade and the restoration of currency convertibility. The latter goal was achieved through the European Payments Union (EPU), formed in 1950, and the European Monetary Agreement (EMA), concluded in 1958.

After it had become clear that with the establishment of the EEC in 1957, responsibilities for the liberalization of trade in goods would be transferred to this new organization, the role of the OEEC in trade diplomacy shrunk considerably. Plans to convert the Paris-based organization into a free trade area were not adopted. When the OEEC was finally replaced by the OECD in 1961, it was charged with very broad but somewhat blurry responsibilities that still characterize the organization's activities today. Apart from a few low key and generally unsuccessful attempts at liberalizing FDI and financial services in later years, the organization has not engaged in international trade policy activities since its foundation in 1961.

A closer look at the beginnings of the OEEC's attempts at trade liberalization in the late 1940s and early 1950s shows that its jurisdiction over financial market liberalization derived directly from its initiatives to liberalize trade in goods. Initiatives to reduce quantitative restrictions on trade in goods, which the OEEC had begun right after its establishment in April 1948, led in 1951 to the enactment of the Code of Liberalization of Trade and Invisible Transactions. The title of this Code already indicates that the OEEC was not only engaged in the liberalization of goods but also in the liberalization of 'invisible transactions', or, in other words, international services trade. This part of the liberalization agenda addressed among other services those of banking, and especially of insurance industries, even though it did so to a very limited degree so that these activities have been largely overlooked in the literature.[6]

The drafters of the Code had by no means intended to create an extensive liberalization programme for the entire insurance or banking industries, let alone for the entire service sector. They focused only on a very few narrowly defined trans-border activities. The main motive for this selective approach was to support the development of international trade in goods which could not function smoothly without the efficient international provision of specific services such as transport services, trade credit or specific insurance services such as transport insurance. Narrow limits were set to these liberalization efforts by the general shortage of foreign exchange, which restricted the entire cross-border exchange of goods and services. Initiatives to liberalize services were further limited by the specific shortages of the post-war economies in many areas of the 'real economy'. These shortages suggested a concentration on liberalization of trade in goods and left little room for manoeuvre in other fields.

The liberalization obligations that the OEEC introduced to insurance trade were listed in an Annex of the Code of Liberalization of Trade and Invisible Transactions. Three chapters covered direct insurance, reinsurance and operations of foreign insurance companies. The chapter on direct insurance comprised liberalization obligations concerning transport insurance, property insurance, life insurance and capacity shortages, that is, situations in which domestic insurance companies were not able to cover all domestic risks. For transport insurance, which was particularly important for international trade in goods, obligations were comparatively far-reaching even though only cargo insurance, i.e. the insurance of goods in transit, was considered and not hull insurance, i.e. the insurance of the means of transport. Since 1954, obligations for cargo insurance had referred both to 'transfers' – restrictions on foreign exchange – which were at the centre of the entire liberalization programme of the OEEC, and to 'transactions' – limitations on the conclusion of individual insurance contracts, the majority of which derived from prudential regulation.

Liberalization of life insurance, which made only little progress in later years in the EEC and the EU, was included in the Annex of the Code because of increased levels of international migration that had begun right after the end of the Second World War. These movements necessitated cross-border payments of life insurance policies in large quantities. The liberalization obligations consequently focused on trans-border payments to migrants, and did not include other trans-border activities such as the signing of new contracts, the licensing of foreign-owned insurance companies or the ongoing activities of already established foreign firms. Moreover, there were strict limits on the total amount of trans-border payments that could be made under life insurance policies.

The consideration of international reinsurance activities can be interpreted as an effort to return to the level of liberalization that had already been achieved in many countries before World War II. Reinsurance has had a strong international orientation right from the start.[7] Consequently, for reinsurance as well, comparatively far-reaching measures were taken. Besides transport insurance, reinsurance was the only other insurance service for which the OEEC did not only address barriers to transfers but also to transactions.

The strict limits to the OEEC's liberalization measures in the insurance sector are best described with respect to liberalization obligations on property insurance, the operations of foreign insurers and shortages of insurance capacity. As in the field of life insurance, obligations on property insurance focused only on existing contracts. Provisions aimed at shortages of insurance capacity were of little practical relevance, since it had already been common practice of supervisory authorities in the past to admit foreign insurers to the domestic market in such situations. Obligations upon foreign commercial presence covered only specific international transfers of foreign subsidiaries and branches with their parent companies. Neither restrictions on market access, for example the restrictive licensing of foreign insurance companies that had emerged in practically all member states on the basis of more or less arbitrary needs tests, nor the national treatment principle, i.e. the equal treatment of foreign subsidiaries vis-à-vis domestically owned companies under national prudential regulations, were addressed.

Even though the progress that the OEEC achieved in the liberalization of insurance markets is by today's standards extremely limited, it is important to recognize that by focusing on some particularly pressing issues the organization met the special needs of the post-war years. The highly selective approach to liberalization was well-suited given the shortage of foreign exchange on the one hand and the pressing challenges to re-establishing trade in goods on the other. More importantly, as limited as the reach of these early measures was regarding lines of business and modes of international service supply, they already contained all the essential elements of modern multilateral trade policy: the principles of progressive liberalization and full reciprocity; a catalogue of concrete liberalization obligations (listed in the Code's Annex); the principle of unconditional most-favoured nation treatment; and institutions and procedures to monitor compliance. In 1954 an Insurance Sub-committee was established to observe the progress of the programme. This sub-committee was to support the Committee on Invisible Transactions which was responsible for all service transactions covered under the Code. In addition, multilateral rules for the insurance sector comprised a number of derogations and reservations, allowing sufficient scope for member states to move towards the agreed-upon objectives at varying speeds and according to specific national economic circumstances.

Taking all these instruments together, there is no doubt that the introduction of the Code of Liberalization of Trade and Invisible Transactions in 1951 represents the first step towards a treaty-based multilateral approach to liberalization of financial services in the history of financial market globalization. There was a crucial aspect, however, in which the liberalization concept applied to financial services did not meet the standards of that applied to trade in goods. The provision for insurance trade did not make use of the 'percentage method' which guaranteed for trade in goods that all countries made similar progress in their liberalization efforts despite differences in the treatment of individual classes of goods. Balance of payments statistics did not provide enough information on 'invisible trade' to make this method applicable to trade in services. Thus an efficient monitoring of the overall liberalization achievements of member countries was not possible in the case of financial services and other services. Surveillance had to rely solely on peer pressure and on a case-by-case evaluation of liberalization commitments. Neither a formal dispute settlement procedure nor sanctions were available and the liberalization process was much less transparent.

By far the most important conceptual weakness of the insurance programme was, however, the little attention paid to the many obstacles that existed in the form of domestic regulation and specifically to prudential regulation.[8] These obstacles were addressed only in the cases of transport insurance and reinsurance, that is, in fields in which domestic regulation was not very stringent to begin with. As in the case of liberalization of trade in goods, the liberalization of the insurance trade was concerned mainly with transfers, and not with transactions and the many ways in which they were limited through prudential regulation.

The harmonization of national prudential regulation in the wake of liberalization initiatives, although every now and then touched upon in the OEEC, was not a realistic policy option in the Bretton Woods Era, in which multilateral trade policy focused almost exclusively on trade in goods, and the regulation of financial services markets was considered the sole domain of nation states. Under these conditions, financial service liberalization had to remain on the fringes of the main policy agenda of the OEEC. More specifically it had to be confined to those trans-border activities which do not present a challenge to the stability of national financial markets. Against this background, insurance services rather than banking services were an ideal target for the Code of Liberalization.

The lack of political support for addressing domestic regulation in the OEEC can best be seen in provisions of the Code which explicitly stated that a member state may take action to deny foreign insurance firms access to their domestic markets through prudential regulation. Even modest steps towards harmonization, for example the introduction of a standardized system of classification for the different lines of insurance business, failed in the Council of Ministers. However, the nearly complete lack of progress had also a positive side to it. While the OEEC was far from developing a broad-based liberalization programme for insurance or any other service, discussions in the organizations had at least led to the firm belief that the major challenge to any broad-based liberalization programme for financial services, if it was ever to be undertaken, was the differences in national prudential regulation and that these differences can only be overcome through harmonization. To that effect the OEEC and the OECD commissioned the first systematic stocktaking of national regulatory systems in the insurance industry in 1956 and 1963.[9] Although these studies showed significant differences in national prudential regulation and their negative effects on trans-border activities, no further action was taken.

It should also be mentioned that not only the OEEC but later on also the OECD became active in the liberalization of insurance trade. This resulted largely from discussions about the future of the OEEC in the years 1956 to 1958. At the request of the US, the OECD, which replaced the OEEC in 1961, was not to take over any responsibility for trade liberalization. The overriding goal of the Americans was to keep trade policy initiatives outside the GATT to a minimum. The only exception that was made in the era of the Cold War for political reasons was the EEC. After its reestablishment in 1961, the Paris-based organization was consequently stripped of the main part of its trade policy agenda, the liberalization of international trade in goods. The organization remained, however, responsible for 'invisibles', a component of the trade policy of its predecessor organization that was obviously not taken seriously enough to come into conflict with demands to end the organization's involvement in international trade policy. On the occasion of the establishment of the OECD in 1961, the Code of Liberalization of Trade and Invisible Transactions was not completely resolved but transformed into a Code of Liberalization of Current Invisible Operations. The organization was to keep its responsibility for trade in services.

Another Code of the OEEC, the Code of Liberalization of Capital Movements, was also carried over into the new organization. This Code had originally been introduced in 1959. It was not aimed at short- or medium-term capital movements, which were off-limits in the Bretton Woods era as they would have threatened the stability of fixed exchange rates, but at long-term movements and especially at foreign direct investment. With these two Codes the OECD was equipped with a surprisingly modern trade policy agenda in 1961 covering international services trade and FDI. In its further development, however, the OECD made no progress in any of these fields. All efforts to develop a modern trade policy agenda, which include services liberalization as well as capital account liberalization, were indeed focused on the EEC and the EU. Interestingly though, the OECD never formally gave up on the work on their two liberalization codes.

In 1976 the organization introduced a National Treatment Instrument that for the first time and somewhat belatedly acknowledged that a foreign subsidiary should not be treated less favourably than domestic companies. However, this instrument was not legally binding. The same is true for the results of a more broad-based overhaul of the two Codes which began in 1979, with financial services now officially at the centre of the initiative. Although quite a few papers were produced and new rules drafted, political support was once again inadequate to give this initiative any relevance for markets. Among other problems, there was once again no support for harmonization of prudential regulation.[10]

From Common Market to Single Market

The EEC, which began its involvement in European economic integration almost ten years later than the OEEC, started out with a remarkably far-sighted trade policy agenda in 1957.[11] Paragraph three of the Treaty of Rome laid out goals for progressive liberalization not only for trade in goods, but also for trade in services, capital movements and the free movement of workers. The treaty also addressed the problems of domestic regulation, which was to be harmonized as far as this was necessary for the integration of the national economies into a Common Market. Even though there was no doubt that this endorsement was to be interpreted as covering prudential regulation, liberalization in the field of financial services turned out to be a painstakingly slow and inefficient process until the implementation of the Single Market programme in the late 1980s and early 1990s. As before in the OEEC, the liberalization of trade in goods had priority over other more challenging trade policy agendas. After the OEEC had focused on quantitative restrictions on trade in goods, the EEC turned its attention to tariffs. In 1957 the six founding members of the EEC had committed themselves to creating a customs union by 1968. The community set to work so diligently that it reached this goal a year early.

Although little progress was made in the liberalization of insurance and banking services until the introduction of the Single Market programme, quite a few efforts were made in this area. In the 1960s and 1970s representatives from national regulatory agencies, financial ministries and central banks engaged in intense discussions of this topic. In the first half of the 1960s the first liberalization measures were introduced in areas in which the OEEC had already been active. The first liberalization directive that was introduced in 1964 for the international insurance trade addressed reinsurance and co-insurance.[12] Further liberalization directives were agreed upon only in 1973 and 1979. They were directives on life insurance and non-life insurance. The most important objective of all these first-generation measures was the freedom of establishment for insurance companies, which was to be accomplished for subsidiaries as well as for branches and agencies. However, the liberalization commitments introduced lacked a broad-based commitment to the principles of market access and national treatment.

Numerous second-generation directives were introduced for insurance services in the late 1980s and therefore already coincided with the first steps of the implementation of the Single Market programme. They were, in particular, the non-life insurance directive of 1988, the automobile liability directive of 1990 and a life insurance directive that was also agreed upon in 1990. The objective of this second generation of directives was to make progress towards the liberalization of cross-border supply of services, or, in the terminology used by the EEC, in the 'free movement of services'.[13] In the absence of any meaningful harmonization of national prudential regulations, the effectiveness of these directives was, however, limited. In order to compensate for the lack of harmonization, provisions for life insurance, for example, included specific customer protection requirements. The signing of life insurance contracts with insurance companies of other member states was only permitted if the foreign company had not actively solicited business, for example through advertisements or sales representatives. Access to foreign markets was only granted on the basis of a so-called 'passive freedom' to provide services. The signing of a contract had to be initiated by the customer, a scenario that was so rare as to be insignificant if not completely irrelevant in the markets.

For private non-life insurance, member states were granted the right to make market access dependent on a test of insurance tariffs of the foreign insurance company, a complex procedure for which no clear guidelines existed. All member states except the Netherlands and Great Britain made such tests mandatory. Insurance companies attempting to serve the Common Market had to thus receive permission for each and every insurance tariff in all member states (except in the Netherlands and Great Britain). Understandably only very few insurance companies found this to be an attractive option so that the liberalization of cross-border supply of insurance services remained ineffective in the case of private non-life insurance as well. The second-generation measures brought progress only in the field of substandard risks for which mutual recognition of national prudential regulations was introduced, a principle of the Single Market programme that was fully applied to international insurance trade only with the introduction of a third generation of insurance directives in the 1990s.

While the EEC's liberalization directives for insurance services built on the OEEC's liberalization efforts, banking services were largely new territory.[14] Main liberalization initiatives for the banking industry started much later than for the insurance industry. In 1973 the Council adopted a first directive on 'The Abolition of Restrictions on Freedom of Establishment and Freedom to Provide Services for Self-Employed Activities of Banks and other Financial Institutions'.

While the main focus of this first directive was to introduce freedom of establishment together with the national treatment principle, it remained ineffective, largely because of a lack of coordination of prudential regulation. It was only in 1977 that a first step towards harmonization of banking regulation was made through the First Banking Directive. However, besides the establishment of the principle of home country control, no significant progress was made towards a common set of regulations. More efficient measures for the integration of banking markets had to wait until the introduction of the Single Market programme.

Although banking services did not receive as much attention as insurance services in the EEC, the examples of the most important liberalization directives show that trade policy initiatives did not focus any longer on a very few narrowly defined financial services. The EEC aimed for a broad-based liberalization programme covering a wide range of financial services as well as both modes of trans-border supply; the cross-border supply of services (or 'free movement of services' as it was referred to in the EEC) and operations of foreign firms (or 'freedom of establishment'). In this respect the EEC's activities mark a clear departure from those of the OEEC. Other serious limitations on multilateral financial market liberalization remained in place, however, so that it is not quite clear what progress the EEC could have made under the best of circumstances. The most important limitation on the creation of a Common Market for financial services, which was obvious right from the start in 1957, was that liberalization of short-term capital movements, a prerequisite for the free movement of banking services, was off limits. As the OEEC's Code of Liberalization of Capital Movements, the EEC's Treaty of Rome left no doubt that short-term movements, or 'hot money', were not to be considered.[15] Two capital liberalization directives adopted in 1960 and 1962 as well as the member states' reactions to the emergence of the Euro-Dollar Market in the 1960s confirmed this view. Far into the 1970s the main economic policy concern of member states was not to open financial markets to more international competition but to limit fast growing activities on Euro-Dollar Markets, which had developed in spite of the existence of unilateral restrictions. As with other short-term capital flows, those of the Euro-Dollar Markets threatened to compromise the stability of the Bretton Woods system of fixed exchange rates.[16]

Another serious limitation on the creation of a Common Market for financial services was the liberalization concept employed. While prudential regulation was now officially on the trade policy agenda, attempts at coordination were made rule by rule with a view to covering all aspects of very complex national regulatory systems, a process that lacked political support from main actors on the national level. The negotiations on harmonization were left to finance ministries, central banks and regulatory agencies, whose main responsibility was not to introduce more international competition to national markets but to guarantee stability, safety and soundness. By and large, the Common Market represented a threat to sovereign economic policies of these institutions. In the 1960s and 1970s they were indeed much more successful in expanding domestic financial market regulation than in opening up markets to foreign competition. One of the reasons that the Common Market programme was not more successful, not only in financial services but also in many other areas, is that it coincided with one of the greatest expansions of the interventionist state.

Only in the late 1970s and early 1980s, when it became clear that the new era of flexible exchange rates would lead to vigorous financial market globalization, and when doctrines of deficit spending and tight national regulatory control were replaced with those of supply-side economics and deregulation, was a new chapter for multilateral financial services liberalization opened. The Single Market programme, which was initiated through the White Paper of 1985 and the Single European Act of 1986, did not only make necessary changes to the liberalization concept; it also led to coordinated efforts for capital account liberalization.[17]

The most important conceptual innovation introduced in the Single Market programme for financial services was that by far not all rules of the complex national regulatory systems had to be addressed in the harmonization process but, through a process of minimum harmonization, only a very few significant ones. Subject to harmonization efforts in the new programme were only a few regulations that were indispensable for guaranteeing stability, safety and soundness. The focus of the third generation of insurance directives, the Second Banking Directive of 1989 and further banking directives, was on crucial aspects of prudential regulation such as capital adequacy standards, solvency standards, large exposure rules and deposit guarantee schemes. The great majority of domestic prudential regulations was not harmonized but became subject to mutual recognition, the other one of the two main principles of the Single Market programme. Countries had to recognize rules from other member countries as being equivalent to their own. Consequently, a financial firm signing a contract with a customer from another member country could do so on the basis of (a) core rules of prudential regulation harmonized on the basis of the principle of minimum harmonization and (b) individual domestic regulations that had to be acknowledged by other member states as equivalent. Based on the new liberalization principles, firms were granted a single license which made it possible for them to offer services in all member states through trans-border supply of services and also through foreign branches.[18] Subsidiaries, on the other hand, remained subject to the regulation of the host countries in which they were licensed.

The new approach to liberalization comprising the two key elements of minimum harmonization and mutual recognition had the advantage that quite a few differences in the complex national regulatory systems did not have to be dealt with on the EU level but only in the member countries, which could decide individually whether to leave them as they were or engage in a process of deregulation. Of course, with the increasing cross-border competition that the Single Market programme was finally to introduce to financial markets, it was in the best interest of member countries to keep a critical eye on regulations that would unnecessarily burden domestic financial firms vis-à-vis competitors from other countries. The introduction of minimum harmonization and mutual recognition to the liberalization process resulted in a situation in which not only companies but – to a certain degree – also regulatory agencies had to compete with each other in providing favourable conditions for an efficient provision of financial services. The Single Market programme created a much-needed incentive for national regulatory agencies not only to liberalization but also to deregulation on the national level. At the same time minimum harmonization prevented member states from engaging in a destructive race to the bottom.

Even though the new liberalization principles applied to the banking and insurance industries through the Single Market programme were quite successful, it is worth mentioning that they were not geared specifically towards the financial sector but towards broad new trade policy agendas for services, Foreign Direct Investment and behind-the-border barriers to trade in the form of domestic regulation. The principle of mutual recognition, for example, which was first introduced by the Supreme Court, was originally applied to a case in the field of international trade in goods. In the case of Cassis de Dijon the judges had ruled in 1979 that the Federal Republic of Germany could not reject the import of a French currant liqueur on the basis of national foodstuffs regulation, which stipulated that liqueurs have to have a specific alcohol content that the French beverage failed to meet. The court emphasized in its judgement that a commodity that was legally produced and sold in one of the member states could also be sold in other member states. Only in 1986 was the concept of mutual recognition applied by the Court to trade in insurance services. Taken together, the decisions of 1979 and 1986 provided a basis for introducing the principle of mutual recognition to a broad field of industries in the service and manufacturing sectors. The emergence of new concepts for financial services liberalization in the Single Market programme once again demonstrates that this particular branch of modern trade policy has been an inseparable part of greater trade policy agendas and not – as assumed in the finance literature – a stand-alone endeavour which answers only to the specific demands of this sector.[19]

Besides the introduction of a new and successful liberalization concept, a fundamental change in the macroeconomic policy environment also contributed to the success of the Single Market for financial services. The 1980s brought clarity that the new era of flexible exchange rates would lead to capital account liberalization in OECD countries and subsequently to financial market globalization. Quite a few OECD countries had already liberalized their capital accounts unilaterally in the late 1970s and early 1980s, among them Great Britain (1979) and Germany (1981). For the success of the Single Market for financial services it was important that all member countries formally agreed to the same principles of full liberalization of capital movements. To this end, two capital liberalization directives were adopted in 1986 and 1988. In 1994 all requirements for capital account liberalization were met by the twelve member states. The two capital liberalization directives provided the macroeconomic foundation for a liberalization programme that for the first time aimed seriously and successfully at the free movement of banking services. While the capital liberalization directives focused largely on the freedom of capital movements from a macroeconomic point of view as it is relevant for central banks and finance ministries, banking directives such as the Second Banking Directive aimed at eliminating supervisory barriers to the provision of the many individual financial services that come along with free short-term capital movements.[20]

Onwards to the World Trade Organization

In the GATS, financial services became subject to negotiations for the first time during the Uruguay Round (1986–94) as part of an effort to systematically liberalize the many different service industries. When the agreement came into effect on 1 January 1995, financial services were not covered because of controversies over the strength of liberalization commitments. As a consequence, negotiations on insurance and banking had to be continued after the official completion of the Uruguay Round. They led to an agreement in December 1997, which will be in effect until a new negotiating round has been successfully completed. Since the Doha negotiations stalled in 2008, there are currently no expectations that the agreements reached in 1994 and 1997 will be developed further in the near future. Unlike the EU, which is making continuous efforts to fine-tune the Single Market programme, the WTO cannot alter agreements unless it officially enters into a new trade round.

The impulse for including services in the Uruguay Round had originally come from the US, where financial firms such as Citicorp and American Express had lobbied for such an initiative for quite some time.[21] Developing countries and the majority of Western European countries were at first not particularly interested in pursuing this topic. The overall perception of services negotiations in developing countries was that they are a defensive trade policy issue or, in other words, that there would be little to gain from such negotiations. Europeans on the other hand had a preference for a narrower agenda for the Uruguay Round than Americans. According to their view, complex issues such as services liberalization jeopardized the outcome of the whole negotiating round. Another reason for Europe's reluctance to engage in services negotiations was bad timing. When the Uruguay Round was officially launched in 1986 the EU had just taken its first steps with the Single Market programme. The Commission had introduced its proposal to finally complete the Common Market with the publication of the White Book in 1985. Taking on two extremely ambitious trade policy projects at the same time might have simply overburdened the Union.

There was moreover no doubt that liberalizing services would turn out to be far more difficult in the WTO than in the EU. The most obvious difference between service liberalization in the Single Market programme and in the GATS is that WTO agreements are not confined to a comparatively small number of like-minded countries. The WTO that emerged from the GATT in 1995 currently has 153 members representing not only all industrialized countries but also transition and developing countries, the great majority of which had to participate in the service negotiations if they were to be concluded successfully. The large number of potential signatories is at the same time the biggest advantage and the most significant disadvantage of any WTO agreement. An obvious advantage of this large number is the much wider reach of the MFN principle. Although regional initiatives such as the Single Market programme have a clear advantage when it comes to finding common ground for new and complex trade policy agendas, any agreement reached will exclude – and probably actively discriminate against – the great majority of countries worldwide. Only the WTO offers the basis for agreements which provide a level playing field on a global basis.

On the other hand, the large number of potential signatories makes it very difficult for the WTO to reach a meaningful consensus, especially with regard to the many new and complex trade policy issues that have emerged worldwide once quantitative barriers and tariffs were successfully removed. Member states of the WTO show, for example, dramatic differences regarding their levels of and philosophies for prudential regulation and their willingness to open financial markets to foreign competition – not least because of different stages of capital account liberalization. Although the great majority of developing countries gave up on protectionist strategies of import substitution a long time ago, and quite a few of them have also pursued the cautious opening of their financial service sectors, their policy regimes in these sectors are in no way comparable to those of industrialized countries. Opening up financial services markets is one of the key challenges to development policies. Because of a comparatively low level of development of financial institutions and regulatory agencies, and an unstable macroeconomic environment, limits and challenges to liberalization are manifold. Financial liberalization carries not only a high risk of destabilization for these countries, but also offers significant welfare gains given the central role that financial services play in the development process.[22]

How did the drafters of the GATS cope with this difficult situation? First and foremost, the WTO framework agreement was not aimed at full reciprocity, that is, at reaching the same absolute level of liberalization commitments for all signatories, but at first-difference reciprocity, i.e. at moving towards the common goal of progressive liberalization with approximately the same speed. The two crucial liberalization obligations of the agreement – market access and national treatment – are not general but specific obligations. Signatories are free to choose to what extent they want to take on such specific obligations – with respect to the different fields of financial services and other services and regarding four modes of international service supply; the two main modes of supply and two more modes, which involve the cross-border movement of individuals (or natural persons). A single liberalization commitment, for example a commitment for any narrowly defined insurance service in any one of the four modes of supply, is already sufficient for a WTO member country to officially become a signatory to the GATS and thus to have access to the specific liberalization commitments of other member countries under the MFN principle, which is one of the general obligations of the agreement.

The à-la-carte approach to liberalization commitments was undoubtedly a necessary condition to reach an agreement on trade in services among the very diverse membership of the WTO.[23] This approach meant, however, that it was very difficult to arrive at meaningful liberalization commitments in the trade negotiations between member states once the framework agreement was drafted. The great freedom offered to signatories left the negotiating process without much orientation as to what commitments to expect from individual member countries. The main reason for the prolongation of the financial services negotiations beyond the official conclusion of the Uruguay Round was that quite a few countries – especially in Asia – had not even come close to offering the status quo of their unilateral liberalization process in crucial fields of financial service markets.[24]

The other notable effect that the large and heterogeneous group of signatories had on the GATS framework agreement was in the area of domestic regulation. The main emphasis of the relevant provisions of the framework agreement (Article VI, GATS) is on guaranteeing signatories the greatest possible freedom to pursue independent regulatory policies.[25] This goes back to a demand of developing countries that made sovereignty over regulatory policies a prerequisite for their participation in the GATS negotiations right at the beginning of the Uruguay Round. As in the case of liberalization commitments, this freedom was undoubtedly another necessary condition for reaching an agreement on trade in services. There was no way that the WTO could have dealt with the vast differences in domestic regulations of many service industries of member countries, neither through traditional harmonization, i.e. rule by rule, nor through minimum harmonization and mutual recognition. This is even clearer with respect to financial services, for which sovereignty over domestic regulation is emphatically ensured in sector-specific provisions of an Annex on Financial Services in its so-called prudential carve-out. One the other hand, both provisions, Article VI, GATS and the sector-specific prudential carve-out, leave wide open the question as to what extent changes in prudential regulation may be used as an excuse for protectionist backsliding.

In spite of all these obvious weaknesses the GATS has been regarded as one of the more promising results of the Uruguay Round.[26] It was, for example, argued that the fact that such a broad agreement could be formed under the auspices of the WTO is in itself a remarkable achievement and that the GATS marks a first and necessary step towards a more meaningful global agreement. For financial services this conclusion is, however, questionable. There are very few provisions in the framework agreement and the Annex on Financial Services which indicate that the GATS could help to integrate the two main functions of an international financial market regime: guaranteeing stability, safety and soundness on the one hand and securing open markets on the other. Because the framework agreement leaves the responsibility for prudential regulation firmly in the hands of individual member states, there is no strategy for coping with the many conflicts that come from different regulatory systems in a globalized financial sector.

Conclusion

What progress has the multilateral liberalization of trade in financial services made in the last sixty years? What contributions have trade policy initiatives by the OEEC, EEC, EU and WTO made to an emerging global financial architecture? The answer to these questions depends largely on where we look – at the European experience leading to the Single Market programme or at the GATS of the WTO.

The Single Market programme is so far the only programme that adequately performs the two main functions of an international financial order: guaranteeing stability and securing open markets. The achievements of the EU can be best understood against the background of exceptionally strong intergovernmental institutions and a learning process that started long before the formulation of the White Book in 1985. While early initiatives in the OEEC and the EEC only made progress in specific, narrowly-defined areas, they introduced multilateral rules to financial service liberalization and raised awareness among policymakers of the extraordinary challenges that would face them if they were ever to make a serious attempt at broadening and deepening this branch of modern trade policy.

The breakthrough came in the 1980s in the form of a liberalization concept consisting of two elements: minimum harmonization and mutual recognition. While mutual recognition introduced a much-needed incentive to national regulators to evaluate the burden of domestic prudential regulation on domestic firms, minimum harmonization prevents a race to the bottom. The breakthrough was made possible not only by strong intergovernmental institutions and a learning process covering almost four decades of European integration, but also by two other factors: monetary regime change and a broadening of the trade policy agenda. Monetary regime change in the 1970s opened the path to coordinated capital account liberalization in the 1980s, which in turn allowed for liberalization of the many banking services that come along with free short-term capital flows. With the Single Market programme the EU extended liberalization efforts for the first time to cross-border supply of banking services, the core of international trade in financial services, which had been off-limits for the OEEC and the EEC due to the restrictions of the Bretton Woods system of fixed exchange rates. The broadening of the trade policy agenda that came with the introduction of the Single Market programme on the other hand facilitated trade policy issues in areas that are highly relevant for financial service liberalization, such as domestic regulation and FDI. In the wake of a liberalization programme that was strongly focused on the freedom of establishment also the second important mode of trans-border supply of services that is important for financial services made considerable progress.

Financial services' move onto the world stage in the GATS in the late 1990s was an indispensable step in the development of modern trade policy for financial services. While financial market liberalization has dominated economic globalization for more than twenty years now, the development of international organizations governing international finance is still lagging behind.[27] The WTO is the only international organization that offers the basis for agreements which provide a level playing field on a global basis. In its current form the GATS is, however, problematic; in many ways it is an antipode to the Single Market programme.

Although the GATS framework agreement represents the broadest and most systematic approach to financial service liberalization to date, the agreement's liberalization commitments are weak and sketchy. More importantly, prudential regulation, the single most important body of regulation determining market access for financial firms and the stability of financial markets, is largely ignored in this agreement. The GATS leaves authority over prudential regulation firmly in the hands of states. In this important respect the agreement is reminiscent of early West European trade policy initiatives in the OEEC. The reason for this remarkable weakness of the WTO agreement lies not only in a lack of strong inter-governmental institutions on the global level, compared to those that have developed in Western Europe, but also in the fact that WTO negotiations are one-off endeavours which can only be improved with the successful conclusion of another negotiating round. By far the most important impediment to the development of a strong WTO agreement is, however, the different developmental stages of member states' financial services sectors. Stark differences in capital account liberalization pose a very serious challenge to a coordinated liberalization process. While first-difference reciprocity is the correct answer to this challenge in the sphere of liberalization, a corresponding concept for guaranteeing stability, safety and soundness has not yet been implemented on the global level. Given the experience of the last 60 years, there is no doubt that such a concept will have to consist of various forms of minimum harmonization and mutual recognition, the two liberalization principles of the Single Market programme which have been applied in the EU successfully not only to Western European member states but through Eastern enlargement in the early 1990s also to transition economies.

Currently it is international organizations, which focus predominantly on stability, safety and soundness, from which the most important impetus comes for the development of a global financial architecture. Since the onset of the global financial crisis in 2007 organizations such as the Basel Committee of the Bank for International Settlements are updating and strengthening standards for prudential regulation and supervision. There is no doubt however, that liberalization and especially multilaterally coordinated liberalization will remain the other driving force behind institution-building in international finance in the future. Whether the GATS can be a vehicle for further trade policy initiatives for financial services is not quite clear, not least because the prospects for another successful negotiating round in the WTO look dim.

8 SOMETHING OLD AND SOMETHING NEW: NOVEL AND FAMILIAR DRIVERS OF THE LATEST CRISIS

Adair Turner

Beginning in 2007, the developed world has suffered a major financial and economic crisis, the latest stages of which we are still seeking to manage. It is certainly the biggest financial crisis since the Great Depression and by some measures, in its global reach, the biggest financial crisis in the 200-year history of the modern capitalist system. So far – and I am confident that this will continue to be true – the real economic consequences have been nothing like as severe as the Great Depression, but they are still large, in lost wealth, lost income, lost employment.

What went Wrong and Why?

We have to learn the lessons of why this crisis occurred so that we can reduce the probability and the severity of a repetition. One thing is clear: the primary causes of this crisis came from within the financial system and not from the factors which lay behind, for instance, the crisis of the 1970s – inflationary fiscal and monetary policies, inflexible labour markets and over-powerful trade unions, and politically induced swings in commodity prices. True, in some countries – Greece in particular – long-term unsustainable public finance has played an important role; but in most what is striking is how rapidly public deficits and debt burdens which appeared sustainable before the crisis have become onerous in the face of financial turmoil. And what is equally striking is that the financial system from which this crisis sprang had been positively lauded before the crisis as a driver not only of economic efficiency but stability, dispersing risk into the hands of those best able to manage it, creating new and flexible mechanisms for the hedging of risk, enhancing market discipline through the increased transparency of prices in increasingly liquid markets. The new financial system of credit securitization and credit derivatives was seen as a key contributor to 'the Great Moderation'.

We must understand why we were so wrong. That requires theoretical analysis, empirical analysis of this crisis and analysis of past history. Financial and economic history, together with theory, tells us three key things.

First, that financial markets and systems, and more broadly still, monetary relationships and the artifice of money itself, play a central role in market economies. The economic transformation of the last 200 years is in part the history of real developments, technologies and productivity growth; but it is also crucially a history of the development of complex financial relationships. And the financial system plays a far larger relative role in the modern market economy than it did in the pre-industrial economy. Increasing prosperity has tended to be accompanied by increasing financial intensity.

Second, however, that financial intensity itself creates the potential for instability, and one key driver of that potential instability is that financial markets are inherently susceptible to momentum and herd effects, to over-shoots, to self-reinforcing irrational exuberance and then to irrational despair. Charles Mackay's classic work on the *Madness of Crowds* (1841) and Charles Kindleberger's on *Manias, Panics and Crashes* (1978) – have documented that inherent susceptibility, from the Dutch tulip mania of 1635–7 to the Wall Street boom of the 1920s.[1] And we have an increasingly rich theoretical understanding of why these over-shoots occur. The behavioural economics of Daniel Kahneman and others provide explanations from psychology and evolutionary biology, with people acting in instinctive or emotional ways which, even at the individual level, might reasonably be described as irrational, with 'animal spirits' sometimes a key driver of market dynamics.[2] But theories of imperfect principal/agent relationships and decision making under conditions of imperfect information and inherent irreducible uncertainty, also explain how even the most rational of people might participate in a collectively irrational boom, calculating that they will be among those clever enough to get out just in time.[3] Both sets of explanation are important to our understanding.

Thirdly and crucially, however, it is clear that some booms and busts matter more than others, and that in particular, booms and busts in credit pricing and credit supply are far more important than those in specific commodities or in equities. The internet boom and bust of 1998–2001, while large enough to move equity indexes in a dramatic fashion and to create wealth gains and losses which were significant relative to US GDP, had only a slight impact on US or global growth. But throughout modern economic history, in the nineteenth-century banking crises, in the many banking collapses of the 1930s and in the numerous crises of the past thirty years, it was volatility in credit supply within the economy, surges and sudden stops of credit – whether to governments, to other banks, or to the non-bank private sector, which have had a peculiar ability to cause real economic harm. As the International Monetary Fund (IMF) figures illustrate, banking crises are far more likely than other financial crises to have severe real economic impact.

And we have a fairly good understanding of the features which make credit contracts different and potentially more disruptive than, for instance, equity contracts. Four features are important: specificity of tenor, specificity of nominal value, the irreversibility and rigidities of default and bankruptcy, and the credit/asset price cycle.

Specificity of tenor, the fact that a debt contract has to be repaid at a particular date, and that at any time there are large debt repayments due in the next month or the next year, means that a continual supply of new credit is essential to the working of the economy in a way which is not true of equity finance. Equity prices can collapse, and firms may be unable to raise new equity, but they are not also required to repay existing equity; and economies could operate for sustained periods of time with no new primary equity issues: they cannot operate without new lending to refinance old. Portfolio equity flows to Asian countries prior to the 1997 crisis, if measured as the purchases or sales of secondary equities by foreign investors, show volatile equity flows but, measured as the net flow of new money, they were less volatile because sales of secondary equities are not repayments. Debt flows by contrast can go from net new credit provision to large debt repayments. Credit is different because if the financial machine suddenly stops lending, the economy can go into reverse.

Specificity of nominal value – debt contracts in nominal value money terms – is an equally important feature, harmless as long as generalized inflation is maintained at a relatively stable and predictable level, but potentially destructive in the face of unanticipated inflation or deflation. Unanticipated inflation and hyper-inflation can destroy financial wealth and social cohesion, but it is unanticipated deflation, such as that of 1930–3 in the US, which has arguably even greater capacity to wreak real economic harm through its impact on the real value of debt, via the mechanisms which Irving Fisher set out in his classic article on debt-deflation.[4]

Thirdly, rigidities of default and bankruptcy, which generate economic costs even in the absence of debt-deflation or financial crisis, but which if combined with either debt-deflation or banking crisis (banks as well as corporates going bankrupt) can have an enormously destructive effect. As Ben Bernanke points out in one of his essays on the Great Depression, the existence of debt default and bankruptcy are direct contradictions of any theory of smoothly adjusting economic relationships: 'In a complete markets world, bankruptcy would never be observed – Bernanke notes – because complete state contingent loan agreements would uniquely define each party's obligations in all possible circumstances.'[5] As firms approach default, economic rationality and perfect information would dictate a smoothly operating write-down of debt claims or translation of debt claims to equity claims. The fact that instead we have large legal and administrative costs and fire sales of assets illustrates how far from the Arrow Debreu nirvana of complete markets our real world economy actually is.

Fourth and finally, credit plays a specific and potentially destabilizing role because of its interaction with real asset prices, its ability to drive speculative bubbles in real assets, such as equities, but above all in real estate. Increased credit supply can drive capital appreciation which appears to both the borrower and the lender to make further borrowing and lending safer. In Hyman Minsky's terms, credit supply can become first 'speculative', relying on the anticipation of capital gain to pay back the capital of the loan and then ultimately 'Ponzi' in nature, relying on the anticipation of capital gain to raise new loans not just to pay back existing loans but also to service interest payments.[6] Without credit there could still be irrational exuberance in real estate or other real asset markets, but with the implicit put option of a credit contract, the potential is hugely increased. And the extent to which the banking system is involved, for instance, in the financing of real estate investment has, at least in the UK, increased dramatically over the last twenty years.

So credit claims are different in economic substance from equity claims; and volatility in credit markets has far greater potential to drive volatility in the real economy than volatility in equity markets. Between 1998 and 2001 internet and IT related stocks soared and then collapsed. Between 2002 and 2008 confidence in the credit markets soared and then collapsed, spreads on many categories of credit falling to historically low levels, underpricing risk – before soaring to excessive levels. But the former boom and bust did little real economic harm; the latter produced a financial and economic crisis.

But it is not just credit which is different; it is bank credit which is even more specific. The characteristics of credit mentioned above – specificity of tenor and nominal value, the rigidities and irreversibilities of default and bankruptcy, and the potential for credit driven asset cycles – apply to non-bank credit securities as well as to bank intermediated credit – and indeed one crucial issue to which I will return later is whether a non-bank system of credit extension introduces some specific drivers of instability which are not present to the same extent in a bank based credit system. But it is certainly the converse case that bank credit intermediation introduces specific additional risks not present in the non-bank case.

Essentially, what leveraged fractional reserve banks do is to increase the range of potential contracts available to both users and suppliers of funds, by making it possible for suppliers to hold assets with different combinations of risk, return and maturity from those which users of funds face in their liabilities. Essentially they tranche by risk and return and they transform maturity.[7]

Those transformation functions in turn appear to deliver significant economic benefits, at least at some stages of economic development. Economic historians of nineteenth-century Britain have often argued that Britain's more developed banking system was one of the factors driving superior economic performance, facilitating the mobilization of savings which would have been more difficult if savers had been linked to users of funds through untransformed contracts, in which the risk, return and maturity of the issuers' liabilities had to match precisely the aggregate risk, return and maturity of the savers' assets. Walter Bagehot certainly believed so arguing in Lombard Street that Britain enjoyed an economic advantage over France because the UK's more advanced banking system fostered the productive investment of savings rather than leaving them 'dormant'. 'Much more cash', he wrote, 'exists out of banks in France and Germany and in the nonbanking countries than can be found in England or Scotland, where banking is developed. But this money is not ... attainable ... the English money is "borrowable money"'.[8]

Clearly these benefits of leveraged and fractional reserve banks also bring with them significant risks. For one, banks facilitate greater leverage in the real economy and they are leveraged themselves, increasing the dangers that arise from the specific characteristics of credit rather than equity contracts. Secondly, they introduce maturity transformation risks, and related confidence and contagion risks, rooted in the simple fact that banks create a set of contractual liabilities which legally have a right to simultaneous execution, but which banks could never simultaneously honour, given the contractual tenor of their assets. Banks are therefore inherently risky institutions, which can only be made safe through the combined effect of capital and liquidity regulation and central bank liquidity insurance. Finally, Minsky's cyclical process of asset price appreciation driving credit demand and supply, which in turn drives further asset price inflation, while possible to some degree in a world of non-bank credit extension, is hugely facilitated in a world of bank credit. Bank credit creates bank money in a cyclical process, and periods of low loan losses, facilitated by collateral price appreciation, swell bank capital reserves thus removing constraints on further credit growth. Until, that is, the self-reinforcing cycle swings into reverse. Bank credit extension has deeply embedded tendencies to self-reinforcing procyclicality.

Something Old and Something New

These specific characteristics and risks of credit supply were central to the latest financial crisis. The specific forms through which these risks manifested themselves, however, combined some which were novel and some very familiar – and it is vital that we understand this mix of the new and the old in order to think through the required policy response.

The new element, compared with many previous banking crises, was the increased role of securitized credit, of credit in the form of marketable securities, traded in at least somewhat liquid markets, and continually marked-to-market against prices in those markets. Marketable credit securities of course are not new. Simple marketable credit securities, corporate or government bonds, have existed for almost as long as bank credit to corporates or governments; covered bonds have existed since the Pfandbriefe emerged in late eighteenth-century Germany. But what was new from the 1970s on was the steady growth and then in the 1990s the explosion of complex packaged credit securities, using the techniques of pooling and tranching to extend securitized credit to new market segments, encompassing a rising share of mortgage market debt in many countries, significant shares of commercial real estate debt, and various categories of personal unsecured credit – credit cards and student loans. And what was new from the 1990s onwards was the emergence of credit derivatives to hedge credit risk and to take credit risk in a synthetic form.

Together these changes made the marginal price of credit more transparent, and that greater transparency was lauded by many as bringing the disciplines of transparent liquid markets to the world of credit extension. Thus the IMF Global Financial Stability Report of April 2006 noted with approval that 'credit derivatives enhance the transparency of the market's collective view of credit risks ... [and thus] ... provide valuable information about broad credit conditions and increasingly set the marginal price of credit'. But a marginal price of credit set by a liquid market in credit derivatives is only economically valuable if we believe, as per the efficient market hypotheses, that the market's collective view of credit risks is by definition a correct one. If instead we note the movement in the CDS spreads for major banks, with spreads falling relentlessly to reach a historic low in early summer 2007, and providing no forewarning at all of impending financial disaster, we should be worried that an increased reliance on market price information to set the marginal price of credit, could itself be a source of credit and asset price volatility, particularly when combined with marked-to-market accounting. A crucial issue to consider is therefore whether the increased role of securitized credit, and its potential for self-referential credit pricing and credit risk evaluation, has introduced a new driver of volatility into the financial system.

However, if the importance of securitized credit and credit derivatives was something new in this crisis, it also had some deeply familiar features. HBOS, one of the UK banks which got into most trouble, was not extensively involved in risky proprietary trading, complex structured credit and credit derivatives. But it was extensively involved in what turned out to be poor bank lending against commercial real estate, one of the most familiar and most recurring features of recent banking crises – the Japanese and the Swedish crises of the early 1990s, the savings and loan crisis of 1980s America, the early 1970s secondary banking crisis in Britain, or the Thai crash of 1997. Minsky's insight into the inherent dangers of bank lending against assets whose value can move in line with the value of bank finance extended, must be central to a policy response which ensures that we do not repeat the pattern yet again in another fifteen or twenty years' time.

Finally, it is worth noting that the more recent phase of the crisis, the sovereign debt crisis that surfaced during 2010, also takes us into familiar territory. For most countries the cause of the rapid increase in sovereign debt has been the financial crisis itself and the tax implications of property booms and busts which derived from financial system excess. More than in some past crises, this sovereign debt crisis has its origin in financial system deficiencies. But the dynamics of the market for sovereign debt are displaying long familiar patterns of the sort described by Carmen Reinhardt and Ken Rogoff[9] – with sudden switches in market willingness to provide new credit to sovereign borrowers, and sudden shifts in the perceived probability of defaults. That reflects of course the inherently fragile and multiple nature of sovereign debt market equilibria once debt levels go above some threshold. With default probabilities strongly influenced by the cost of debt, which in turn reflects the perceived default probability in a self-reinforcing cycle. And with the inherently uncertain and political nature of decisions on sovereign debt restructuring and the extreme uncertainty of loss given default estimates. This uncertainty is inherent to contracts where creditors have no rights to seize underlying business assets and attempt to recover value, and thus where the bounds which somewhat constrain Loss Given Default estimates for non-sovereign debt contracts are entirely absent.

So we have both old and new factors in our latest crisis, but all of them rooted in the highly specific nature of credit contracts.

Policy Implications

The crucial question is how we design policy to reduce the likelihood or the severity of a similar crisis in future. Three broad categories of policy response can be envisaged – in choosing between them, or combining them, we should be guided by insights from history as well as from theory.

The first approach focuses on parametric reform – on changing the numeric rules which govern capital leverage and liquidity. Such reform is at the core of the global regulatory agenda, with major decisions made or to be made by the Basel Committee, the Financial Stability Board and the G20. What history tells us is that banking systems in the past have operated with capital and liquidity levels not just slightly but far above current levels, suggesting that we should at least consider quite radical change. One thing theory and models tell us, however, is that transition to higher capital and liquidity standards needs to be managed carefully if we are not to slow recovery from the recession which excessive leverage and maturity transformation has produced – an issue to which I will return later.

The second category of approach focuses on issues relating to the structure of the banking system. One clear priority is to address the problem of banks which are too big to fail and which, if the market perceives this, are free from the market discipline which might otherwise constrain their risk taking. And there is popular pressure to fix this problem, given anger at the sight of tax payer money bailing out large banks. But we also need to recognize that addressing the too big to fail issue is a necessary but not sufficient response. The direct tax payer cost of rescue – adding up the capital injections and the Treasury guarantees, and any central bank losses on liquidity provision – are likely, as the IMF's latest estimate show, to be the small change of the cost of this crisis – 2 per cent to 4 per cent of GDP maybe, perhaps less, versus 50 per cent or more added to many countries debt to GDP ratios.[10] The far bigger issue is volatility in the supply of credit, first over-exuberantly supplied at too low a price and then restricted – and it is possible that such volatility could arise in a system of multiple small banks as much as in a system of large ones. And multiple small banks can fail as much as large and with as harmful effects: the US banking crisis of 1931–3 was a crisis of a fragmented banking system. We must learn enough from history to know that common underlying problems can manifest themselves in multiple different forms.

The third category of response, which we may call macro-prudential, would focus on the most important underlying problem – the volatility of credit extension and its relationship to asset prices, a problem which lies at the interface between central banking and prudential regulation, an interface which in the years before the crisis we allowed to become a gap. The conventional wisdom of developed world policy, before the crisis, was that monetary policy should be exclusively focused on the inflation target, pursued through the use of the interest rate policy lever; and that the regulation of banks and other financial institutions should entail enforcing a clear set of rules applicable continuously over time. The idea that either the central bank or the regulator should be willing to make judgements on the sustainability of lending and asset prices in, say, the commercial real estate sector, has been outside the conventional intellectual framework. But a historical perspective tells us that we used to pull such levers; and an international perspective tells us that many emerging markets still use such levers today, having resisted our over-simplistic preaching in favour of our apparently more advanced approach. We need, I believe, new policy levers which can take away the punch bowl before the party gets out of hand – levers such as countercyclical capital requirements, which a macro-prudential authority can pull on a discretionary and possibly sector specific basis.[11] We need, as Stefan Ingves, Governor of the Swedish Riksbank recently put it, to 'extend the punch bowl principle into the financial sector'. But we also need the historical and international perspective to remind us that such policy levers are not actually new.

Economic Benefits of Increased Financial Intensity?
A Historical Perspective

So we need fundamental analysis, rooted in theory, empirical analysis and history to help decide the appropriate balance of parametric reform, structural reform and new macroprudential approaches which should form our response to the latest financial crisis. But we also need to ask fundamental questions about the role and size of the financial system in the real economy. I mentioned earlier that one of the key things we know is that the financial system plays a crucial role in a market economy, and that, if we look over a 200-year perspective, increasing prosperity has tended to be accompanied by increasing financial intensity. Broadly speaking, richer countries have higher financial assets and liabilities and large bank balance sheets relative to GDP than poorer countries, and a wider array of financial markets and products – both greater financial intensity and greater financial sophistication.

The financial intensity and complexity of developed economies indeed grew very rapidly in the thirty years running up to the crisis. Financial assets relative to GDP grew rapidly in many countries, with significant increases in non-financial sector leverage, but what was even more startling was a dramatic increase in intra-financial sector leverage, in the aggregate value of claims between one financial institution and another. Financial innovation produced an explosion of new derivative contracts, with the nominal value of over-the-counter (OTC) interest rate contracts rising from around zero in 1987 to over £400 trillion in 2007. And the value of financial trading in multiple markets soared relative to real underlying values – the growth of FX trading far outstripping growth in real trade or long-term capital flows; oil futures trading swelling from far less than the total value of physical oil produced and consumed in 1980 to about ten times today.

At least until the crisis, the dominant conventional wisdom of economic theory was that this increase in financial intensity was value-creative, enabling the economy both to improve efficiency and to disperse risk more effectively, completing more markets and thus taking us closer to the nirvana of an Arrow Debreu equilibrium. The correlation between increasing financial intensity and increasing prosperity was assumed to apply limitlessly over time: if nineteenth-century Britain gained an economic advantage from increased financial intensity and sophistication, then still further financial intensity and sophistication beyond today's levels was also assumed to be beneficial.

However, we need to consider whether this assumption is true, whether the financial deepening and financial innovation of the last thirty years truly has delivered economic benefits, and whether it is possible to distinguish elements of financial deepening and sophistication which are more or less useful. We cannot assume that the existence of financial activity proves axiomatically that its economic impact is beneficial; we cannot assume, as the Greenspan doctrine did, that what exists is necessarily optimal. Once we move away from the simplistic elegance of the economics of always efficient markets and always rational expectations and introduce imperfect information, complex principal/agent relationships and inherent irreducible Knightian uncertainty, it becomes clear that financial activity, far more than other categories of economic activity, has a theoretical potential to swell beyond its economically optimal level.[12]

And high level historical analysis – which should provoke more detailed exploration – at very least casts doubt over whether increased financial intensity over the last thirty years has truly delivered economic benefits.

Carmen Reinhardt and Ken Rogoff characterize the mid-twentieth century – the 1930s to the 1970s – as a period of relative 'financial repression' both in developed economies and in developing. And in some emerging countries – for instance India – it probably was the case that 'financial repression' was one among a package of market restrictive policies which hampered economic growth. But equally, there were countries which in that period achieved historically rapid growth with fairly 'repressed' financial systems (for instance Korea). And in the developed economies – US, Europe and Japan – this period of financial repression was one of significant and relatively stable growth, comparing fairly well with the subsequent thirty years of increased financial activity and financial liberalization.

A recent paper by Moritz Schularick and Alan Taylor poses a fundamental question, one to which economics has not yet provided adequately clear answers: what is the relationship between financial deepening in its most straightforward form – increased credit outstanding relative to nominal GDP – and economic growth?[13] A number of studies have in the past illustrated either cross-sectional or time series correlations between the development of basic banking systems and related credit aggregates, and the early stages of economic growth.[14] But Schularick and Taylor's paper suggests that any positive relationship may break down beyond the level of financial intensity reached in advanced countries thirty or forty years ago. It documents the growth of leverage and credit extension which liberalization and innovation have facilitated, but finds little support for the proposition that this liberalization and innovation has led to a corresponding increase in real growth rates for the countries in their sample.

A finding which perhaps should not surprise us, given the changing functions which credit extension plays within developed economies, and the fact that perpetual growth in credit intensity must produce major financial risks.

Over the last fifty-five years for instance, private sector debt to GDP in the UK has grown from around 30 per cent of GDP to over 120 per cent of GDP, with that growth almost entirely dominated by growth in household mortgage debt and commercial real estate financing. Both forms of finance of course perform some useful economic functions; but it is clearly not the case that further growth of such credit intensity is essential for economic growth; further intensity of this sort, for instance, does not drive increased fixed capital formation.[15] And it is also clear that the higher the leverage the greater the fragility of the system, the more vulnerable it is to the specific risks induced by debt contracts which I documented earlier. Neither economic logic nor time series data nor cross-country correlations suggest that increased credit intensity is essential to drive superior economic performance once some basic threshold has been achieved.

That may seem so obvious as to be not worth saying. But in fact the implicit assumption that further credit growth is economically beneficial and limitlessly so has played a pervasive role in debates about financial liberalization and regulation. Arguments for the social benefit of complex securitization and credit derivatives, and therefore against tight regulation which might restrict their growth, have often asserted that these are beneficial because they will 'facilitate credit extension'. And in the debates about the Basel II capital adequacy regime, there was an overt argument that the more sophisticated risk management techniques used by banks moving on to the Advanced Internal Ratings Based approach, should be rewarded and should make possible more 'efficient use of capital' (i.e. lower but still safe capital requirements). But this more 'efficient use of capital' is only economically valuable if we assume that the extra leverage thereby enabled will be economically beneficial. And in the current debates about future capital adequacy requirements, arguments are being advanced against the tightening of requirements which explicitly assume that private credit growth is essential and which implicitly assume that once a certain level of leverage is attained, it is impossible to reduce it. Thus, for instance, several of the private sector contributions to the debate clearly assume that if private sector credit growth is reduced, nominal GDP growth falls roughly *pari passu*. Now of course that may be at least partially true as a statement of transition dynamics, particularly if other potential drivers of demand growth – fiscal or monetary – have reached their limit. But if it is true in the long term, we have a big problem because we face a ratchet effect, in which it is possible to have periods in which private sector credit growth significantly outpaces nominal GDP growth, thus producing the growth in debt to GDP, but in which any attempt to de-leverage will produce slower growth, thus at the limit making smooth deleveraging completely impossible.[16] Under these circumstances, deleveraging would require debt default and restructuring. To the extent that any such ratchet does exist, it reinforces the vital importance of policies which prevent the build-up of excessive debt in the first place.

Conclusion

The long-term dynamics and impact of changing credit intensity in developed economies are subjects on which far more empirical, theoretical and historical analysis is essential if we are to make sensible decisions both about long-term policy frameworks and about how we transition towards them. We need therefore to ask fundamental questions about the role and economic value added of financial systems, as well as about their tendency to stability or instability. Such questions were too often swept aside in the years before the crisis by a dominant conventional wisdom which asserted that increased financial activity and innovation must be beneficial because otherwise the market would not sustain it, which assumed that technically efficient liquid markets were always collectively rational, and which went along with the sloppy logic that if financial innovation 'facilitated credit extension' this was by definition beneficial.

To answer these questions we need new approaches within economics. Too much of recent economics has involved the development of mathematically elegant results based on assumptions about rational economic man, rather than on observation of human decision-making in the real world. Too much financial and monetary economics has treated the specific structure of the financial system itself – the balance sheets of banks, insurance companies, investment banks, mutual funds, hedge funds, as unimportant. And too much of economics has ignored economic history.

The history of financial systems and financial markets has a crucial role to play in our understanding of how economics work. It can illustrate what happened in the past and help us think through how far the problems we now face are similar to those faced before, and how far and in what way they have subtly changed. And within financial history the history of banking systems and of the dynamics of credit extension have a particular importance because banks are very specific institutions and credit contracts have very specific and important characteristics. Unless we study the past we are condemned, if not to repeat it, at least to suffer new variants of old problems.

One of the greatest benefits we had as we entered this financial crisis was that economists and economic historians had thought deeply about the history of the Great Depression, and about the mistakes which then turned financial crisis into economic and political disaster. Amid the crisis of autumn 2008, as we were trying to think out how to stabilize our banking systems, the two most useful books I found time to read were Ben Bernanke's *Essays on the Great Depression* (2000) and the chapter on 'The Great Contraction' from Friedman and Schwartz's *A Monetary History of the United States* (1963).[17] The good news was that the most important decision maker that autumn didn't need to read the former collection, because he had, sometimes with others, written them. The insights of economic history helped the world respond to the latest financial crisis. We now need to use them to help design a less fragile financial system for the future.

9 TO REGULATE OR NOT TO REGULATE: NO EASY FIXES FOR THE FINANCIAL SYSTEM

William R. White

Should Lax Financial Regulation be Blamed for the Crisis?

Lax financial regulation certainly bears part of the blame, not least with respect to undocumented mortgage loans, the emergence of a huge shadow banking system and the decision to allow banks to put into their trading books financial instruments which had never been traded, and indeed never could be traded. The fact that regulators have acted more recently to address these issues is a statement that they recognize these earlier shortcomings. That said, the regulators bear only part of the blame. Still more fundamental was the explosion of credit globally that was made possible by very easy monetary conditions, and the decision of bankers and others to ease credit standards in the pursuit of easy profits.

In sum, everyone involved is guilty of failing to see how the risks were building up and, in consequence, of not taking action to help avoid or even mitigate the ensuing crisis. Perhaps even worse, no one made any effort to prepare for managing the crisis when it did hit. In most countries, deposit insurance regimes were inadequate, insolvency regimes for financial institutions were non-existent and agreements for cooperation between various official bodies had real shortcomings.

Too Big to Fail: Should the Size of Financial Institutions be Regulated?

Behind this question is the assumption that the disorderly failure of some financial institutions could cause so much systemic damage that it could not be allowed to happen. Regulating 'size' has some superficial attractions but also some downsides. First, measuring 'size' would be difficult given the variety of activities carried out by many large financial institutions. Of course, some of those activities might be banned or regulated, but that is another issue. A more important qualification is that, while size is likely related to the capacity to cause systemic damage, other considerations like complexity, the extent of interrelationships with other institutions and concentration in certain markets also matter. A lot of effort is now being put, and rightly so, in trying to identify which institutions are 'systemic' and which are not.

Of course, this immediately leads on to the question of how to handle such systemically important institutions. One road is to take measures to reduce the probability of their failing. Much of the Basel III regulatory framework is designed to do this, as are recommendations that such institutions should be subject to closer regulatory oversight than others. A second road is to reduce the damage caused in the event of a failure. This leads on to suggestions for 'living wills' (perhaps better described as assisted euthanasia) and explicit bankruptcy regimes to ensure an orderly rather than a disorderly outcome.

Finally, I would note that a financial system made up of only small institutions can also be subject to systemic risks. If many of these institutions have similar portfolios, are subject to similar shocks, and would likely react in the same way in extremis, then a highly disorderly outcome might also be the order of the day. In short, there are no magic bullets in this area.

Should We Ban Some Derivatives?

My instinctive reaction is to say no. Virtually all forms of derivatives have real usefulness for somebody. We should, however, ensure that the risks associated with certain kinds of derivatives are made very clear, both to those who sell them and those who buy them. I do not think this has always been the case. I think the same point could also be made for structured products. However, it is now obvious that even very sophisticated investors failed to appreciate the implications for the prices of structured products of increases in the correlations of defaults in the underlying securities. This implies the problem was not one of failing to share an understanding of the risks but one of sheer ignorance. I am not sure how to deal with that problem.

The BIS in its 2009 Annual Report made the intriguing suggestion that all new financial products ought to be licensed, like pharmaceuticals. Presumably such a process would include an evaluation of the possible systemic implications of the use of new types of instruments. Whether this suggestion is practical, given the sheer number of new innovations in any given year, remains to be seen.

A Central Clearing House for All Transactions

I am not an expert in 'plumbing' issues, which I regret because they are very important. Failures in the infrastructure supporting clearing and settlement can have important systemic implications.

I think there is a consensus that many more transactions should be standardized such that they can go through central clearing houses. This will reduce bilateral exposures to counterparty risk, and potential knock on effects with systemic implications. One caveat, however, is that the costs to customers, particularly non-financial institutions doing normal hedging, should not rise excessively. Another caveat is that the continued good functioning of the central clearing house then becomes ever more crucial. Its failure must become unthinkable.

Finally, as with my thought about derivatives, there can be real value added with customized financial instruments of various sorts, and these would likely have to continue to trade 'Over the Counter' (OTC). The trick will be to achieve a better balance than we currently have between OTC and exchange traded transactions. This rebalancing will have to be done in spite of strong opposition from financial institutions that make large profits from customized products, and the need for cross country harmonization of such developments.

Are Policymakers Overreacting? Will we get Regulatory Overkill?

With respect to some of the new instruments and the new business practices that contributed to the current crisis, there could well be an overreaction. The fundamental concern is regulation and legislation that is essentially designed to be punitive. Here, the danger is one of throwing out the baby (useful innovations) with the bathwater. Personally, I find the focus on unregulated hedge funds, private equity funds and suchlike somewhat overdone. The real damage was in fact done by institutions that were regulated, at least in principle.

I hope that the driving force behind global financial reform will be the Basel III process now taking place in Switzerland. Some form of globally agreed way forward is required to avoid the serious complications and inefficiencies associated with different governments deciding to go their own way. This Basel process is now well underway, and the resulting recommendations have been taken on board by the G20. These, rightly, include proposals for more bank capital and better bank capital, as well as proposals for banks to hold more and better liquid assets.

There are also proposals for capital requirements to move counter cyclically, and for capital surcharges to be imposed on systemically important institutions. Personally, I feel these latter measures are very important. The trick, however, will be to find the right balance between too easy rules that will encourage excessive speculation, and too onerous rules that will stifle normal lending for productive purposes. Evidently, the Basel Committee is doing and will continue to do research to allow it to avoid either extreme. In this sense, both overreaction and underreaction are still possibilities.

Financial Regulation Reform: Concluding Remarks

We must deal with the too big to fail problem, as I have suggested above. It is important to note that government support measures in the crisis have led to some 'too big to fail' banks emerging from the crisis even bigger (and sometimes more complex) than they were before. Moreover, big banks with assumed government support have funding advantages over others, which can only lead to their becoming even bigger. This is a very bad path, and we must get off it as soon as possible.

NOTES

1 Clement, James and Van der Wee, 'Financial Innovation, Regulation and Crises: A Historical View'

1. See, for instance, S. Kates (ed.), *The Global Financial Crisis: What Have We Learnt?* (Cheltenham: Edward Elgar, 2011).
2. T. F. Geithner, *Reducing Systemic Risk in a Dynamic Financial System* (Federal Reserve Bank of New York, 2008), at http://www.newyorkfed.org/newsevents/speeches/2008/ tfg080609.html [accessed September 2012]. An insider's plea for reducing the complexity of financial products and the excessive levels of market leverage can be found in R. Bookstaber, *A Demon of Our Own Design, Markets, Hedge Funds, and the Perils of Financial Innovation* (Hoboken: John Wiley & Sons, 2007).
3. H. Minsky, *Can It Happen Again? Essays on Instability and Finance* (Armonk: M. E. Sharpe, 1984).
4. R. G. Rajan, 'Has Financial Development Made the World Riskier?', NBER Working Paper Series, Working Paper 11728 (National Bureau of Economic Research, MA, 2005).
5. S. Das, *Traders, Gus and Money: Knowns and Unknowns in the Dazzling World of Derivatives* (Englewood Cliffs: Prentice Hall, 2010), p. 333.
6. N. Gennaioli, A. Shleifer and R. Vishny, *Financial Innovation and Financial Fragility* (Harvard, MA: Harvard University research paper, 2010).
7. 'Derivatives and new techniques for risk management have benefited society by providing better means of sharing risks ... However, [they] have also expanded the scope for gambling, and they can be used in ways that increase rather than reduce risks in the system'. A. Admati and M. Hellwig, *The Bankers' New Clothes, What's Wrong with Banking and What to Do about It* (Princeton, NJ: Princeton University Press, 2013), p. 70.
8. B. Eichengreen, 'The Crisis in Financial Innovation', remarks on the occasion of the award of the Schumpeter Prize of the International Schumpeter Society, Vienna, 20 January 2010, p. 3.
9. M. Haliassos (ed.), *Financial Innovation, Too Much or too Little?* (Cambridge, MA: MIT Press, 2013), p. ix.
10. D. A. Moss, *When All Else Fails, Government as the Ultimate Risk Manager* (Cambridge, MA: Harvard University Press, 2004). Moss argues that the introduction of limited liability as early as 1811 in New York State corporate law, was essential in reassuring investors and thereby in generating a supply of risk capital.

11. A. Kern, J. Eatwell and A. Persaud, 'The Nature of Modern Credit Markets, Banking and Financial Innovation', in K. Alexander and R. Dhumale (eds), *Research Handbook on International Financial Regulation* (Cheltenham and Northampton, MA: Edward Elgar, 2012), pp. 11–16.

12. As cited by Eichengreen in 'The Crisis in Financial Innovation'. Indeed, the same argument can be said to apply to an earlier age too. See, for instance, H. Van der Wee, 'European Banking in the Middle Ages and in the Early Modern Times (476–1789)', in H. Van der Wee and G. Kurgan-Van Hentenryck (eds), *A History of European Banking* (London: EIB, 2000), pp. 71–266.

13. C. A. E. Goodhart, 'Financial Regulation' (2011), in S. Eijffinger and D. Masciandaro (eds), *Handbook of Central Banking, Financial Regulation and Supervision* (Chelthenham: Edgar Elgar, 2011), pp. 326ff.

14. M. Baily, R. Litan and M. Johnson, *The Origins of the Financial Crisis*, Brookings Paper, Fixing Finance Series, 3 (2008), as quoted in J. Stewart, 'Financial Innovation and the Financial Crisis', paper presented at the International Schumpeter Society Conference, Aalborg, 21–4 June 2010, p. 6.

15. H. Van der Wee (ed.), *Cera 1892–1998: The Power of Co-operative Solidarity* (Antwerp: CERA, 2002).

16. H. James, *The Creation and Destruction of Value: The Globalization Cycle* (Harvard, MA: Harvard University Press, 2009).

17. In other words, to fall for the 'this time is different' fallacy. C. Reinhart and K. Rogoff, *This Time is Different: Eight Centuries of Financial Folly* (Princeton, NJ: Princeton University Press, 2009).

18. Eichengreen, 'The Crisis in Financial Innovation'.

2 Petram, 'Contract Enforcement on the World's First Stock Exchange'

1. In Amsterdam alone, 1,143 investors signed up for ƒ3,679,915; slightly more than 57 per cent of the company's total stock: Henk den Heijer, *De geoctrooieerde compagnie: de VOC en de WIC als voorlopers van de naamloze vennootschap* (Deventer: Kluwer, 2005), p. 61. The VOC (Verenigde Oost-Indische Compagnie or Dutch East-Indies Company) consisted of six semi-independent chambers, each with its own stock and subscription in 1602. Amsterdam was the largest chamber and as a result the Amsterdam market for VOC shares became the most active. I will therefore focus on Amsterdam.

2. The States General of the Dutch Republic granted the VOC a charter for a period of twenty-one years. It stated that all company belongings would be liquidated after ten years (i.e. in 1612) and again at the end of the charter, but this never happened. It is true, however, that the shareholder only gradually learned that they could sell their share on the secondary market if they wanted to liquidate their investment.

3. That is, shareholders' accounts on which at least one purchase or sale was registered.

4. Number of active accounts: 1609 – 276, 1639 – 264. Nationaal Archief, The Hague (hereafter NA), VOC, inv. nrs 7066, 7068.

5. In 1691, Rodrigo Dias Henriques stated explicitly that he aimed for a gain of a quarter or half a percentage point of the nominal value of the shares he traded: Dias Henriques to Levy Duarte, 1 November 1691, Stadsarchief, Amsterdam (hereafter SAA), Archief van de Portugees-Israëlitische Gemeente te Amsterdam (hereafter PIG), inv. nr 677, pp. 897–8. On a share with a nominal value of ƒ3,000, which were traded most frequently, this would amount to a profit of ƒ15–30. Also: Dias Henriques to Levy Duarte, 16 January 1697, SAA, PIG, inv. nr 681a, pp. 534–5.

6. Admittedly, part of the transactions will have been merely inspired by a compulsion to gamble.

7. M. O'Hara, 'Optimal Microstructures', *European Financial Management*, 13 (2007), pp. 825–32, on pp. 831–2.

8. See, for example, H. Van der Wee, *The Growth of the Antwerp Market and the European Economy (Fourteenth–Sixteenth Centuries)*, 3 vols (The Hague: Nijhoff, 1963), vol. 2. Oscar Gelderblom, *Cities of Commerce: The Institutional Foundations of International Trade in the Low Countries, 1250–1650* (Princeton, NJ: Princeton University Press, 2013).

9. D. de Ruysscher, 'Handel en recht in de Antwerpse rechtbank (1585–1713)', (PhD thesis, K.U. Leuven, 2009).

10. See note 32 below.

11. Heleen Kole generously shared her notes for Oscar Gelderblom in the Court of Holland archives with me. She used a sample of court cases over the period 1585–1630 in which litigants appeared whose last names started with B, M or P. In addition to her sample, I used the name index (NA, Court of Holland, inv. nr 1077) to look up all cases whose litigants are known to also have been share traders. There are no share-trade-related court cases available prior to 1610; which can be explained by the facts that it took several years before the court pronounced judgement, that there were relatively few trades in the first years after 1602 and that share traders started using more advanced financial techniques (forward trading, short-selling) only from 1607 onwards.

12. There are twenty so-called extended sentences of lawsuits dealing with share-trade-related conflicts available for the period 1640–1700. I have used the name index (NA, Court of Holland, inv. nr 1078) to look up all cases for which I knew that the litigants (or their close relatives) traded shares. Additionally, I have checked all lawsuits listing names of Portuguese Jews.

13. In the case between the directors of the VOC and Abraham de Ligne c.s., for example, the costs for the report made by one of the councillors of the High Council already amounted to ƒ126; each party had to pay half. This sum does not include the costs of lower courts, the process server, the solicitors' fee and taxes. NA, High Council, inv. nr 642, 7 December 1621. These reports usually constituted half of the court's total costs; a bill in the Cardoso family's estate shows that the report constituted about 60 per cent of the court's costs: ƒ36 on a total of ƒ59.20. Rachel Cardoso had to pay half of this amount (ƒ28.40), to which a total of ƒ12.90 taxes were added: bill Parnassim of the Jewish community of Amsterdam *vs.* Rachel Cardoso, 2 November 1712, estate David Abraham Cardoso, SAA, PIG, inv. nr 654. The reports of the Court of Holland's *commissarissen* (e.g. NA, Court of Holland, inv. nr 1355, for the year 1672) sometimes also include the bill of the court's process server. He charged ƒ3.75 for every summons. The clerk of the court's office charged ƒ6.20 per document. The bill could become steep if a lawsuit involved several litigants who all had to be served summons individually.

14. The main factor of influence on the variation in duration was the amount of time litigants let go by before they submitted a request for appeal. The Court of Holland of course employed a maximum term to request an appeal, but the court could make exceptions for special cases. Moreover, a lower court's judgement could be suspended for the duration of the appeal (*mandement in cas van appel*) only if the appeal had been requested within a short period: M.-Ch. le Bailly, *Hof van Holland, Zeeland en West-Friesland: de hoofdlijnen van het procederen in civiele zaken voor het Hof van Holland, Zeeland en West-*

Friesland zowel in eerste instantie als in hoger beroep (Hilversum: Verloren, 2008), p. 26. Le Bailly does not mention the maximum periods before lodging an appeal.

15. Diego d'Aguirre, Duarte Rodrigues Mendes, Antonio do Porto and Isaack Gomes Silvera, for example, referred to a judgement of the Court of Holland in a claim they submitted to the Court of Aldermen (18 September 1672): SAA, Notaries, inv. nr 4075, pp. 186–9.

16. D. C. North, *Institutions, Institutional Change and Economic Performance* (Cambridge: Cambridge University Press, 1990), p. 27.

17. The full text of the ban (27 February 1610) can be found in: Cornelis Cau (et al.), *Groot placaet-boeck, vervattende de placaten, ordonnantien en-de edicten van de … Staten Generael der Vereenighde Nederlanden, ende van de … Staten van Hollandt en West-Vrieslandt*, 9 vols (The Hague: Weduwe, ende erfgenamen van wylen Hillebrandt Iacobsz van Wouw, 1658), vol. 1, pp. 554–5. The ban of 1610 was reissued in 1623, 1624, 1630, 1636 and 1677. Placard 3 June 1623: Cau, *Groot placaet-boeck*, vol. 1, pp. 555–9. Placard 20 May 1624: ibid., pp. 665–7. Placard 1 October 1630: ibid., p. 667. Placard 27 May 1636: ibid., p. 667. Placard 16 September 1677: Cau, *Groot placaet-boeck*, vol. 3, p. 1307.

18. SAA, PIG, inv. nrs 687–8. The values given are market values; the currency is Dutch guilders.

19. Interestingly, their nominal position in the VOC fluctuated between *f*9,000 and *f*27,000 in the years 1680 and 1681: NA, VOC, inv. nr 7072, fols 235, 383. Unfortunately, their forward trading activity during these years is unknown.

20. R. C. van Caenegem, *Geschiedkundige inleiding tot het privaatrecht* (Ghent: Story-Scientia, 1981), p. 51.

21. Gelderblom, *Cities of Commerce*, p. 366.

22. S. Banner, *Anglo-American Securities Regulation* (Cambridge: Cambridge University Press, 1998).

23. A. Greif, 'Reputation and Coalitions in Medieval Trade: Evidence on the Maghribi Traders', *Journal of Economic History*, 49 (1989), pp. 857–82.

24. M.-Ch. le Bailly and Chr. M.O. Verhas, *Hoge Raad van Holland, Zeeland en West-Friesland (1582–1795): de hoofdlijnen van het procederen in civiele zaken voor de Hoge Raad zowel in eerste instantie als in hoger beroep* (Hilversum: Verloren, 2006), p. 7.

25. This is based on the *insinuaties* in the protocols of Amsterdam's notaries. An *insinuatie*, or notarial summons, was usually the first step in legal action. The protocols of 1672 and 1688, two years with large price fluctuations and consequently many conflicts between share traders, contain high numbers of *insinuaties*. It is very well possible that these conflicts were also brought before the local court. Only one conflict stemming from a transaction in 1672 and one from a transaction in 1688 reached the Court of Holland, however.

26. For the types of evidence accepted by the courts, see Gelderblom, *Cities of Commerce*, pp. 272–3.

27. See A. van Meeteren, *Op hoop van akkoord: instrumenteel forumgebruik bij geschilbeslechting in Leiden in de zeventiende eeuw* (Hilversum: Verloren, 2006), pp. 172–3. According to Van Meeteren, for an attestation to be credible, it had to be attested to a notary public as soon after the event had happened as possible (p. 181).

28. For example, NA, Case files, inv. nr IIT39.

29. NA, Case files. Normally, litigants received the contents of the case file back when the court procedure was finished. However, some litigants did not collect the case files.

30. NA, Court of Holland, inv. nrs 1552, 1559.

31. The first page of the Amsterdam chamber's subscription book stated this rule. For a transcript of this page (followed by the entire book), see J. G. van Dillen, *Het oudste aandeelhoudersregister van de Kamer Amsterdam der Oost-Indische Compagnie* (The Hague: Nijhoff, 1958), pp. 105–6.

32. The *Consultatien*, a famous compilation of early-modern Dutch jurisprudence, confirms that the courts treated shares as immovables in the winding up of estates (*Consultatien, advysen en advertissementen, gegeven ende geschreven by verscheyden treffelijcke rechtsgeleerden in Hollandt*, 6 vols (Rotterdam: Joannis Næranus, 1645–85), vol. 1, pp. 77, 139–40). In England, it had been unclear after the foundation of the first joint-stock companies whether common law treated shares as real or personal property. This had implications for the transferability of shares. Subsequent incorporation acts added a clause that declared shares to be personal property. See R. Harris, *Industrializing English Law: Entrepreneurship and Business Organization, 1720–1844* (New York: Cambridge University Press, 2000), pp. 117–8. In the Dutch Republic, there were no impediments to the transfer of unmovable goods other than the obligation to officially register a transfer.

33. H. de Groot, *Inleidinge tot de Hollandsche Rechts-Geleerdheid* , 2 vols (1631) vol. 2, *Aantekeningen*, ed. S. J. F. Andreae (Arnhem: Gouda Quint, 1939), p. 236.

34. *Allert van Balck* vs *Jan Hendricksz. Rotgans*, 22 December 1622, NA, High Council, inv. nr 715. The *insinuatie* that preceded the court case has been published by Van Dillen: J. G. van Dillen, 'Isaac le Maire en de handel in actiën der Oost-Indische Compagnie', *Eco-nomisch Historisch jaarboek*, 16 (1930), pp. 1–165, on p. 101 (doc. nr 46). Pieter Symonsz van der Schelling ended up in a similar situation after transferring shares to Hans Bouwer: Van Dillen, 'Isaac le Maire', 108 (doc. nr 57).

35. Van Dillen, 'Isaac le Maire', p. 121.

36. D. L. C. Miller, 'Transfer of Ownership', in R. Feenstra and R. Zimmerman (eds), *Das römisch-holländische Recht. Fortschritte des Zivilrechts im 17. und 18. Jahrhundert* (Berlin: Duncker & Humblot, 1992), pp. 521–40, on pp. 527, 532–4.

37. P. van Dam, *Beschryvinge van de Oostindische Compagnie* 1A (1701), ed. F. W. Stapel (The Hague: Nijhoff, 1927), pp. 144–5.

38. *Abraham Abelijn* vs *Pieter Overlander*, NA, Court of Holland, inv. nr 632, nr 1614–50 and NA, High Council, inv. nr 708, 30 July 1616. Dirck Semeij *vs.* Abraham Abelijn, NA, Court of Holland, inv. nr 632, nr 1614–73 and NA, High Council, inv. nr 708, 30 July 1616. Maerten de Meijere *vs.* Dirck Semeij, NA, Court of Holland, inv. nr 632, nr 1614–76 and NA, High Council, inv. nr 708, 30 July 1616. The traders also appealed the judgements of the Court of Holland to the High Council, but the trial before the High Council did not reveal any new information. The motivations behind these appeals were of a more pragmatic nature: since Bouwer had fled from Amsterdam, the last person in the chain – Semeij – had no one to lay a claim on. He therefore tried once more to be released from De Meijere's claim.

The cases concerning the chain of transactions starting with Pieter Overlander are almost identical; the Court of Aldermen pronounced judgement around late November or early December 1611, the appeals came up before the Court of Holland in 1614 and before the High Council in July 1616.

There was a similar lawsuit between Maerten de Meijere and Pieter van Duynen. Van Duynen had traded with Maerten de Meijere, who had an unsettled transaction with Bouwer. The share transfer from Bouwer to Van Duynen settled both transactions. *Maerten de Meijere* vs *Pieter van Duynen*, 27 January 1612, NA, Court of Holland, inv. nr 626, nr 1612–6.

39. J. H. Munro, 'The Medieval Origins of the Financial Revolution: Usury, Rentes, and Negotiability', *International History Review*, 25 (2003), pp. 505–62, on p. 553. Van der Wee, *The Growth of the Antwerp Market*, vol. 2, pp. 340–3, 348. Veronica Aoki Santarosa is preparing a PhD thesis in which she argues that the incentive to monitor the counterparty becomes smaller as the number of endorsers increases. The maximum number of endorsers in share transactions is two, so in my opinion, the negative effects of endorsements on monitoring would not have played a significant part on the seventeenth-century share market.

40. For an example of an endorsed contract, see the options contract in the case file of the lawsuit between Willem Hendrick Tammas *vs.* Antonio Alvares Machado, 1689, NA, Case files, 11T39. The earliest endorsements I have found date from 1609. In the chaotic aftermath of Le Maire's bear raid, many forward traders wanted to be sure who their counterparty was. Several notarial deeds show that forward contracts had been resold, e.g. *insinuatie* 10 August 1610, SAA, Notaries, inv. nr 120, fol. 99v; *insinuatie* 16 August 1610, SAA, Notaries, inv. nr 209, fol. 181v; *insinuatie* 21 August 1610, SAA, Notaries, inv. nr 120, fols 99v–100r.

41. Adriaen van der Heijden and Daniel van Genegen *vs.* Abraham Abelijn, NA, inv. nr 633, nr 1614–118.

42. For example, Isaac le Maire *vs.* Louis del Beecke, NA, Court of Holland, inv. nr 633, 1614–134 and Isaac le Maire *vs.* Louis del Beecke, NA, Court of Holland, inv. nr 664, 1624–64. (In spite of the fact that the same litigants appear in both cases, these are different lawsuits.)

43. For example, Philips de Bacher *vs.* Frederick van Schuijlenburch (20 December 1641), NA, Court of Holland, inv. nr 739, nr 1641–166. This lawsuit shows that the market custom had already become established, but the court did not yet rule accordingly: the buyer had waited a month before he requested delivery of the share, but the court still ruled in favour of his claim to get the share delivered.

44. Attestation (11 July 1659), SAA, Notaries, inv. nr 2207, p. 95.

45. Samuel Cotinho *vs.* Vincent van Bronckhorst, 1689, NA, Case files, 11K98.

46. See note 43 above.

47. Forward contract 14 June 1688, SAA, PIG, inv. nr 654. The bottom lines of this contract stipulated that it should be settled within twenty days after the original settlement date. If the seller did not comply, the price would thereafter be reduced by a quarter of a percentage point a day. If the buyer did not comply, the price would be increased by a quarter of a percentage point a day. In any case, the contract would lose its legal validity three months after the original settlement date.

48. M. F. J. Smith, *Tijd-affaires in effecten aan de Amsterdamsche beurs* (The Hague: Nijhoff, 1919), pp. 57–60.

49. *Samuel Cotinho* vs *Vincent van Bronckhorst*, 1689, Court of Holland, Case files, 11K98.

50. *Severijn Haeck* vs *Andries Polster* (28 March 1633), NA, Court of Holland, inv. nr 703, nr 1633–36–1. The court pronounced the same judgement in a similar case between Severijn Haeck and Dirck van der Perre, which came up in court on the same day: *Severijn Haeck* vs *Dirck van der Perre* (28 March 1633), NA, Court of Holland, inv. nr 703, nr 1633–36–2.

51. During the period June–August 1664, the share price fluctuated between 490 and 500 per cent: SAA, Merchants' accounts, inv. nr 39, fol. 73.

52. SAA, Deutz, inv. nr 291, fol. 46.

53. This would have been the maximum possible loss per share.

54. *Sebastiaen da Cunha* vs *Michiel Rodrigues Mendes c.s.* (27 May 1667), NA, inv. nr 784, nr 1667–60. This case was brought before the Court of Holland in first instance, but it is unclear to me why Da Cunha did not take the case to the Court of Aldermen first. Foreign merchants were allowed to litigate directly before the Court of Holland, but a plausible explanation may also be that one of the defendants (Joan Corver) was himself one of the judges in the Court of Aldermen in 1666; see J. E. Elias, *De Vroedschap van Amsterdam, 1578–1795*, 2 vols. (Haarlem: Loosjes, 1903), vol. 1, p. 521. Names of the defendants as follows: Michiel Rodrigues Mendes, Isaack Mendes da Silva, Moses de Silva (also acting on behalf of Moses Machado, Joan Corver, Louis Gonsales d'Andrada, Manuel Lopes Villareal, Gerrit van Beuningen and Cornelis Lock).

    Da Cunha could prove that the forward contracts were short sales because the sellers had placed the shares on Da Cunha's 'time account' in the course of the terms of the contracts, thus trying to make the sales appear legal.

55. Please note that Sebastiaen da Cunha *vs.* Michiel Rodrigues Mendes c.s. was not an appeal case either, see note 54 above.

56. These buyers did not ask for *aanwijzinge* because they wanted to be relieved from their contractual obligations – this was before the ban on short-selling – but because they feared that they would miss out on the first dividend distribution if their counterparties did not actually own the shares they had sold.

57. See, for example, A. Goldgar, *Tulipmania: Money, Honor, and Knowledge in the Dutch Golden Age* (Chicago, IL: Chicago University Press, 2007).

58. When, for example, the shareholder explains the use of options, he says: 'Even if you do not gain through the "opsies" the first time, you do not risk your credit, and do not put your honor in danger'. J. P. de la Vega, *Confusión de confusiones* (1688), trans. and ed. H. Kellenbenz (Boston, MA: Baker Library, 1957), p. 77 (p. 24 in the 1688 edition, p. 7 in Kellenbenz's English edition).

59. George Morton Pitt to Lord Londonderry, 23 April 1720, quoted in L. Neal, 'Reflections from the Mirror of Folly: The Adventures of Lord Londonderry in the Stock Markets of Paris, Amsterdam, and London in the Bubbles of 1719–1720', *Working Paper* (2010), pp. 13–4. George Morton Pitt characterized these disreputable traders as 'Scrub Jews'.

60. The organization of the Amsterdam trading clubs bears close resemblance to the London Stock Exchange in the eighteenth century. Both were closed associations of traders characterized by a high degree of self-regulation. See L. Neal, 'The Evolution of Self- and State-Regulation of the London Stock Exchange, 1688–1878', in D. Ma and J. L. van Zanden (eds), *Law and Long-Term Economic Change: A Eurasian Perspective* (Stanford, CA: Stanford Economics and Finance, 2011), ch. 14.

61. Without the possibility of exclusion, the free-rider problem arises. The possibility of exclusion was therefore key to the functioning of the trading clubs. J. M. Buchanan, 'An Economic Theory of Clubs', *Economics*, 32 (1965), pp. 1–14.

62. North, *Institutions*, p. 33.

63. Attestation 9 January 1704, SAA, Notaries, inv. nr 6956, fol. 23. Names of the attestants: Henri Alvares, Jacob Gabay, Moises Coronel and Daniel Dias de Pas. It is unclear why these four men made this attestation before notary Van Velen.

64. Goldgar, *Tulipmania*, pp. 191–2.

65. Smith, *Tijd-affaires*, pp. 135–8. It is unknown when this regulation was put into effect, but this is likely to have happened before 1 May 1764.

66. SAA, PIG, inv. nrs 687–8.

67. In June 1672, Balthasar da Cunha (not to be confused with Sebastiaen da Cunha – see note 54), one of the largest stock traders on the Amsterdam exchange, transferred the ownership of two houses and a ƒ6,000 share in the Enkhuizen chamber of the VOC to Miguel Netto de Paiva: deed of conveyance and transfer (28 June 1672), SAA, Notaries, inv. nr 4074, fols 485–7. He had obviously financial difficulties, but did not renege on his forward deals.

68. Frans Pardicque became insolvent in October 1688. He was unable to fulfil his obligations because he did not receive payment on an unsettled transaction with Coenraet van Beuningen. He did not, however, try to let the courts declare his forward purchases null and void, but rather let his counterparties lay claims on his insolvent estate: record containing the unsettled forward deals of Pardicque (22 October 1688), SAA, Notaries, inv. nr 4135, fols 712–4.

69. *Insinuaties* Raphael Duarte (18 May 1672) and Manuel Mendes Flores (19 May 1672): SAA, Notaries, inv. nr 2239, fols 183, 199. Gaspar Mendes de Garvoijs gave a similar answer to an *insinuatie* requesting him to receive a share at 530 per cent on 1 July: *insinuatie* Antonio and Miguel Guitieres Martines (1 July 1672): SAA, Notaries, inv. nr 2239.

70. The share price decreased from 560 to 460 in August and further to 416 in October.

71. Goldgar, *Tulipmania*, pp. 237–51. E. H. Krelage, *Bloemenspeculatie in Nederland: de Tulpomanie van 1636–'37 en de Hyacintenhandel 1720–'36* (Amsterdam: Van Kampe, 1942), p. 96. The reasons why the courts refused to do so remain unclear. Goldgar eagerly uses the courts' refusal to support her argument that civic harmony stood at the basis of Dutch society: the courts encouraged traders to settle their conflicts in the friendliest way. It is undoubtedly true that arbitration and mediation were important in the Dutch legal system, but why would the courts refuse to attend to these cases? Their number could have clogged the system, as Goldgar put forward, but these cases were all similar: one judgement would have created a precedent. I think the principal motivation for the courts was that the tulip trade had attracted large numbers of new participants only months before the bubble burst. The courts might have argued that the tulip contracts were invalid because the new entrants to the market were unaware of its rules and customs; more experienced traders might have misled them to pay the exorbitantly high prices.

3 Mooij, 'Co-operative Banking in the Netherlands in pre-Second World War Crises'

1. See CBS, *Overzicht van den omvang van het coöperatiewezen in Nederland op 1 jan. 1938* ('s-Gravenhage, 1939).

2. See, as one example, J. L. Van Zanden and A. Van Riel, *Nederland 1780–1914, Staat, Instituties en economische ontwikkeling* (Uitgeverij Balans, 2000), pp. 362–76.

3. Van Campen, Ph. C. M., P. Hollenberg and F. Kriellaars, *Landbouw en Landbouwcrediet 1898–1948: vijftig jaar geschiedenis van de Coöperatieve Centrale Boerenleenbank* (Eindhoven, 1949), pp. 33–5.

4. J. Kymmell, *De algemene banken in Nederland*, and P. A. Geljon, *De algemene banken en het effectenbedrijf 1860–1914* (Amsterdam: dissertatie VU, 2005).

5. See J. Stoffer, *Het ontstaan van de NMB; De geschiedenis van haar voorgangers in de jaren 1900 tot 1927* (Deventer: Kluwer, 1985), ch. 1. The German economist and liberal politician F. H. Schultze-Delitzsch (1808–83) was a pioneer in the development of co-operatives in Germany.

6. J. De Vries, *De geschiedenis van De Nederlandsche Bank. Vol. V: De Nederlandsche Bank van 1914 tot 1948* (Haarlem: Enschedé, 1994), pp. 203–66. See also W. Vanthoor, *The King's Eldest Daughter. A History of the Nederlandsche Bank, 1814–1998* (Amsterdam: Boom, 2005).

7. See J. Mooij and H. Prast, 'A Brief History of the Institutional Design of Banking Supervision in the Netherlands', in T. Kuppens, H. Prast and S. Wesseling (eds), *Banking Supervision at the Crossroad* (Cheltenham: Edward Elgar Publishing, 2003), pp. 10–37.

8. M. Van Nieuwkerk and C. Kroeze (eds), *Bubbels: spraakmakende financiële crises uit de Geschiedenis* (Amsterdam: Stichting Vereniging voor de Effectenhandel/Arnhem: Sonsbeek Publishers, 2007), p. 64.

9. F. A. G. Keesing, *De conjuncturele ontwikkeling van Nederland en de evolutie van de economische overheidspolitiek 1918–1939* (Nijmegen: Socialistische Uitgeverij Nijmegen, 1978), p. 93, and F. de Roos, 'De gave gulden', in A. Knoester (ed.), *Lessen uit het verleden: 125 Jaar Vereniging voor de Staathuishoudkunde* (Leiden [ets.]: Stenfert Kroese, 1987), pp. 122–3.

10. H. A. M. Klemann, *Nederland 1938–1948: economie in de jaren van oorlog en bezetting* (Amsterdam: Boom, 2002), chs 2 and 6.

11. There was no specific legislation in this area until 1988. See I. Van Dooren and J. van IJperenburg, 'The Structure and Corporate Governance of Rabobank Nederland', *International In-house Counsel Journal*, 2:7 (Spring 2009), pp. 21–108.

12. ARN, Terugblikker, G. K. Van Wijk, 'Banken tussen twee zeeën', in *De Rabobank* (1978), pp. 35–37.

13. C. Colvin, 'Interbank Competition and Financial Stability: The Case of Dutch Cooperative Banks in the Early Twentieth Century', in *Economic History Society Annual Conference* (University of Durham, Session I/E, 26 March 2010).

14. G. W. M. Huysmans, 'Het landbouwcrediet in Nederland', *De Economist*, 7:8 (1941), p. 392.

15. Sluyterman, *Het coöperatieve alternatief*, p. 55.

16. See CBS, *Overzicht van den omvang*, p. 11.

17. Van Campen, 'Heden, verleden, toekomst', pp. 13–15.

18. De Vries, *Geschiedenis*, vol. 5, table 43. See also pp. 203–30 and pp. 259–63.

19. Sluyterman, *Het coöperatieve alternatief*, p. 41.

20. CCB, *Jaarverslag* (annual report) 1924.

21. Ibid., p. 29. For further details, see C. J. A. Borst, De Coöperatieve Centrale Christelijke Boerenleenbank C.C.C.B gevestigd te Alkmaar 1904–19, unpublished graduate thesis, Hogeschool, Holland, 2004

22. G. Weststrate, *Gedenkboek uitgegeven tgv het vijftigjarig bestaan der Coöperatieve Centrale Raiffeisen-Bank te Utrecht 1898–1948* (Utrecht: Coöperatieve Centrale Raiffeisen-Bank, 1948), pp. 191, 200–1; Van Campen, *Landbouw en landbouwcrediet*, pp. 238–9.

23. J. De Vries, *De Coöperatieve Raiffeisen- en Boerenleenbanken in Nederland 1948–1973: van exponent tot component* (Utrecht: Coöperatieve Centrale Raiffeisen- en Boerenleenbank G.A., 1973), p. 15.

24. A breakdown of the causes: merger, winding up/liquidation, bankruped. DNB, *Nederlandse financiële instellingen in de twintigste eeuw: balansreeksen en naamlijst van handelsbanken*, Statistische Cahiers Nr 3 (Amsterdam: NIBE/SVV, 2000), table 1, and De Vries, *Geschiedenis*, vol. 5, table 8, p. 50.

25. CCB, *Jaarverslag* (annual report) 1929, p. 8.

26. De Vries, *De Coöperatieve Raiffeisen-en Boerenleenbanken*, p. 28.

27. De Vries, *Geschiedenis*, vol. 5, table 5, p. 46.

28. '*De betekenis van de landbouwcredietcoöperatie in Nederland*' (conclusion), p. 90.
29. CCB, *Jaarverlagen* (annual reports) 1923 and 1942; *Maandelijkse Mededeelingen*, 1926, p. 12.
30. CCRB, *Raiffeisenbode*, July 1923, p. 4.
31. E. Schilte, *Menselijk kapitaal. Honderdtien jaar personeelsbeleid bij de Rabobank* (Utrecht: Rabobank, 2009), p. 41.
32. CCB, *Jaarverslag* (annual report) 1925.
33. Weststrate, *Gedenkboek*, p. 211. See also: J. Mooij and W. Boonstra (eds), *Raiffeisen's Footprint* (Amsterdam: VU University Press 2012), ch. 7.
34. J. Mooij, 'Statistics: A Means of Communication. De Nederlandsche Bank (1850–1940)', in I. H. Stamhuis, P. M. M. Klep and J. G. S. J. van Maarseveen (eds), *Statistical Mind in Modern Society: The Netherlands 1850–1940*, 2 vols (Amsterdam: Aksant, 2008), vol. 1, pp. 383–406.
35. De Vries, *Geschiedenis*, vol. 5, pp. 166–9.
36. T. P. Bergsma, *Das niederländische Bankwesen, unter besonderer Berücksichtigung der Entwicklung seit dem Beginn der Weltwirtschaftskrise* (Gelnhausen: Kalbfleisch, 1939), p. 76.
37. Weststrate, *Gedenkboek*, p. 68.
38. CCB, *Mededeelingen*, June 1933.
39. CCRB, Minutes of the Board, 7 April 1933.
40. Mooij and Prast, 'A Brief History'.
41. T. J. Visser, *Het landbouwcrediet in de afgeloopen 25 jaar, 1914–1939* (Utrecht, 1940), p. 18.
42. Huysmans, 'Het landbouwcrediet', p. 395.
43. Ibid., p. 392.

4 Straumann, 'The Discreet Charm of Hidden Reserves: How Swiss Re Survived the Great Depression'

1. See, for example, the comparison between then and now by Barry Eichengreen and Kevin O'Rourke at http://www.voxeu.org/index.php?q=node/3421 [accessed 31 March 2010].
2. 'Swiss Re ditches Foray into Financial Markets', *Financial Times*, 5 February 2009.
3. C. Trebilcock, *Phoenix Assurance and the Development of British Insurance, Volume II: The Era of the Insurance Giants, 1870–1984* (Cambridge: Cambridge University Press, 1998), p. 592.
4. Major works on the history of reinsurance include: C. E. Golding, *A History of Reinsurance* (London, 1927); C. H. Hollitscher, *Internationale Rückversicherung* (Berlin, 1931); A. Manes, *Versicherungswesen: System der Versicherungswirtschaft*, 3 vols (Leipzig und Berlin, 1930–2), vol. 2, pp. 290–308; P. L. van der Haegen, *Der internationale Rückversicherungsmarkt unter besonderer Berücksichtigung des schweizerischen Angebots* (Berne, 1956); B. Mossner, *Die Entwicklung der Rückversicherung bis zur Gründung selbständiger Rückversicherungsgesellschaften* (Berlin, 1959); L. Arps, *Auf sicheren Pfeilern: Deutsche Versicherungswirtschaft vor 1914* (Göttingen, 1965); K. Gerathewohl, *Rückversicherung: Grundlagen und Praxis*, 2 vols (1976; Karlsruhe, 1979); P. Koch, 'Über die Anfänge der professionellen Rückversicherung in der Schweiz', in *Zeitschrift für Versicherungswesen*, 21 (1990), pp. 554–7; W. Werner, *Die späte Entwicklung der amerikanischen*

Rückversicherungswirtschaft: Eine Branchenstudie zur internationalen Wettbewerbsfähigkeit (Berlin, 1993); R. Pearson, 'The Development of Reinsurance Markets in Europe during the Nineteenth Century', *Journal of European Economic History*, 24 (1995), pp. 557–71; R. Pearson, 'The Birth Pains of a Global Reinsurer: Swiss Re of Zürich, 1864–79', *Financial History Review*, 8 (2001), pp. 27–47; P. Borscheid and R. Pearson (eds), *Internationalisation and Globalisation of the Insurance Industry in the Nineteenth and Twentieth Centuries* (Marburg: Philipps University, 2007). As for SR, there are three unpublished master theses worth citing: L. Feldmann, 'Die Schweizerische Rückversicherungs-Gesellschaft in den 30er Jahren' (Master thesis, University of Zurich, 1996); R. Bach, 'Die wirtschaftliche und soziale Entwicklung des Unternehmens Schweizerische Rückversicherungs-Gesellschaft in der Zeit von 1900–1929' (Master thesis, University of Zurich, 2006); E. Rohland, 'The Swiss Re Fire Branch 1864–1906: Riks – Fire – Climate' (Master thesis, University of Berne, 2008).

5. This approach to financial crises has been reinvigorated by the 'Flandreau school'. See for example J. Flores, 'Information Asymmetries and Conflict of Interest during the Baring Crisis, 1880–1890', *Financial History Review*, 18:2 (2011), pp. 191–215.

6. SR Archives Zurich (Switzerland), 10.101 501: Allgemeine Versicherungs-Gesellschaft Helvetia St. Gallen, Auszug aus dem Protokolle der LIV. Sitzung des Verwaltungsrates vom 10. Juli 1863 im Beisein des Spezial-Directors Herrn Grossmann ('Gutachten zu Handen der Tit. Schweizerischen Creditanstalt in Zürich über eine von derselben, unter Mitwirkung der Allgemeinen Versicherungsgesellschaft in St. Gallen zu gründende Rückversicherungsgesellschaft').

7. An account of the struggle for survival in the 1860s and 1870s is given by Pearson, 'The Birth Pains'.

8. A modern history of Generali remains to be written. On the link of Generali to the Rothschilds, see M. A. López-Morell and J. M. O'Kean, 'A Stable Network as a Source of Entrepreneurial Opportunities: The Rothschilds in Spain, 1835–1931', *Business History*, 50:2 (March 2008), pp. 163–84.

9. See the comparison of SR with Munich Re and Cologne Re by H. Kluge, 'Der Einfluss des Geschäfts der "Allianz" auf die Entwicklung der "Münchener Rückversicherungs-Gesellschaft" in deren ersten fünfzig Jahren (1880–1930)', *Jahrbuch für Wirtschaftsgeschichte*, 2 (2006), pp. 217–46.

10. A. de Mestral, *Charles Simon: humaniste et réassureur, 1862–1942* (Zurich, 1947), p. 16.

11. SR Archives Zurich (Switzerland), 10.107 760: Protokolle des Verwaltungsrats, 24 August 1928.

12. Schweizerische Rückversicherungs-Gesellschaft AG, Geschäftsbericht 1930, S. 3. The report was finalized in May 1931.

13. Hollitscher, *Internationale Rückversicherung*, pp. 69–70.

14. SR Archives Zurich (Switzerland), 10.107 760: Protokolle des Verwaltungsrats, 31 May 1930, and 14 October 1930.

15. SR Archives Zurich (Switzerland), 10.107 760: Protokolle des Verwaltungsrats, 26 September 1931.

16. SR Archives Zurich (Switzerland), Bericht des Präsidenten zum Abschluss 1931, 11.5.1932, S. 13: 'Darum leben wir, seit die Pfundabwertung stattfand und die Wirtschaftskrise weiter zunahm, in einem steten Hangen und Bangen'.

17. Schweizerische Rückversicherungs-Gesellschaft AG, Geschäftsbericht 1931, S. 3: 'Die katastrophale Entwicklung, welche die Wirtschaftskrise besonders in der zweiten Hälfte des Jahres nahm, hat kein Unternehmen, das international tätig ist, verschont'. The report was finalized in May 1932.

18. SR Archives Zurich (Switzerland), P. Guggenbühl, *Hausstatistik der Schweizer Rück*, 2 vols (Zurich, 1939 and 1964), vol. 1, p. 378: 'Nur dank einer vorsichtigen Reservepolitik gelang es der Gesellschaft, die Erschütterungen einzelner Jahre, ohne dauernden Schaden zu nehmen, zu überwinden'.

19. SR Archives Zurich (Switzerland), 10.107 760: Protokolle des Verwaltungsrates, 26 September 1931.

20. Feldmann, *Rückversicherungs-Gesellschaft*, p. 97. According to Feldmann the drop of the share price in late 1931 was the turning point bringing the board to make a radical change in the investment strategy.

21. SR Archives Zurich (Switzerland), 10.107 760: Protokolle des Verwaltungsrates, 15 October 1931 and 18 December 1931.

22. C. Feinstein, P. Temin and G. Toniolo, *The European Economy between the Wars* (Oxford: Oxford University Press, 1997).

23. SR Archives Zurich (Switzerland), 10.106 983 Bericht an den Verwaltungsrat zum Abschluss 1938. For a discussion of the causes and the course of the crisis of 1937–8, see F. R. Velde, 'The Recession of 1937 – a Cautionary Tale', *Chicago FRB Economic Perspectives*, Q4 (2009), pp. 16–37.

24. SR Archives Zurich (Switzerland), 10.107 760: Protokolle des Verwaltungsrates, 15 May 1934 and 16 May 1934.

25. SR Archives Zurich (Switzerland), 10.107 760: Protokolle des Verwaltungsrates, 14 December 1934.

26. SR Archives Zurich (Switzerland), 10.107 910: Protokolle des Verwaltungsratsausschusses, 1 December 1933.

27. SR Archives Zurich (Switzerland), 10.107 910: Protokolle des Verwaltungsratsausschusses, 25 June 1934.

28. Pioneering research has been undertaken by F. Capie and M. Billings, 'Profitability in English Banking in the Twentieth Century', *European Review of Economic History*, 5 (2001), pp. 367–401.

5 Barbiellini Amidei and Giordano, 'The Redesign of the Bank–Industry–Financial Market Ties in the US Glass–Steagall and the 1936 Italian Banking Acts'

1. We consulted the historical archives of the Bank of Italy (ASBI), Comit (ASBCI), IMI (ASIMI), IRI (ASIRI) and Ufficio Italiano Cambi (UIC).

2. F. Amatori and A. Colli, *Impresa e industria in Italia dall'Unità a oggi* (Venice: Marsilio, 1999), p. 89.

3. G. Conti, 'Finanza di impresa e capitale di rischio in Italia (1870–1939)', *Rivista di storia economica*, 3 (1993), pp. 307–32, on p. 317.

4. S. Baia Curioni, *Regolazione e Competizione. Storia del Mercato Azionario in Italia (1808–1938)* (Bologna: Il Mulino, 1995).

5. G. Siciliano, 'La regolamentazione delle Borse valori in Europa e negli USA agli inizi del Novecento', *Rivista di Storia Economica*, 2 (2002), pp. 131–51.

6. F. Barbiellini Amidei and C. Impenna, 'Il mercato azionario e il finanziamento delle imprese negli anni Cinquanta', in F. Cotula (ed.), *Stabilità e sviluppo negli anni Cinquanta. 3. Politica bancaria e struttura del sistema finanziario* (Rome-Bari: Laterza, 1999), pp. 657–883.

7. All these provisions were, however, enforced only in 1925.
8. H. E. Krooss and R. B. Blyn, *A History of Financial Intermediaries* (New York: Random House, 1971).
9. For detailed accounts of the development of investment banks in the US, see V. P. Carosso, *Investment Banking in America. A History* (Cambridge, MA: Harvard University Press, 1970), and P. G. Mahoney, 'The Political Economy of the Securities Act of 1933', *Journal of Legal Studies*, 30 (January 2001), pp. 1–31.
10. E. J. Kelly, 'Legislative History of the Glass–Steagall Act', in I. Walter (ed.), *Deregulating Wall Street. Commercial Bank Penetration of the Corporate Securities Market* (New York: Wiley, 1985), pp. 42–3.
11. D. M. Kotz, *Bank Control of Large Corporations in the United States* (Berkeley, CA: University of California Press, 1978), p. 43.
12. B. J. Klebaner, 'Banking Reform in the New Deal Era', *Banca Nazionale del Lavoro Quarterly Review* (September 1991), pp. 319–41.
13. R. S. Kroszner, 'The Evolution of Universal Banking and its Regulation(s) in Twentieth Century America', in A. Saunders and I. Walter (eds), *Universal Banking. Financial System Design Reconsidered* (New York: Stern New York University Salomon Center, 1996), p. 74.
14. E. N. White, 'Banking Innovation in the 1920s: The Growth of National Banks' Financial Services', *Business and Economic History*, 12 (1984), pp. 92–104, on p. 102.
15. Ibid., p. 95.
16. P. G. Mahoney, 'The Political Economy of the Securities Act of 1933', *Journal of Legal Studies*, 30 (January 2001), pp. 1–31, on p. 8.
17. J. Barron Baskin and P. J. Miranti jr, *A History of Corporate Finance* (Cambridge: Cambridge University Press, 1997).
18. Mahoney, 'The Political Economy of the Securities Act', p. 18.
19. R. S. Kroszner and R. G. Rajan, 'Is the Glass–Steagall Act Justified? A Study of the US Experience with Universal Banking Before 1933', *American Economic Review*, 84:4 (1994), pp. 810–32, on p. 812). Interlocking directorates and overlapping officers were also common.
20. W. N. Peach, *The Security Affiliates of National Banks* (Baltimore, MD: Johns Hopkins Press, 1941), p. 83.
21. Ibid., p. 20.
22. Carosso, *Investment Banking in America*, p. 287.
23. Ibid., p. 282.
24. C. Williams, 'Investment Trusts under the Microscope', *Magazine of Wall Street*, (29 October 1932), p. 26.
25. Carosso, *Investment Banking in America*, p. 291.
26. Kotz, *Bank Control of Large Corporations in the United States*, p. 48.
27. Conti, 'Finanza di impresa e capitale di rischio in Italia (1870–1939)', p. 323.
28. P. Sraffa, 'The Bank Crisis in Italy', *Economic Journal*, 32:126 (1922), pp. 178–97, on p. 195.
29. Ibid., p. 196.
30. R. Mattioli, 'I problemi attuali del credito', *Mondo economico*, 17:2 (1962), pp. 27–31, on p. 28. *Catoblepismo* is untranslatable, but it implies the pathological manifestation of a perverse auto-referential concentration and entanglement of powers (see M. Onado, 'La lunga rincorsa: la costruzione del sistema finanziario', in P. Ciocca and G. Toniolo (eds),

Storia Economica d'Italia. 3. Industrie, mercati, istituzioni. 2. I vincoli e le opportunità (Rome-Bari: Editori Laterza, 2003), p. 404.

31. P. Ciocca and G. Toniolo, 'Industry and Finance in Italy, 1918–1940', *Journal of European Economic History*, 13:2 (1984), pp. 113–36; H. P. Minsky, 'Banking and Industry between the Two Wars: The United States', *Journal of European Economic History*, 13:2 (1984), pp. 235–72.

32. Minsky, 'Banking and Industry', p. 247.

33. S. Battilossi, 'Banche miste, gruppi di imprese e società finanziarie (1914–1933)', in G. Conti and S. La Francesca (eds), *Banche e reti di banche nell'Italia postunitaria. Vol I. Persistenze e cambiamenti nel sistema finanziario e creditizio* (Bologna: Il Mulino, 2000), pp. 307–52.

34. ASIRI, fascicolo carte Softit, 'Atto costitutivo della società', in G. Toniolo, *L'economia italiana (1861–1940)* (Rome-Bari: Laterza, 1978), p. 293.

35. Royal decrees of 7 September 1926, No. 1511 and 6 November 1926, No. 1830.

36. Underwriting and distributing securities (bonds and stocks) beyond the banks' home cities was still forbidden by branching restrictions; again, state-chartered affiliates were organized to circumvent this ban.

37. M. Friedman and A. Schwartz, *A Monetary History of the United States 1867–1960* (Princeton, NJ: Princeton University Press, 1963); M. D. Bordo and J. G. Haubrich, 'Credit Crises, Money and Contractions: An Historical View', NBER Working Paper 15389 (2009).

38. Up to that time most bank failures had occurred in rural areas; furthermore, the Bank of United States had over $200 million of deposits, as well as a distinctive name which made it resemble more an official bank than an ordinary state-chartered commercial bank. See M. Friedman and A. Schwartz, *The Great Contraction 1929–1933* (Princeton, NJ: Princeton University Press, 2008), pp. 26–7.

39. Report of a Subcommittee of the Senate Committee on Banking and Currency of 1931, cited in E. J. Kelly, 'Legislative History of the Glass–Steagall Act', in I. Walter (ed.), *Deregulating Wall Street. Commercial Bank Penetration of the Corporate Securities Market* (New York: Wiley, 1985), pp. 41–65, on p. 45. In general, the Federal Reserve System stressed that the bank failures (which mostly involved small or non-member banks) were due to bad bank management or to inevitable reactions to prior speculative excesses. The influential leading banks had in the past clashed with the rural banks mainly over branching issues and thus also showed little concern for their failures. See E. N. White, 'A Reinterpretation of the Banking Crisis of 1930', *Journal of Economic History*, 44:1 (1984), pp. 136–7).

40. T.-K. Go, *American Commercial Banks in Corporate Finance 1929–41. A Study in Banking Concentration* (New York: Garland, 1999).

41. Friedman and Schwartz, *The Great Contraction 1929–1933*, pp. 31–2.

42. M. Friedman and A. Schwartz, *A Monetary History of the United States 1867–1960* (Princeton, NJ: Princeton University Press, 1963).

43. 'I think it is fair to say that what happened in Germany, in England, and in Central Europe generally has been a cause of disturbance in the mental attitude of bankers and business men in this country ... We cannot control conditions in foreign countries, but we can do our best to counteract their disastrous effects on our own industries by providing a bulwark for the banks upon which the strain falls most heavily' (Remark by Walcott, Congressional Record-Senate, 7 January 1932, p. 1465).

44. The RFC was funded mainly through the Treasury which, in turn, sold bonds to the public.
45. 'The two developments may have been unrelated' (Friedman and Schwartz, *The Great Contraction*, p. 45). See J. R. Mason, 'Do Lender of Last Resort Policies Matter? The Effects of Reconstruction Finance Corporation Assistance to Banks during the Great Depression', *Journal of Finance Services Research*, 20:1 (2001), pp. 77–95, for an empirical assessment of the impact the RFC had on the US economy, in a political economy perspective.
46. Remark by Glass, Congressional Record-Senate, 3 March 1932, p. 5245.
47. The required publication of the names of banks borrowing from RFC led in fact to bank runs and proved to be a huge disincentive against using this facility.
48. R. W. Goldsmith, *Financial Institutions* (New York: Random House, 1968).
49. Kotz, *Bank Control of Large Corporations in the United States*, p. 52.
50. Goldsmith, *Financial Institutions*.
51. Banca Commerciale Italiana, *Relazione annuale di bilancio*, 1931.
52. *Convenzione* of 20 February 1931, in ACS, ASIRI, serie nera, cart.1 and *Convenzione* of 31 October 1931, in ASBCI, Sofindit, cart. 374, fasc. 1. The latter is also published in G. Guarino and G. Toniolo (eds), *La Banca d'Italia e il sistema bancario 1919–1936* (Rome-Bari: Laterza, 1993).
53. Royal legislative decree of 13 November 1931, No. 1398.
54. ASBI, Fondo Beneduce, b. 9, fasc. 4.
55. G. Lombardo, *L'Istituto Mobiliare Italiano. Modello istituzionale e indirizzi operativi: 1931-1936* (Bologna: Il Mulino, 1998), pp. 38–9.
56. A. Confalonieri, 'Il ruolo delle istituzioni creditizie nella canalizzazione del risparmio agli investimenti produttivi', in *Atti del convegno internazionale di studi per il 50° anniversario della fondazione dell'IMI* (Rome: IMI, 1983).
57. 'Memorandum by Comit to the Minister of Finance, Jung' of 14 November 1932, in ASBCI, Carte Mattioli, cart. 1; 'Letter by Toeplitz to Jung' of 6 December 1932, in ASBCI, Carte Mattioli, cart. 1.
58. The IMI management believed it had to use this instrument gradually in financial markets 'which almost totally lacked in experience and traditions' (remark by Mayer, Meeting of IMI Board of Directors, in ASIMI, Verbali del Consiglio di Amministrazione-IMI, vol. 1, 1931–4, II session, p. 18). Mutual funds only developed in Italy many decades later, in the 1980s.
59. Law of 23 January 1933, No 5.
60. Speech of Steagall in the House of Representatives on 20 May 1933, reported in Congressional Record-Appendix, 22 May 1933, p. 4039.
61. While commercial banks were removed from the field of investment banking, they retained their trust activities, as these were recognized as traditional banking services. As a result, commercial banks could purchase and sell equity securities on behalf of fiduciary customers and could also vote the securities they held in trust.
62. 'The unholy alliance between the brokerage office and the bank must be broken. Up to now it has been possible for directors and officers of a brokerage house to be directors of a national or member bank. This has grave dangers. It violates the fundamental principle of the lawyers' code of ethics – that of undivided allegiance. In banking as elsewhere, no man can serve two masters ... If the men who are to determine the type and character of the banks' investments are at the same time promoters and sellers of these securities, the

bank will be prevented from acting with untrammelled judgement' (Remark by Kopple-
man, Congressional Record-House, 22 May 1933, p. 3996).

63. Extension of remarks by Bacon in the House of Representatives on 22 May 1933,
reported in Congressional Record-Appendix, 23 May 1933, p. 4148.

64. 'The Future of the Banking Investigation' by D. U. Fletcher, chairman of the Senate
Committee on Banking and Currency, published in *Today* on 30 December 1933 and
printed in the Congressional Record-Appendix on 11 January 1934, p. 494.

65. Cited in C., 'Roosevelt's First Year: Twelve Epochal Months', *New York Times*, 4 March
1934, p. 21; emphasis added.

66. Remark by Kelly, Congressional Record-House, 15 January 1934, p. 642.

67. Remark by Steagall, Congressional Record-House, 29 January 1935, p. 1146.

68. Société des Nations *Rapport au Conseil sur les travaux de la Soixante-huitième Session du
Comité Financier*, 15–20 June, Geneva, p. 17; E. N. White 'Lessons from the History of
Bank Examination and Supervision in the United States, 1863–2008', in A. Gigliobi-
anco and G. Toniolo (eds), *Financial Market Regulation in the Wake of Financial Crises:
The Historical Experience*, Banca d'Italia, Workshops and Conferences No. 1 (2009), pp.
15–44, on p. 28.

69. Carosso, *Investment Banking in America*, p. 384.

70. What is commonly defined as the Italian Banking Act of 1936 is actually made up of the
law 7 March 1938, with amendments made by the successive 7 April 1938 law. These two
laws were the result of the conversion of two legislative decrees respectively of 12 March
1936 (No. 375) and of 17 July 1937 (No. 1400). The long parliamentary *iter* was not due
to any particular opposition but to administrative delays and deadlines.

71. On this topic see A. Gigliobianco and C. Giordano, 'Does Economic Theory Matter in
Shaping Banking Regulation? A Case-Study of Italy (1861–1936)', *Accounting, Economics and Law*, 2:1, art. 5 (2012), pp. 1–72.

72. The separation was formally reversed in 1947 when supervisory responsibilities were
again assigned directly to the Bank of Italy.

73. Istituto per la Ricostruzione Industriale, 1937; emphasis added.

74. S. Cassese, *Come è nata la legge bancaria del 1936* (Spoleto : Banca Nazionale del Lavoro,
1988).

75. In 1946, Title V was extended by law to the medium- and long-term institutions created after 1936, such as Mediobianca, and thus not enumerated in the original Title VI
(DLCPS 23 August 1946, No. 370). Hence within this category there were those created
before 1946 which continued to be regulated by their founding laws and by the few articles of Title VI and others which were instead under the penetrating control of Title V.

76. Royal legislative decree of 12 March 1936, No. 376, 'Esercizio del credito mobiliare da
parte di istituti di diritto pubblico', converted into the law of 18 January 1937, No. 169.

77. G. Lombardo and V. Zamagni, *L'Istituto Mobiliare Italiano, 1931–1998* (Bologna: Il
Mulino, 2009), p. 59.

78. See, for example, the Report by the Fascist Confederation of Workers of Credit and
Insurance Institutions of May 1935, p. 8, reported in Cassese, *Come è nata la legge bancaria del 1936*.

79. Camera dei deputati, 1939: vol XIII, doc. 1137, p. 4.

80. Ministero per la Costituente, Ministero per la Costituente, *Rapporto della commissione
economica presentato all'Assemblea Costituente, IV: Credito e Assicurazione, I: Relazione*
(Roma: Istituto Poligrafico dello Stato, 1946), p. 217.

81. Ibid., p. 236.

82. The latter two sources of funds could not exceed 15 times the equity of the institutions (Bank of Italy instructions, 'Mediobanca – disposizioni di massima', 22 October 1949, pratica 2/8, p. 1 in ASBI).
83. Letter from Menichella, Governor of the Bank of Italy to the Treasury, 14 December 1946, p. 4, in ASBI.
84. Letter from Banca di Credito Finanziario to Associazione Nazionale per le Casse di Risparmio, dated 28 April 1947, p. 2, in ASBI.
85. Letter from the Inspectorate to Banca di Credito Finanziario, 1 May 1946, p. 2 in ASBI, and the subsequent reply, 18 July 1946, p. 2, in ASBI. However, the divide between short and long-term within savings banks and *Istituti di diritto pubblico* was more blurry.
86. Discussion at the Camera on 23rd May 1936.
87. G. Ferri and P. Garofalo, 'La crisi finanziaria nella Grande Depressione in Italia', *Ricerche per la storia della Banca d'Italia*, 5 (Roma-Bari: Laterza, 1994), pp. 97–151, on p. 138.
88. However, there was a loophole in the Act: banks could attend the shareholder meetings of the firms whose stocks they held in their portfolio as collateral, due to contango loans, or as temporary deposits by clients. This possibility was abolished by law only in 1974 (law No. 216 of 7 June 1974).
89. Kotz, *Bank Control of Large Corporations in the United States*, p. 54.
90. Barbiellini Amidei and Impenna, 'Il mercato azionario e il finanziamento delle imprese negli anni Cinquanta'.
91. F. Allen and D. Gale, *Comparing Financial Systems* (Cambridge, MA: Massachusetts Institute of Technology Press, 2000), p. 34.
92. Remark by Steagall, Congressional Record-House, 1 May 1935.
93. Deposit banks in Italy could only 'flank long-term credit institutions with pre-funding operations' (Ministero per la Costituente, *Rapporto della commissione economica presentato all'Assemblea Costituente, IV*, p. 237).
94. Only in 1956, with the Bank Holding Company Act, was the ownership of banks by industrial firms more strictly regulated. This act required each company to register with the Federal Reserve and to obtain the Federal Reserve's approval to acquire stock in a bank if the purchase would result in ownership of more than 5 per cent of the bank's voting shares.
95. See, for example, J. G. Haubrich and J. A. C. Santos, 'Alternative Forms of Mixing Banking with Commerce: Evidence from American History', *Financial Markets, Institutions & Instruments*, 12:2 (2003), pp. 121–64, for a survey of the relationship between banking and commerce in the history of the US.
96. Go, *American Commercial Banks in Corporate Finance 1929–41*.

6 Ferguson, 'Regulation and Deregulation in a Time of Stagflation: Siegmund Warburg and the City of London in the 1970s'

1. See, for example, P. Krugman, 'Reagan Did It', *New York Times*, 31 May 2009.
2. P. Krugman, 'Financial Reform 101', *New York Times*, 1 April 2010. See also 'Punks and Plutocrats', *New York Times*, 28 March 2010.
3. P. Krugman, 'Making Banking Boring', *New York Times*, 9 April 2009.
4. R. A. Posner, *The Crisis of Capitalist Democracy* (Cambridge, MA: Harvard University Press, 2010).

5. S. Johnson and J. Kwak, *Thirteen Bankers: The Wall Street Takeover and the Next Financial Meltdown* (New York: Vintage, 2010).

6. See, for example, Lord Turner, 'After the Crises: Assessing the Costs and Benefits of Financial Liberalisation', Fourteenth C. D. Deshmukh Memorial Lecture, Mumbai, 15 February 2010.

7. B. Kelly Diary, 17 June 1971; 11 October 1971; 12 November 1971.

8. D. Kynaston, *The City of London. Vol. IV: A Club No More, 1945–2000* (London: Pimlico, 2001).

9. F. Capie, *The Bank of England: 1950s to 1979* (Cambridge: Cambridge University Press, 2010), pp. 589ff.

10. See N. H. Dimsdale, 'British Monetary Policy since 1945', in N. F. R. Crafts and N. W. C. Woodward (eds), *The British Economy since 1945* (Oxford: Oxford University Press, 1991), p. 108.

11. In 1960 there were seventy-seven foreign banks with branches in London, by 1970, 159, and by 1978, 395.

12. What follows is based on N. Ferguson, *High Financier: The Lives and Time of Siegmund Warburg* (London: Penguin Press, 2010).

13. Siegmund Warburg papers, London (henceforth SGW) VME/CL/CZ../2, Siegmund Warburg (henceforth SGW) to Philipson, 29 September 1945.

14. SGW VME/CL/CZ../2, SGW to Philipson, 17 January 1946.

15. R. Chernow, *The Death of the Banker: The Decline and Fall of the Great Financial Dynasties and the Triumph of the Small Investor* (New York: Vintage, 1997).

16. SGW Box 62, SGW 'Thinking Aloud about a Ten-years' Plan for K.L. & Co', 24 April 1953.

17. P. Stormonth Darling, *City Cinderella: The Life and Times of Mercury Asset Management* (London: Orion, 1999), pp. 112f.

18. Bank of England (henceforth BoE) C48/51, [D.E.B.] to the Chief Cashier, 22 May 1951.

19. BoE C48/291 45, Memorandum to Sir Kenneth Peppiatt, 20 July 1953.

20. *Economist*, 27 April 1957.

21. 'Warburg's Record', *Sunday Times*, 30 July 1961.

22. Barclays Capital, *Equity Gilt Study 2007* (London, 2008).

23. *Economist*, 13 September 1969, p. 95.

24. SGW Box 13, Fraser and Kelly, 'Note to the Bond Team', 4 February 1965. See also SGW to Sir Eric Roll, 22 February 1965.

25. J. H. Hambro and SGW, 'Action that Must be Taken Now; *The Times*, 20 November 1965. See also 'Crisis Warning from City Bankers', *Daily Telegraph*, 22 November 1965.

26. SGW Box 20, SGW to all Executive Directors, 31 October 1967.

27. K. Fleet, 'Modern Attitudes in Merchant Banking', *Sunday Telegraph*, n.d.

28. 'What Next for Merchant Banks', *Economist*, 21 June 1969, p. xlv.

29. A. Maddison, *The World Economy: A Millennial Perspective* (Paris: OECD, 2001), Table A1-d.

30. SGW VME/CL/CZ../2, SGW to Schubart, 26 September 1949.

31. SGW VME/CL/CZ../2, SGW Aphorisms.

32. Capie, *Bank of England*, p. 742.

33. R. Crossman, *The Backbench Diaries of Richard Crossman* (London: Holmes & Meier, 1981), pp. 606f.

34. G. O'Hara, *From Dreams to Disillusionment: Economic and Social Planning in 1960s Britain* (Basingstoke and New York: Palgrave Macmillan, 2007), p. 42. See in general, A. Cairncross, *The British Economy since 1945: Economic Policy and Performance, 1945–1990* (Oxford/Malden: Wiley, 1995), pp. 139–61.

35. Public Record Office/ UK National Archives (henceforth PRO) PREM 13/3153, Le Cheminant note, 19 September 1968. See also PRO PREM 13/2670, Note of a meeting, 10 December 1969.

36. 'DM's at 6½pc for Gas Council', *Daily Telegraph*, 18 March 1969.

37. SGW & Co. memorandum, 'UK Balance of Payments: Long-term Borrowing', 15 October 1971.

38. See most recently G. O'Hara, '"Dynamic, Exciting, Thrilling Change": The Wilson Government's Economic Policies, 1964–70', in G. O'Hara and H. Parr (eds), *The Wilson Governments 1964–1970 Reconsidered* (London and New York: Routledge, 2006), pp. 79–98.

39. Cairncross, *British Economy since 1945*, p. 175.

40. SGW VME/MA../ZZ../4, SGW Diary, 5 February 1942; 11 February 1944.

41. SGW Box 8, SGW to Mazur, 21 July 1962. Cf. Box 5, SGW to James Meade, 3 January 1961; SGW to Mazur, 18 January 1961; SGW to Furstenberg, 30 June 1961; Box 8, SGW to Leonard Keesing, 27 August 1962.

42. SGW Box 27, SGW to Dilworth, 30 April 1971. See also Box 28, SGW to Mazur, 13 November 1971; SGW to McConnell, 29 December 1971; DME/AA../CNZZ/5, SGW to Furstenberg, 31 December 1971.

43. SGW Box 29, SGW to Mazur, 25 March 1972.

44. PRO T 312/1849, Bancroft note, 18 January 1965.

45. C. King, *The Cecil King Diary: 1970–1974* (London: Jonathan Cape, 1975), pp. 106f.

46. SGW Box 34, SGW to Scholey, 17 July 1974.

47. Capie, *Bank of England*, pp. 716–27.

48. Ibid., pp. 488f.

49. Ibid., pp. 510f.

50. Dimsdale, 'British Monetary Policy', pp. 114–20. See also Cairncross, *British Economy since 1945*, p. 191.

51. Capie, *Bank of England*, p. 651.

52. Ibid, p. 527.

53. Ibid., pp. 519f.

54. M. Reid, *The Secondary Banking Crisis, 1973–75: Its Causes and Course* (London: Macmillan, 1982).

55. Capie, *Bank of England*, pp. 535ff.

56. Ibid., pp. 544, 549.

57. Ibid., p. 572.

58. Ibid., p. 577.

59. SGW Box 33, SGW to Wilson, 5 March 1973. See also the draft of a speech by Warburg, intended for Wilson's use, n.d., *c.* June 1973. Warburg gave Wilson the draft when they met on June 10: see SGW to Roll, 11 June 1973.

60. SGW Box 33, SGW to Roll, Grunfeld, Korner, et al., 1 March 1974.

61. SGW Box 33, SGW to Freddie Rubinski, 6 April 1974.

62. SGW Box 33, SGW to Roll, 11 June 1973.

63. SGW Box 35, SGW to Roll, Grunfeld, Korner et al., 21 January 1975.

64. SGW Box 36, SGW to Steiner, 18 March 1976.

65. See K. Burk and A. Cairncross, *Goodbye, Great Britain: The 1976 IMF Crisis* (New Haven, CT: Yale University Press, 1992).
66. E. Dimson, P. Marsh and M. Staunton, *Triumph of the Optimists: 101 Years of Global Investment Returns* (Princeton, NJ: Princeton University Press, 2002), p. 303, table 32–2.
67. J. Wechsberg, *The Merchant Bankers* (Boston, MA and Toronto: Pocket Books, 1966), p. 220.
68. SGW VME/CL/CZ../2, SGW to Goldmann, 5 and 6 August 1970.
69. Grunfeld interview.
70. SGW Box 29, SGW to Roll, Kelly, Spira et al., 10 April 1972.
71. SGW Box 33, SGW & Co. Memorandum, 'Index Linked Bonds', 10 June 1974; SGW to Harold Lever and Robert Armstrong, 11 June 1974; SGW to Roll et al., 11 June 1974. See also Lewisohn to SGW et al., 17 June 1974; SGW to Roll, Grunfeld, Seligman et al., 26 June 1974; DME/CO../RPBZ/6, Armstrong to SGW, 9 August 1974.
72. SGW VME/CL/CZ../2, Grunfeld to SGW, 11 February 1970.
73. SGW VME/CL/CZ../2, SGW to Grunfeld, Korner, Seligman et al., 24 February 1971; P. J. Mann note, 2 April 1971.
74. SGW VME/CL/CZ../2, Mann note, 9 June 1971.
75. SGW VME/CL/CZ../2, SGW to George Warburg, 17 March 1972.
76. SGW VME/CL/CZ../2, Grunfeld to Roll, 10 January 1973.
77. SGW Box 31, George Warburg to Grunfeld, 6 March 1973; Grunfeld to George Warburg, 6 March 1973.
78. SGW Box 34, SGW to Scholey, Grunfeld, Roll et al., 27 August 1974.
79. SGW Box 34, SGW to Scholey, Grunfeld, Roll et al., 20 July 1974. See also VME/CL/CZ../2, Scholey to SGW, 22 July 1974; Scholey to SGW, Grunfeld and Seligman, 22 July 1974; 23 July 1974.
80. SGW Box 34, SGW to Scholey, Grunfeld, Roll et al., 23 July 1974; VME/CL/CZ../2, SGW to Scholey, 24 July 1974.
81. SGW VME/CL/CZ../2, SGW Note, 29 July 1974.
82. SGW Box 34, SGW to Scholey, Grunfeld, Roll et al., 27 August 1974; VME/CL/CZ../2, George Warburg to SGW, 20 February 1975; SGW to George Warburg, 20 February 1975; Box 36, SGW to Roll, Grunfeld, Seligman et al., 6 May 1976.
83. SGW VME/CL/CZ../2, Scholey to SGW, Grunfeld and Seligman, 29 July 1974.
84. SGW VME/CL/CZ../2, Dalton to SGW and Scholey, 28 May 1976.
85. SGW Box 43, SGW to Roll, Scholey and Chairman's Committee, 14 January 1981.
86. 'Merchant Banking Renaissance', *Economist*, 31 March 1979.
87. Ibid., pp. 50–65.
88. SGW Box 42, SGW to Doris Levy, 9 December 1980.
89. Capie, *Bank of England*, pp. 600ff, 619.
90. Ibid., pp. 629–38.
91. T. Sargent, 'The Ends of Four Big Inflations', in R. E. Hall (ed.), *Inflation: Causes and Effects* (Chicago, IL: University of Chicago Press, 1982), pp. 41–97.
92. SGW DME/AA/CMZZ/5/, Scholey to Thatcher, 16 February 1981.
93. SGW Box 43, SGW to Joseph, 5 May 1981.
94. P. M. Williams (ed.), *The Diary of Hugh Gaitskell* (London: Jonathan Cape, 1983), p. 524.
95. SGW Box 43, SGW to Fisher, Smithers and Chairman's Committee, 16 March 1981.

96. SGW Box 42, SGW to Spira, 18 December 1980. See also Box 43, SGW to Roll, Scholey and Chairman's Committee, 14 January 1981.
97. SGW Box 43, SGW to Grunfeld, Fisher, Garmoyle et al., 15 January 1981.
98. SGW Box 43, SGW to Sir Edwin Leather, 15 January 1981.
99. SGW DME/CO../RPBZ/6, Keith Joseph to SGW, 10 March 1981.
100. SGW Box 43, SGW to James Leigh Pemberton, 1 June 1981.

7 Financial Market Integration: An Insurmountable Challenge to Modern Trade Policy?

1. See W. Werner, *Handelspolitik für Finanzdienste*, Schriften zur Monetären Ökonomie (Baden-Baden: Nomos, 2004).
2. The main focus of this paper is on the emergence of trade policy initiatives for financial services in Europe and the WTO in the latter half of the twentieth century. There have, however, been other preferential trade agreements, such as the North American Free Trade Agreement (NAFTA), that have included financial services in the last fifteen years. For an overview of the service sector provisions of the many preferential trade agreements that have been concluded more recently see H. Lim, J. Marchetti and M. Roy, *Services Liberalization in the New Generation of Preferential Trade Agreements (PTAs): How Much Further than the GATS?* World Trade Organization, Staff Working Paper ERSD-2006-07 (Geneva: World Trade Organization, 2006).
3. The terminology used in this paper regarding forms of and barriers to international trade in financial services is derived from the GATS agreement, the most broad-based and systematic approach to insurance liberalization to date. International activities, including 'cross-border supply of services' (or trade) and the 'operations of foreign firms' (or commercial presence), is restricted by barriers to market access and national treatment. Besides these two economically significant modes of trans-border supply of services, the GATS framework agreement makes reference to two more modes, which involve the cross-border movement of individuals (or natural persons): 'consumption abroad' and 'presence of individuals'.
4. For a historical treatise on the monetary policy trilemma (or 'impossible trinity'), see M. Obstfeld, J. C. Shambaugh and A. M. Taylor, 'The Trilemma in History: Tradeoffs among Exchange Rates, Monetary Policies, and Capital Mobility', *Review of Economics and Statistics*, 87 (2005), pp. 423–38.
5. In 1948, sixteen states belonged to the OEEC: Austria, Belgium, Denmark, France, Greece, Great Britain, Iceland, Italy, Ireland, Luxembourg, Netherlands, Norway, Switzerland and Turkey. The Federal Republic of Germany and Spain became full members of the organization in 1949 and 1959 respectively. Canada and the US were associated members as of 1950.
6. The OEEC's early liberalization initiatives on insurance trade were discussed almost exclusively in the legal literature. See, for example, Lorenz-Liburnau, who reported regularly on changes in the insurance provisions of the Code of Liberalization of Trade and Invisible Transactions. H. Lorenz-Liburnau, 'Integration der Europäischen Versicherungswirtschaft in Vergangenheit, Gegenwart und Zukunft', *Die Versicherungsrundschau*, 17 (1962), pp. 70–85. An exception is Dürr, who offers an analysis from an economic point of view. E. Dürr, *Die Liberalisierung des Internationalen Versicherungsverkehrs* (Berlin, 1956). For an unabridged analysis of the development of multilateral

trade policy for insurance services see W. Werner, 'Multilateral Insurance Liberalization, 1948–2008', in R. Pearson (ed.), *The Development of International Insurance* (Pickering & Chatto, 2010), pp. 85–102.

7. For a discussion of the early development of European reinsurance markets, see R. Pearson, 'The Development of Reinsurance Markets in Europe during the Nineteenth Century', *Journal of European Economic History*, 24 (1995), pp. 557–71. After the end of the Second World War liberalization of reinsurance trade was strongly supported by industry representatives. See M. Grossmann, 'Rückversicherungszahlungen in Drittlandwährungen', *Schweizerische Versicherungs-Zeitschrift*, 17 (1949/50), pp. 331–7.

8. The protectionist effects of prudential regulation are analysed by H. D. Skipper, 'Protectionism in the Provision of International Insurance Services', *Journal of Risk and Insurance*, 54 (1987), pp. 55–85; D. L. Bickelhaupt and R. Bar-Niv, *International Insurance. Managing Risk in the World* (New York, 1983); R. Carter and G. M. Dickinson, *Obstacles to the Liberalization of Trade in Insurance* (London: Thames Essay 58, 1992). For examinations of the role of prudential regulation in the multilateral liberalization of insurance trade, see R. K. Shelp, *Beyond Industrialization* (New York: Praeger, 1981), p. 131; Carter and Dickinson, *Obstacles*, p. 40; H. D. Skipper, 'International Trade in Insurance', in C. E. Barfield (ed.), *International Financial Markets. Harmonization versus Competition* (Washington, DC: AEI Press, 1996), pp. 151–224, at p. 209.

9. Another trade policy initiative of the OECD which focused on FDI was the Multilateral Agreement on Investment (MAI). This agreement was to become a broad-based legally binding instrument covering a large number of industries. Negotiations, however, were cancelled in 1998. For more details on the MAI and the National Treatment Instrument see Werner, *Handelspolitik für Finanzdienste*, p. 118.

10. See Carter and Dickinson, *Obstacles*, p. 126; W. Witherell, 'The Liberalization of International Service Transactions. The Experience of Developed Countries', in United Nations Centre on Transnational Corporations, *Services and Development, The Role of Foreign Direct Investment in Trade*, ST/CTC/95 (New York, 1989), pp. 143–50, on p. 147.

11. The six founding members of the EEC are Belgium, the Federal Republic of Germany, France, Italy, Luxembourg and the Netherlands.

12. For a discussion of this directive and other insurance directives see M. D. Bordo, 'The Bretton Woods International Monetary System. A Historical Overview', in M. D. Bordo, and B. Eichengreen (eds), *A Retrospective on the Bretton Woods System: Lessons for International Monetary Reform* (Chicago, IL: University of Chicago Press, 1993), pp. 3–108; Swiss Re, *Deregulation and Liberalization of Market Access. The European Insurance Industry on the Threshold of a New Era in Competition* (=Sigma 7/1996); Swiss Re, *The Path to the Single Insurance Market. An Economic Retrospective* (= Sigma 7/1996).

13. While concepts used for the liberalization of services trade in the EEC and the EU are not identical to those used under the GATS framework agreement, the following terms are roughly equivalent: (a) cross-border supply of services: free movement of services, (b) operations of foreign firms: freedom of establishment, (c) service consumption abroad by a natural person and (d) service provision abroad by a natural person: free movement of persons.

14. For a discussion of the banking directives see Bank of England, 'The Developing Single Market in Financial Services', *Bank of England Quarterly Bulletin*, 34 (November 1994), pp. 341–6.

15. See A. F. P. Bakker, *The Liberalization of Capital Movements in Europe. The Monetary Committee and Financial Integration 1958–1994* (Dordrecht: Kluwer Academic Publishers, 1996).

16. See D. J. Mathieson and L. Rojas-Suàrez, *Liberalization of the Capital Account. Experiences and Issues*, International Monetary Fund, Occasional Paper 103 (Washington, DC, 1993).

17. Capital account liberalization was also a prerequisite for the introduction of the Economic and Monetary Union in the Treaty of Maastricht in 1992. See J. Delors, *Report on Economic and Monetary Union in the European Community* (Luxemburg: OOPEC, 1989); D. Servais, *Ein Europäischer Finanzraum*, Kommission der Europäischen Gemeinschaften (Luxemburg, 1988).

18. Consequently, quite a few authors count as principles of the Single Market programme not only mutual recognition and minimum harmonization, but also home country control. For a discussion of the application of the liberalization principles of the Single Market to financial services, see S. J. Key, *Mutual Recognition. Integration of the Financial Sector in the European Community*, Federal Reserve Bulletin, 75 (Washington, DC, 1989), pp. 591–609.

19. For an example to the contrary see S. J. Key, *Financial Integration in the European Community*, Board of Governors of the Federal Reserve System, International Finance Discussion Papers 349 (Washington, DC, 1989).

20. See Bakker, *Liberalization*.

21. The position of the US in the GATS negotiations is presented in US Department of the Treasury, *National Treatment Study. Report to Congress on Foreign Government Treatment of U.S. Commercial Banking and Securities Organizations* (Springfield, 1986, 1990); US Department of the Treasury, *Report on the Status of Financial Services Negotiations under the General Agreement on Trade in Services* (Washington, DC, 1995).

22. The sequencing and coordination of financial market reforms in developing countries is discussed in C. Karacadag, et al., *Managing Risks in Financial Market Development. The Role of Sequencing*, IMF Working Paper 03/116 (Washington, DC, 2003). For an overview of developing countries' protectionist views on international trade in insurances, see early studies by the United Nations presented in UNCTAD, *Insurance in the Context of Services and the Development Process* (TD/B/1014) (Geneva, 1984). For a more liberal view, United Nations presented in UNCTAD, *Services and the Development Process* (TD/B/1008) (New York, 1985); United Nations presented in UNCTAD, *The Outcome of the Uruguay Round. An Initial Assessment, Supporting Papers to the Trade and Development Report 1994* (UNCTAD/TDR/14) (New York, 1994), pp. 145–84.

23. W. Werner, *Das WTO-Finanzdienstleistungsabkommen* (Munich: Oldenbourg, 1999)

24. M. Kono et al., *Opening Markets in Financial Services and the Role of the GATS*, World Trade Organization (Geneva, 1997); S. Claessens and T. Glaessner, *Internationalization of Financial Services in Asia*, World Bank, Policy Research Paper 1911 (Washington, DC, 1997).

25. See B. Hoekman and P. Sauvé, *Liberalizing Trade in Services*, World Bank, Discussion Paper 243 (Washington, DC, 1994); A. Mattoo, 'Financial Services and the WTO. Liberalisation Commitments of the Developing and Transition Economies', *World Economy*, 23 (1990), pp. 351–86; K. Nicolaids and J. P. Trachtmann, 'From Policed Regulation to Managed Recognition in GATS', in P. Sauvé and R. M. Stein (eds), *GATS 2000. New Directions in Services Trade Liberalization* (Washington, DC: Center for Business and Government, 2000), pp. 241–82.

26. See, for example, J. J. Schott, *The Uruguay Round: An Assessment* (Washington, DC: Institute for International Economics, 1994).

27. E. Helleiner, 'A Bretton Woods Moment? The 2007–08 Crisis and the Future of Global Finance', *International Affairs*, 86:3 (2010), pp. 619–36.

8 Something Old and Something New: Novel and Familiar Drivers of the Latest Crisis

1.   C. Mackay, *Extraordinary Popular Delusions and the Madness of Crowds* (1841; Radford: Wilder Publications, 2008). C. Kindleberger, *Manias, Panics and Crashes* (1978; New York: Wiley, 2000).
2.   G. Akerlof and R. Shiller, *Animal Spirits, How Human Psychology Drives the Economy and Why it Matters to Global Capitalism* (Princeton, NJ: Princeton University Press, 2009). See D. Kahneman, P. Slovic and A. Tversky, *Judgement under Uncertainty Heuristics and Biases* (Cambridge: Cambridge University Press, 1982), for a discussion of how economic agents made decisions on the bases of rough heuristics, i.e. rules of thumb. The widespread application of these rules by multiple agents can then generate self-reinforcing herd effects.
3.   See D. Vayanos and P. Woolley, *An Institutional Theory of Momentum and Reversal* (London: LSE, 2008), and G. Soros, *The New Paradigm for Financial Markets, The Credit Crisis of 2008 and What It Means* (New York: PublicAffairs, 2008).
4.   I. Fisher, 'The Debt-Deflation Theory of Great Depressions', *Econometrica* (1933), pp. 337–57.
5.   B. S. Bernanke, *Non-monetary Effects of the Financial Crisis: Essays on the Great Depression* (Princeton, NJ: Princeton University Press, 2000).
6.   H. Minsky, *Stabilising an Unstable Economy* (New Haven, CT: Yale University Press, 1986).
7.   See A. Turner, 'What Do Banks Do, What Should They Do?' Lecture at Cass Business School, 17 March 2010 for a more detailed analysis of this characterization of bank functions.
8.   W. Bagehot, *Lombard Street: A Description of the Money Market* (London, 1873).
9.   C. Reinhardt and K. Rogoff, *This Time is Different – Eight Centuries of Financial Folly* (Princeton, NJ: Princeton University Press, 2009).
10. IMF, *A Fair and Substantial Contribution by the Financial Sector*, Interim Report to the G20, April 2010.
11. See Turner, 'What Do Banks Do, What Should They Do?' for a detailed exposition of the case for macro-prudential levers.
12. See, for instance, J. Stiglitz, 'Using Tax Policy to Curb Speculative Short Term Trading', *Journal of Financial Services Research* (1989), pp. 101–15.
13. M. Schularick and A. M. Taylor, *Credit Booms Gone Bust: Monetary Policy, Leveraged Cycles and Financial Crises 1870 to 2008*, NBER working paper number 15512 (November 2009).
14. I. R. G. King and R. Levine, 'Finance and Growth: Schumpeter Might Be Right', *Quarterly Journal of Economics* (1993), pp. 717–37, or P. L. Rousseau and R. Sylla, *Emerging Financial Markets and Early US Growth*, NBER Working Paper 7448 (December 1999).
15. See Turner, 'What Do Banks Do, What Should They Do?'
16. Thus if attempted deleveraging, driven by regulatory intervention, produces a slower growth in private credit, and if this slower private credit growth is matched pari passu with a reduction in nominal demand growth, the ratio of the stock of private credit to nominal demand can never reduce.
17. M. Friedman and A. Schwartz, *A Monetary History of the Unites States 1867–1960* (1963; Princeton, NJ: Princeton University Press, 1993).

INDEX

Abelijn, Abraham, 22–3, 24–5
agricultural sector
    banks, Netherlands, 2, 9, 37, 39–54
    co-operatives, crisis/ recovery, 1930s,
        50–3
    credit, 38–9
    depression, Netherlands, 38
    protective measures, 39
    unions, and co-operative banks, 39
Allgemeine Versicherungs-Gesellschaft
    Helvetia, 56–7
American Express, 120
Amidei, Federico Barbiellini, ix
    on US vs. Italy banking legislation, 10,
        65–83
Amsterdam
    Court of Aldermen, 23, 26, 29
    stock exchange, 2
    trading community, 18–19
Anglo-American securities regulation, 18
Anglo-Dutch War, Second, 28
Arrow Debreu equilibrium, 130, 135
asset management, Warburg and, 89
asset price appreciation, driving credit sup-
    ply, 131
Athias, Jacob, 17, 31
auctions, co-operative, 38
audits, co-operative banks, 47–8
Austrian Credit-Anstalt, 59

Banca Commerciale Italiana (Comit), 70,
    72, 73
Banco di Napoli, Special Credit Section, 78
Banco di Roma, 70, 73
Banco di Sicilia, Special Credit Section, 78
Bank for International Settlements (BIS),
    12, 107

on new financial products licensing, 140
    see also Basel Committee
Bank of England
    credit controls relaxation, 95
    and regulation, 87
    and secondary banks failure 1970s, 97–8
    on Warburg, 88–9
Bank of Italy, 66, 72, 73
    and Banking Act 1936, 78
Bank of United States, failure, 71
bank–industry links
    market ties, 10, 65–83
    US/ Italy comparison, 82
banking industry
    alternative governance culture, 2, 37–54
    credit intermediation, and risk, 130–1
    crises
        1930s, 65–6, 71–3
        Dutch, 1920s, 43–4
    economic crises and, 2
    EEC liberalization directives and,
        116–20
    holding companies (BHCs), Glass–
        Steagall 1933 provisions, 74–5
    legislation, US vs. Italy, 10, 65–83
    Netherlands, structure, 38
    policy, central co-operatives, 50–2
    system, structural reform, 134
banking/ insurance crisis, 1920s, Nether-
    lands, 39
bankruptcy/ default rigidity, effects, 129–30
banks
    big, and government support, 142
    capital/ liquidity ratios, 3
    central, financial policies, 2, 8, 11–12
    inherently risky institutions, 1, 130–1

lending against commercial real estate, and crises, 132–3
    leveraged/ fractional reserve, 130–1
    and structured credit market, 7
    too big to fail issue, 134, 139–40, 142
Banks of National Interest, (BINs), 76, 77
Banner, Stuart, on Anglo-American securities regulation, 18
Barber, Anthony, Warburg on, 94, 104
Barings Crisis 1890, 98
Basel Committee, BIS, 107
    Basel II capital adequacy regime, 137
    Basel III regulatory framework, 140, 141
    and capital leverage/ liquidity rules, 133
Basler Handelsbank, 56
Belgium
    Antwerp, commercial contracting history, 16–18
    co-operative banking sector, 9
Bernanke, Ben
    on bankruptcy, 129
    Essays on the Great Depression, 138
Besso, Giuseppe, 57
Besso, Marco, 57
blame, no consensus, 2
Boerenhypotheekbank NV, 41
bonds to stocks shift losses, SR, 60
Bouwer, Hans, 21, 22–3
Bretton Woods system, 10, 87, 109, 113
    Warburg on, 93
Britain *see* United Kingdom
brokers/ banking separation
    Italy, 66–7
    US, 67

C. W. Capital Ltd (Cripps Warburg), 100–1
Callaghan, James, 92
capital account liberalization, 119–20
capital leverage/ liquidity rules, global regulatory agenda, 133–4
capital/ liquidity ratios, banks, 3
cashiers, co-operative agricultural banks, 40
Cassis de Dijon case, 119
CCB, discount facility revoked, 43
Cedar Holdings, 98
central banks, financial policies, 2, 8, 11–12
central co-operatives (CCB & CCRB), 40–54

conservative banking policy, 50–2
internal controls/ monitoring, 46–9, 54
liquidity policy, 51–2
local credit lending/ savings, trends, 49–50
member banks 1899–1939, 42*f*3.1, 42*t*3.1, 44, 45*t*3.2, 45*t*3.3
Citicorp, 120
City of London, 1970s, 86–7
clearing/ settlement infrastructure, 140–1
Clement, Piet, ix
    historical view, 5–12
clergy, and agricultural co-operative banks, 39
co-operative agricultural banks, 2, 9, 37, 39–54
    administration training, 47
    articles of association, 46–7
    banking supervision, 46–50
    commercial banks, liquidity comparison 1930s, 52
    controls/ monitoring, 46–9, 54
co-operative purchasing associations, 38
collateralized debt obligations (CDO), 5
Collegie vande Actionisten, 29, 30
Collegie vande Blommisten, 30–1
commercial banks
    development, US, 67, 68–9
    see also national banks
    investment banking
        split legislation, 65
        US/ Italy comparison, 80–1
    liquidity comparison 1930s, 52
commercial contracting, Low Countries, 16
commercial law development, north-western Europe, 18
commercial real estate, bank lending against, and crises, 132–3
Common Market
    and financial services industry, 115–20
    and prudential regulation, 117–18
    trade policy initiatives, 108, 115–20
    see also European Economic Community (EEC)
consumer credit regulation, 87
contract enforcement
    Dutch secondary shares market, 8–9, 13–35
    stock exchanges, 2

conveyance rule, VOC shares, 20–1
Coöperatieve Centrale Boerenleenbank
  (CCB), 40–54
Coöperatieve Centrale Christelijke Boerenleenbank (CCCB), 40, 43
Coöperatieve Centrale Raiffeisen-Bank
  (CCRB), 40–54
corporate governance, 2, 3
Cotinho, Samuel, 26–7
Court of Holland, 16–17, 19, 23, 28
  cases summaries, 34–5*t*2.1–2.3
  litigation procedure, 19–20
  sentences, 18
credit
  access, and financial innovation, 6
  contracts, disruption potential, 129–31
  co-operative banks, 41, 44–5, 49–51
  cycle, 1
  default swaps (CDS), 5
  derivatives market, 132
  extension volatility, and asset prices issue,
    134
  markets, volatility effects, 130
  potentially destabilizing effects, 130
  pricing/ supply booms/ busts, impact,
    128–9
credit securities
  marketable, 131–2
  pooling/ tranching, 132
credit-driven asset cycles, 130
Credito Italiano (Credit), 72, 73
Cripps Warburg, 100–1
Cripps, Milo, 100
Cripps, Stafford, Warburg and, 105
crises, co-operative banks performance during, 9, 37, 39–54
crisis 2007, drivers, 127–38
Crockett, Andrew, and credit controls
  relaxation, 95
Crown Agents, rescue, 98

da Cunha, Sebastiaen, 26, 28–9, 31–2
dairy co-operatives, 38
de Groot, Hugo (Grotius), law compilation,
  18
de Meijere, Maerten, 22–3
De Nederlandsche Bank (DNB), 39, 43–4,
  51, 52

de Vries, Johan, on DNB, 39
de-leveraging, 5
debt contracts
  specificity of nominal value, effects, 129
  specificity of tenor, effects, 129
debt default/ bankruptcy rigidity, effects,
  129–30
debt deflation, effects, 129
deflation, economic harm capacity, 129
deposit insurance, 105
deposits use, US/ Italy comparison, 79–80
derivatives, associated risks control, 140
Discount Office Principal, 87
disposals attempts, SR, 63–4
Doha negotiations, 120
dollar assets vs. gold, 62–3
Duarte, Manuel Levy, short sales, 17
Dutch *see* Netherlands
Dutch East India Company (VOC), 8–9,
  13–35
  conveyance rule, 20–1
  share prices, declines, 28, 31–2
  share transfers, 13–18, 14*f*2.1, 15*f*2.2

easy money policies, 1, 2
Economist, on Warburg, 89
economy, real, financial system relation to,
  135–7
Eichengreen, Barry, on financial history, 12
Escher, Alfred, 57
Euro–Dollar Market, 117
Eurobond market, Warburg and, 90, 92
European Economic Community (EEC)
  Common Market
    and financial services industry, 115–20
    and prudential regulation, 117–18
    and tariffs, 115
    trade policy initiatives, 108, 115–20
    transition to single market, 115–20
  First Banking Directive, 117–18
  liberalization directives
    and banking industry, 116–20
    and insurance trade, 116
  Second Banking Directive, 118–20
  Treaty of Rome, 117
  UK and, 104
  see also European Union
European Monetary Agreement (EMA), 110

European Payments Union (EPU), 110
European Recovery Programme (ERP), 110
European Union
    and GATS financial services programme,
      120–1
    Single Market programme (EU),
      115–20, 121, 123–4
    trade policy initiatives, 108, 115–20
exchange-traded forward contracts (futures),
    6

Ferguson, Niall, ix-x
    on regulation and stagflation, 10–11,
      85–106
Fforde, John, and credit controls relaxation,
    95
financial innovation, as positive force, 6–7
financial instability hypothesis, 5
financial intensity, value-creative limits,
    135–6
financial markets
    integration, and trade policy, 107–25
    products licensing, 140
    and stagflation, 99–102
    susceptibility, 128
financial regulation debate, White on, 12,
    139–42
financial services
    EEC liberalization directives and,
      116–20
    GATS negotiations, 120–3
    and open markets, 11, 107–25
financial system
    crisis caused within, 127–38
    evolution and volatility, 11–12, 127–38
    inherent fragility, 1
    relation to real economy, 135–7
Financial Stability Board (FSB), 107
    and capital leverage/ liquidity rules, 133
Financial Times, share indexs, 95, 96, 97*t*6.3,
    99–100
Fisher, Irving, on debt deflation effects, 129
flexible exchange rates, and capital account
    liberalization, 119–20
foreign direct investment (FDI), 110
    EU and, 119
    OECD Code and, 114–15
forward market, Holland, 17–19, 22–35

Frans van Cruijsbergen, 23
Friedman, M. and A. Schwartz, *The Great
    Contraction 1929–1933*, 138
futures, 6

G20, 107
    and Basel III, 141
    and capital leverage/ liquidity rules, 133
Gaitskell, Hugh, on Warburg, 105
General Agreement on Tariffs and Trade
    (GATT), 107, 108, 109
    Tokyo Round, 110
General Agreement on Trade in Services
    (GATS), 108, 120–3, 124, 125
    and independent regulatory policies,
      122–3
    liberalization commitments choices, 122
    negotiations, financial services, 120–3,
      124–5
Genoa stock market, and 1907 crash, 66
Germany
    financial crisis 1931, 39, 59
    reinsurance companies, 56–7
Giordano, Claire, x
    on US vs. Italy banking legislation, 10,
      65–83
Glass–Steagall Act 1932, 71, 74–5, 80
    restoration calls, 85
global regulatory agenda, capital leverage/
    liquidity rules, 133–4
globalization process, and modern trade
    policy, 107–25
Goldman Sachs, 67
Goldmann, Nahum, Warburg and, 100
governance culture, alternative, cooperative
    banking, 2, 37–54
government intervention, Warburg and, 90
governments, financial policies, 8, 11–12
Great Depression, 12, 71–2, 127
    learning from, 138
    Swiss Re and, 1, 9–10, 55–6, 58–64
Great Moderation, 127
Greece, public finance, 127
greed, and good corporate governance, 2
Greenspan, Alan
    Greenspan doctrine, 136
    'irrational exuberance', 8

Greif, Avner, on North Africa/ Italy traders' coalitions, 18
Grossmann, Moritz, 56–7
Grunfeld, Henry
George Warburg and, 100, 101
on Warburg, 100

Haeck, Severijn, 28
Haliassos, Michael, on financial products, 6
Hambro, Jocelyn, 90
Hanzebank, 's-Hertogenbosch, 43
HBOS, and commercial real estate, 132
Heath, Edward, government, 93–9, 104
hedge funds, 138, 141
hidden reserves, Swiss Re, 1, 10, 55–6, 61–4
Hill Samuel, 102
history and crisis prediction, 2–3, 5–12
Holland *see* Netherlands
Hollandsche Consultatiën, 18
honour/ reputation, and unenforceable deals, 29–33
Hoover administration, 71
hostile takeovers, Warburg and, 89
Howe, Geoffrey, Warburg on, 105
Hürlimann, Erwin, 58, 59–62
Huysmans, G. W. M., on 1930s crisis/ recovery, 53

index-linked bonds, Warburg and, 100
industrial firms, banks as holding companies, 68, 69
industrial firms, investment banks representation on boards, 67
inflation rates, selected OECD countries, 94*f*6.1
Ingves, Stefan, on punch bowl principle, 134
innovations, non-transparent, 5
insinuatie, 26
Instituto Mobiliare Italiano (IMI), 72–3, 77
Instituto per la Ricostruzione Industriale (IRI), 65–6
insurance industry
EEC liberalization directives and, 116, 118
hidden reserves, 55–6
national prudential regulation, 113–14, 115
OECD liberalization code and, 111–14

Intercontinentale Anlage-Gesellschaft (IAG), 58
intermediaries, returns increase, 7
international business, Warburg and, 90
International Monetary Fund (IMF), 109
Global Financial Stability Report 2006, 132
and sterling, 91, 92, 99
UK and, 104–5
internet boom/ bust 1998–2001, 128, 130
investment banks, development, US, 67, 68
investment/ commercial banking separation
current calls for, 85
legislation, 65
investment situation 1930s, 62–3
investors, private, US increase, 68, 69
irrational exuberance, 8
Italy
banking
crises, 70, 72–3
financial market relations
Banking Act 1936, 78
separation, 66–7
industry links
comparison, 82
financial relationships, 69–70
system pre–1930s, 66–7, 68, 69–70
Banking Act 1936, 10, 65–6, 74, 76–8, 81, 83
banks
deposits use comparison, 79–80
maturity mismatches, comparison, 81–2
short-term liability banks, 78
specialization/ competition, comparison, 82
commercial banking regulation 1926, 70
commercial vs investment banking, comparison, 80–1
Convenzioni (1934), 73, 74, 76, 77, 82
corporations
banks as holding companies, 68, 69
and financial holdings, 69
financial markets, 1930s, 72
financial regulations 1913, 66–7
industrial output decline 1930s, 72
Industrial Reconstruction Institution (IRI), 73

Inspectorate for Safeguard of Savings/
    Credit Activity, 76
Liquidation Institute, 72
North Africa traders' coalitions, 18
stock market crash 1907, 66
US banking legislation comparison, 10,
    65–83
World War I, and banking systems, 67–8

J. P. Morgan, 67, 72
James, Harold, x
    historical view, 5–12
Japan
    1990s crisis, 2, 132
    rice futures, 6
Joseph, Keith, 106

Kahneman, Daniel, on behavioural econom-
    ics, 128
Kindleberger, Charles, *Manias, Panics and
    Crashes*, 128
King, Mervyn, 1
Kölnische Rückversicherungs-Gesellschaft,
    56
Krugman, Paul, on deregulation and
    2007–10 crisis, 85, 86
Kuhn Loeb, 67, 72

Lamfalussy, Alexandre, 2–3
Latin American 1980s debt crisis, 2
lawsuits, shares trading, Holland, 16–17
legal framework, share transactions, Hol-
    land, 20–33
legal systems, and commercial contracting,
    16–18
Lehman Brothers, 67
leveraged/ fractional reserve banks, 130–1
Levy Duarte, Manuel, 31
liberalization commitments, choices,
    GATS and, 122
life insurance
    OECD liberalization code and, 111–12
reinsurance, 58
limited liability, 6, 7
    co-operative banks, 40
liquidity policy, co-operative banks, 51–2
listing problem CCB banks, 47–9, 48*t*3.4
London and County Securities, 98

Londonderry, Thomas Pitt, Lord, 30
loose monetary policy, 1
Lopes de Castro Gago, Antonio, 32
Low Countries *see* Belgium; Netherlands

Mackay, Charles, *Madness of Crowds*, 128
Macleod, Iain, on stagflation, 94
macro-prudential policy levers, 134, 135
Maes, Ivo, x–xi, 1–3
market ties, bank/ industry, 10, 65–83
marketable credit securities, 131–2
markets, complete, bankruptcy impossible,
    129–30
maturity mismatches, US/ Italy comparison,
    81–2
maturity transformation risks, banks, 131
McFadden Act 1927, 70
Mediobanca, Special Credit Section, 78
merchant bank balance sheets 1973–7,
    103*t*6.1
Mercury Asset Management, 89, 91
Mercury Securities, 89
    profits, regulation effects, 102–3,
        103*f*6.4; 103*t*6.1
    real net profits 1954–94, 103*f*6.4
MFN principle, 121
Minsky, Hyman
    on booms, 5
    on credit supply, 130, 131, 132–3
Mitterrand, François, 105
mixed banks (banche miste), 66–7, 68
modern trade policy and globalization
    process, 107–25
monetary policy, loose, 1
Mooij, Joke, xi
    on Netherlands cooperative banking, 2,
        9, 37–54
mortgage bank, CCB, 41
most favoured nation clause (MFN), 107
multilateral regulations, 107

naïve investors, risk transfer to, 5–6
national banks, Banking Act 1935 provi-
    sions, 75–6
national commercial banks, Glass–Steagall
    1933 provisions, 74, 75
Netherlands
    agricultural crises, 45, 50–3

banking crises, 43–4, 44–5, 50–1
commercial banks, 1930s, 44
commercial contracting history, 16–18
co-operative agricultural banks, 2, 9, 37,
  39–54
Co-operative Associations Act 1876/
  1925, 40
Dutch East India Company (VOC),
  8–9, 13–35
  conveyance rule, 20–1
  share prices, declines, 28, 31–2
  share transfers, 13–18, 14f2.1, 15f2.2
Freedom of Association and Assembly
  Act 1855, 40
Post Office Savings Bank (RPS), 41
secondary shares market, 8–9, 13–35
share transactions, legal framework,
  20–33
New Deal
  legislation, 74–6, 80–1
  restrictions on mortgage lending, 85
New England Merchants National Bank,
  100
Nixon, Richard, ends dollar convertibility,
  94
non-bank credit securities, 130
North Africa/ Italy traders' coalitions, 18

Organisation for Economic Co-operation
  and Development (OECD)
  Code of Liberalization of Capital Move-
  ments, 114–15
  Code of Liberalization of Trade and Invis-
  ible Transactions, 108, 109, 110–15
  liberalization codes, 110–15
  capital account liberalization, 119–20
  and insurance trade, 111–14
Organisation for European Economic
  Co-operation (OEEC)
  replaced by OECD, 110
  trade policy initiatives, 108–15
  and quantitative restrictions, 115
off balance-sheet derivatives, 5
oil shock 1973, 94, 95
open markets, financial services industry
  and, 11, 107–25
'over the counter' trading, 135, 141
Overlander, Pieter, 22–3

parametric reform, 133–4, 135
Paribas, 105
Pellicorne, Hans, 22–3
Petram, Lodewijk, xi
  on Dutch secondary shares market, 2,
  8–9, 13–35
Pfandbriefe, 132
Phoenix, 55–6, 63
Pitt, George Morton, 30
policy, implications for future, 133–4
policy levers, macro-prudential, 134, 135
Polster, Andries, 28
Portuguese Jews, and VOC market, 16
Posner, Richard, on Glass–Steagall Act
  restoration, 85
predictors, current financial crisis, 2–3
preferential trade agreements (PTAs), 107
private enforcement mechanisms, securities
  sub-market, 17–18, 18–19, 26–33
private sector debt to GDP ratio, 136–7
property development control relaxation,
  and inflation, 95
Prudentia, 63
prudential regulation, 113–14, 115, 117–18
public law credit institutions (IDPs), 76
punch bowl principle, 134

Radcliffe Committee 1959, 87
Raiffeisen, Wilhelm, 39–40
rating agencies, and new products, 6
real estate
  commercial, bank lending against, and
  crises, 132–3
  cycle, 1, 2
  financing, and private sector debt to
  GDP ratio, 136–7
  investment, and credit, 130
Reconstruction Finance Corporation
  (RFC), 71, 72
regulation
  deregulation and stagflation, 10–11,
  85–106
  effects, 7–8, 10–12
  policies, national, GATS and, 122–3
  regulatory overkill, 141
Reinhardt, Carmen, on 'financial repression',
  133, 136

reinsurance
    international, OECD liberalization code
        and, 112
    Swiss Re and Great Depression, 1, 9–10,
        55–6, 58–64
Rerum Novarum Papal Encyclical (1891), 39
rescontre meetings, 29, 30–2
reserves, hidden, Swiss Re, 1, 10, 55–6, 61–4
Richardson, Gordon, 98, 104, 105
risk
    management strategies, 7–8
    spread, perception of, 6
    transfer to naïve investors, 5–6
    and uncertainty factoring, 6
Rogoff, Ken, on 'financial repression', 133,
    136
Roman Catholic organization, CCB, 40
Roosevelt, Franklin D., 62, 72, 75
Rotgans, Jan Hendricksz, 21
Roubini, Nouriel, 2–3
Russian Revolution, effect on SR, 57–8

S. G. Warburg & Co., 11, 86–106
    banking in adverse conditions, 99–102
    and Cripps Warburg, 100–1
    innovative management, 89–90
    international business, 90
    in regulated market, 86–91
    profits, 102–3, 103*f*6.4; *t*6.1
    and Treasury, 11, 86–7
sales co-operatives, 38
San Francisco earthquake, SR and, 57, 64
savings balances, interest, 41
savings/ savings interest rates, co-operative
    banks, 53
Scholey, David, 101
Schularick, Moritz, on financial deepening
    and economic growth, 136
Schulze-Delitzsch model, 38
Schumpeter, Joseph, on technological/ com-
    mercial innovations, 7
Schweizerische Kreditanstalt (Credit Suisse),
    56, 57
Scottish Co-operative Wholesale Society
    (SCOOP), 98
secondary banks
    1987 Banking Act and, 105
    and real estate speculation 1970s, 97–8

secondary shares market, Dutch, 8–9, 13–35
securities case law, certainty, 9, 17–19
securities sub-market, private enforcement
    mechanism, 17–18, 18–19, 26–33
securitized credit trading, 131–2
self-governance, stock exchanges, 2
self-regulation, securities sub-market, 17–18,
    18–19, 26–33
Seligman Bros, 89
selling groups, US investment banks, 68
Semeij, Dirck, 22–3
Sephardic community, Amsterdam, 19
settlement terms, share transfer, 25–7
shares
    contract negotiability, 24
    endorsement
        derivatives transactions, 24–5
        forward contract assignment, 24
    ownership/ transfer, 20–35
        case law, 21–2, 22–35
        trading, VOC, 13–18, 14*f*2.1, 15*f*2.2
        related court cases, Holland, 16–17
    transactions, legal framework, Holland,
        20–33
    transfer, terms of settlement, 25–7
Shinwell, Emanuel, Warburg and, 105
short selling 1610 ban, Holland, 17, 27–33
    contracts renunciation clause, 28–33
    private enforcement mechanisms, 17–18,
        18–19
Simon, Charles, 57, 58, 59, 61
Single European Act 1986, 118
Single Market programme (EU), 115–20,
    121, 123–4
Slater, Jim, 98
Slater Walker Limited, 98
small business credit sector, Netherlands, 38
Società Finanziamento Titoli (Softit), 70
sovereign debt crisis 2010, 133
specialization/ competition, US/ Italy
    comparison, 82
Sraffa, Piero, on banks and industry, 69–70
stagflation
    financial markets and, 99–102
    policy failures, Britain, 93–9
    regulation/ deregulation and, 10–11,
        85–106

state-chartered securities affiliates, commercial banks, 68
Steagall, Henry, 74
sterling
crises, 59, 92, 94, 95–103
devaluations, 91, 92
Straumann, Tobias, xi-xii
on Swiss Re and Great Depression, 1,
9–10, 55–64
structured credit market, banks and, 7
subprime mortgages, 5
Sunday Times, on Warburg, 89
Sweden, 1990s crisis, 132
Swiss Re and Great Depression, 1, 9–10,
55–6, 58–64
1930s policies, 61–4
assets composition, 60*t*4.1
and Great Recession, 55
hidden reserves, 62*t*4.2
history, 56–8
share price support, 59, 61
technical/ financial results, 59*f*4.1
and US business, 57–64

Taylor, Alan, on financial deepening and
economic growth, 136
Thailand, 1997 crash, 132
Thatcher, Margaret, government, 104–6
Thatcherism and financial deregulation,
104–6
Thorneycroft, Peter, 91
too big to fail issue, 134, 139–40, 142
trade policy and financial market integration, 107–25
traders' coalitions, North Africa/ Italy, 18
trading clubs, 29, 30–3
trading community, Amsterdam, 18–19
transactions standardized for clearing/ settlement, 140–1
transformation functions, leveraged fractional reserve banks, 130–1
Trebilcock, Clive, *Phoenix Assurance*, 55–6
Triumph Investment Trust, 98
trust companies, US, powers, 67
tulip mania, 128
tulip-trading clubs, 30–1, 33
Turner, Adair, 1, xii
on financial evolution and volatility,
11–12, 86, 127–38

underwriting syndicates, 68
unemployment, Warburg on, 105–6
United Kingdom
Accepting Houses Committee, 86, 89
banking
19th century economic success, 130–1
Banking Act 1979, 105
Banking Act 1987, 105
crisis 1973–5, 95–103
regulation/ crisis, Ferguson on, 10–11,
85–106
retail, 'high street' banks cartel, 87
secondary banking crisis, 132
City of London, 1970s, 86–7
credit controls relaxation 1971, and
inflation, 95
economic crises, 1970s, 86–103
economic malaise, 91–3
Exchange Control Act 1947, 87
Financial Services Authority (FSA), 11
Gold Standard abandoned, 39, 51, 71
house price inflation, 95, 96*f*6.2
In Place of Strife, 93
inflation, 1970–9, 94*f*6.1
merchant banks, 86
minimum lending rate hikes, and inflation, 96
private sector debt to GDP ratio, 136–7
public sector bodies and Eurobond
issues, 92
stagflation/ policy failures, 93–9
sterling
crises, 59, 92, 94, 95–103
devaluations, 91, 92
stock market
'Big Bang' 1986, 87
boom and credit controls relaxation, 95
brokers/ jobbers separation, 87
crash 1974–5, 96, 97*t*6.3
stocks/ bonds, negative returns 1970s,
99–100
'Winter of Discontent' 1978–9, 104
United States
banking legislation
Banking Act 1933 (Glass–Steagall), 10,
74–5, 80, 83
Banking Act 1935, 10, 75–6, 81
comparison, 10, 65–83

Emergency Banking Act 1933, 72
Industrial Advances Act 1934, 75
Investment Company Act 1940, 76
McFadden Act 1927, 70
Securities Act 1933, 75, 81
Securities and Exchange Act 1934, 75,
  81
banking system
  crises 1930s, 71–2
  pre–1930s, 67–9
banks
  commercial
    assets shrink 1929–32, 71–2
    development, 67, 68–9
    vs investment banking, comparison,
      80–1
  deposits use comparison, 79–80
  dump corporate bonds, 71
  industry links, comparison, 82
  investment banks development, 67, 68
  maturity mismatches, comparison,
    81–2
  national
    pre–1913 real estate loans restric-
      tions, 67
    pre–1913 security dealings restric-
      tions, 67
    securities activities 1922–33, 68–9
    National Banking Act 1864, 76
    specialization/ competition, com-
      parison, 82
  corporations, bank loans, 71
  Federal Reserve Bank
collateral, 71
  Federal Reserve Act 1913, 67
  Glass–Steagall 1933 provisions, 74
  financial regulations 1864, 67
  government bonds distribution, banks
    and, 68
  industrial firms, investment banks repre-
    sentation on boards, 67
  investment trusts, 69
  leaves gold standard 1933, 72
  Office of the Comptroller of the Cur-
    rency (OCC), 69
  reinsurance business, SR and, 57–64
  savings and loan crisis 1980s, 132
  trust companies, powers, 67

World War I, and banking systems, 67–9
unsecured credit, pooling/ tranching, 132

Van Balck vs Rotgans (1622), 21–2
van Bronckhorst, Vincent, 26–7, 28
van de Geer, Jacques, 22–3
Van der Heijden and Van Genegen lawsuit,
  24–5
Van der Wee, Herman, xii
  Herman, historical view, 5–12
van Meijert, Hendrick, 26
Vega, Josseph de la, *Confusion de confusiones*,
  29
VOC *see* Dutch East India Company
  (VOC)
Volcker, Paul, on financial innovation, 6, 86

Walker, Peter, 98
Wall Street crash 1929, 39, 58, 71
Warburg, George, and C. W. Capital Ltd,
  100–1
Warburg, Siegmund, 87–94, 99–106
  on inflation fears, 100
  politics, 105
  risk-averse business model, 88
  see also S. G. Warburg
Warburg Investment Management, 89
Warren Buffet, 55
Wechsberg, Joseph, on Warburg, 100
Werner, Welf, xii-xiii
  on financial services industry and open
    markets, 11, 107–25
White, William R., xiii, 2–3
  on financial regulation debate, 12,
    139–42
Williams & Glyn, 100, 101
Wilson, Harold
  governments, 92–3, 99, 104
  Warburg and, 99, 105
World Trade Organization (WTO), 107,
  108
  GATS, 108, 120–3, 124, 125
  trade policy initiatives, 108, 109, 120–5
  Uruguay Round (1986–94), 108, 110,
    120–3
World War I
  and banking systems, 67–9
  effect on Swiss Re, 57–8

For Product Safety Concerns and Information please contact our EU
representative GPSR@taylorandfrancis.com
Taylor & Francis Verlag GmbH, Kaufingerstraße 24, 80331 München, Germany

www.ingramcontent.com/pod-product-compliance
Ingram Content Group UK Ltd.
Pitfield, Milton Keynes, MK11 3LW, UK
UKHW020951180425
457613UK00019B/627